THE OPEN CLASSROOM:

MAKING IT WORK

BARBARA BLITZ
New York University

Allyn and Bacon, Inc.   **Boston**

Second printing . . . August, 1973

Photographs courtesy of Allyn and Bacon staff photographers

Library of Congress Catalog Card Number: **72–86606**

CONTENTS

PREFACE

Traditionally oriented school systems have bred classroom atmospheres of conformity, passivity and joylessness in this country. Increasingly, there are reports of successful attempts to change this traditional pattern of American education. These attempts have various names such as informal classroom, free schools, open corridor, open classroom, etc. Whatever the name of the program or its outward form, the essential concept behind these new educational patterns is that children are unique individuals whose learning needs can be met only in a free, active atmosphere where each child can pursue his particular interests and learning needs as they arise.

Many individual teachers are attracted by glowing tales of the success of these new ventures and many have attempted their own innovations. However, many teachers who share the desire to make their classrooms more vital, humane places for learning find it difficult to venture into unknown territories without some frame of reference or guide. Because so little research has been done on the newer forms of education, it is difficult to be sure what is worthwhile and what is not. We have sparse knowledge about how or why children learn so that we must often resort to trial and error methods in the classroom. In attempting to change classroom patterns it is difficult to throw over all our accepted ideas and attitudes about learning and go forth into unknown and relatively uncontrolled classroom situations. However, it may be that in these less structured situations we will find some answers about how children learn and about how teachers can best facilitate their learning.

In the following chapters I will discuss many of the theoretical and the practical problems of operating an open classroom and variations of it. These discussions will serve as guidelines for those teachers who want to develop teaching behavior which meets the needs of children rather than the needs of educational institutions. It is up to you as a unique individual to use the content of this book to suit your personal needs and those of your students. I have not attempted to provide one right way of teaching an open classroom. This would be the antithesis of the open classroom concept. I have attempted to consider all the relevant factors in operating an open classroom so that each teacher may make her own decisions regarding organization, content and goals.

Having every teacher turn her classroom into an open classroom will not provide all the answers to our varied educational needs. Examining the philosophy behind our educational methods and finding more efficient means of implementing educational goals can be an impetus for more experimentation and creativity by all teachers. As long as you, the teacher, are the basic ingredient in every form of existing classroom, you are in the best position to develop more relevant and successful educational methods upon which tomorrow's schools will be patterned.

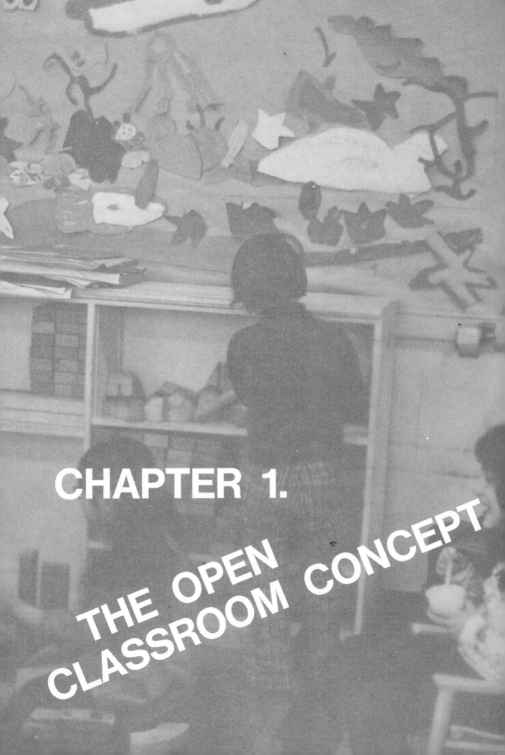

CHAPTER 1.

THE OPEN CLASSROOM CONCEPT

1.

THE AMERICAN CONCEPT OF AN ELEMENTARY SCHOOL CLASSROOM

For most Americans, the concept of classroom life in the elementary school is roughly similar. Thirty to forty children of the same chronological age are gathered in one room with one teacher. They have identical lessons, read the same books, solve standardized problems. At intervals, they are tested and evaluated. Progress reports are given to parents and individual children begin to be known as either good or poor students. The reputation assigned to each child tends to remain constant throughout a child's school career. If we visited classrooms across the country, the rooms would look approximately the same. The behavior expected of students would be roughly similar and the content studied at each age level would be almost identical. This sameness would give most of us a comfortable sense of familiarity. We would know exactly what goes on in those rooms because most of us experienced it during our student years. Our personal experiences comprise our concept of what school is and what it should be.

The Quality of American Schools Today

In recent years insightful critics of this comfortable and familiar concept have wrenched us away from such a nostalgic and simple view of classroom life.

During the 1950's educators, interested scholars and laymen became concerned about the low academic performance of many students in our schools and about the poor quality of scientific knowledge offered in most school curricula. In 1964, John Holt[1] gave us a devastating picture of the meaning of school routines and teaching methods from the individual child's point of view. With the rise of concern for civil rights in the 60's, sensitive teachers such as Kozol[2] presented the bleak life of the urban black child in our modern schools.

The boredom, futility, hypocrisy and hopelessness which exist in our schools have been well documented by Jackson,[3] Henry[4] and Silberman.[5] These men have completely shattered the acceptability of our long held concept of school. They have forced us to look beyond the neat rows of well-groomed children, the orderly behavior of students and the familiar ring of lessons. They have made us sense the feelings of passivity, confusion, hatred and despair that are also a part of a concept of school for present-day students.

THE OPEN CLASSROOM AS AN ALTERNATIVE TO TRADITIONAL CLASSROOMS

Most of us are searching for different concepts of school which are more consistent with the ambitions and dreams we have for our children. Educators and parents throughout the country are trying alternative forms of education which are less restrictive and more beneficial to the growth of children's minds and spirits. Their main concern is that classrooms become more humane and involving places for children. They want every child to be treated with respect. They want every child to be given reasonable choices concerning his own education, so that each child will develop his intellectual and emotional abilities. These classrooms vary in their approaches to implementing their aims and they are called by different names: "open corridor," "open school," "free school," "integrated day," "open education" and "open classroom."

Many of these attempts to find new forms of educational methods share similar interpretations of ways in which some basic needs of children can best be met. Most would agree that 1. children should have the right to pursue individual interests and activities; 2. that they need to be actively engaged with their environment and other people in order for meaningful learning to occur; 3. that the environment is of major importance in structuring the learning of the child; 4. that children learn at their own pace and with their own particular learning styles; 5. that learning should be exciting and enjoyable; and 6. that the teacher's role should be that of diagnostician, guide and stimulator. With these basic building blocks,[6] other ingredients may be quite variable, depending upon the philosophy and personality of the teacher and upon the available facilities. Classrooms can be nongraded. They may utilize the entire school building and the community as a learning environment rather than just one room. They may rely heavily upon materials for stimulation and teaching or they can include group lessons and some standard curriculum. They can involve team teaching.

Whatever the particular outward form of the open classroom, the essential thought behind it is that children are unique, physically active individuals, and that their learning needs can only be met in a free, active atmosphere which tailors the learning environment to the specific needs and abilities of each child. Because I believe the form should remain flexible and open to change at all times, I will refer to a general form of teaching which embodies the above principles as the *open classroom*.

There has been an almost parallel growth of open classroom techniques in this country and in England. The integrated day of the English Primary School is well known to Americans, and in the last ten years it has become standard practice in approximately 25 percent[7] of English Primary Schools. Although the open classroom concept has gained popularity in the United States and its practice is steadily increasing, the number of open classrooms is still quite small.

Psychological Foundations for the Open Classroom

The foundations of the present open classroom concept were being laid at the beginning of this century by the work of Froebel, Montessori, Dewey, Isaacs and Piaget. Froebel had demonstrated that play is the learning vehicle for the young child, and by the early 1900's it became respectable for young children to learn through play. The work of Montessori[8] alerted educators to the importance of materials and surroundings for structuring the learning of young children. It raised questions about the long held assumptions that young children have brief concentration spans and that their interest in learning is transitory if it even exists. John Dewey's extensive writings initiated the progressive movement[9] in elementary education in this country which briefly was very successful but then disappeared after much abuse by practitioners and laymen. Dewey's ideas that children learn best by doing real things and involving themselves in real situations have had lasting effects even in traditional classrooms in this country. His ideas of the curriculum as a whole entity rather than separate subject areas, and of the world outside the classroom as material for learning certainly provide impetus for the open classrooms of today. Susan Isaacs[10] and Jean Piaget[11] moved away from the study of children by normative methods to observe and question them in their play and, in the case of Piaget, in prescribed tasks. Piaget formulated a theory of development which is influencing all educators today. His view that the individual's interaction with his environment changes the structure of his intelligence gives education an importance and significance it did not have previously.

The Changing View of Man

The work of these educators and psychologists has furthered the changing view of man. In recent decades, advances in knowledge have forced us to view ourselves and our development differently. Gordon[12] discusses this change as a movement from a Newtonian frame of reference to an Einsteinian one. The Newtonian view holds intelligence as being fixed genetically and unfolding in an orderly manner, relatively unaffected by environmental factors. The Einsteinian view sees man as possessing a self-organizing system based on a modifiable intelligence. Intelligence can be created through transactions with the environment, and the organism is continually active and searching. Thus, the role of the environment and the experiences it provides become of much greater importance.

Obviously, these two models of viewing man call for very different types of school experiences. With the Newtonian model of man, the school simply teaches the child information and then evaluates his ability to absorb it. The school bears little responsibility for the child's success, since genetic intelligence will predetermine his success or failure in the tasks presented. Most of our traditional classrooms are organized on the basis of this outdated view of man. With the Einsteinian model, however, it is the school which bears responsibility for the experiences it provides for the child. These transactions can modify the intellectual structure and potential of that child. The content of lessons and the very organization of the classroom will communicate things to students which will change and structure the formation of their intelligence and expand or limit the possibilities of their mental development.

Educating the Einsteinian Man

The open classroom concept is aimed at educating the Einsteinian man. Its emphasis upon the active involvement of children with the environment attempts to increase the importance of the transaction which occurs in the school setting. A wide variety of materials, and individual freedom to choose materials and activities also encourages maximum use of the transaction as a means of growth. The active, searching mind of the child is constantly stimulated and developed by the varied and unique transactions which occur. As a relatively new approach in education, we have little research to guide us in the effectiveness of open classroom techniques. This can only come through continued development of techniques and testing of these techniques. Our lack of knowledge should not be a deterrent to establishing open classrooms, since we have no proof that current teaching methods are effective.

CONTEMPORARY EDUCATIONAL MOVEMENTS

In both England and America the motivating factor for recent educational change has not been due primarily to a shift in the philosophical view of man. It has resulted from an attempt to meet the needs of children in unusual environmental situations. In England, the displacements and limited facilities created by wartime conditions forced teachers to teach in unusual situations,[13] often without books or educational tools of any kind. The props of the traditional schoolroom were removed from most teachers, forcing them to seek flexible educational methods. Teachers were able to bring some of these new methods back into the classrooms after the war and, with gradual government support, there has been a marked change in the English Primary School.[14]

In America the prime force in recent change and educational experimentation has stemmed from the civil rights movement, which initiated many questions regarding the equality of American education. As educators attempted to upgrade education in the poverty-stricken ghettos of this country, it became clear that they were dealing with unusual environmental situations. More precise and accurate educational techniques were needed if there was to be any communication with the culturally deprived child. Gradually the validity of our educational approaches with all children came under attack.

It is easy to draw the conclusion that special methods are needed for special instances, such as in wartime or with particular groups of students. From this background of unusual environmental conditions, however, we have come to find that student apathy, passivity and conformity occur in our schools under normal conditions. Even white middle-class schools in wealthy suburbs have been affected by our outmoded educational philosophies and techniques. Instead of producing eager, involved and independent students, our educational practices are producing bored, passive students who are unenthusiastic or openly rebellious about taking roles in society.

New Patterns in American Education

A brief discussion of the better known movements in this country will give you an idea of the direction in which educational patterns are developing. The changes which have occurred in England have been well documented elsewhere.[15]

Many innovative plans developed as sensitive and creative teachers in this country began to search for more successful techniques of educating our young, particularly our disadvantaged young. One such venture was that of Mrs. Lore Rasmussen in 1964.[16] Realizing the hopelessness, the confusion, the intellectual and emotional damage that school creates for poor, black, urban children, Mrs. Rasmussen used her job as a math coordinator to change this bleak prospect. Working in Philadelphia in a black ghetto, she set up a math workshop in an empty basement room. Teachers were invited, not coerced, to bring their students for an hour, during which time they could have unscheduled free time. Mrs. Rasmussen took over the class and children were encouraged to work with math materials which were interesting and which they could manipulate. Their activities were focused in one conceptual area but they worked freely with the materials, learning individually about the focused area of study. Soon teachers became excited by the enthusiasm and learning of their students and they stayed to learn and participate also. This initial success led Mrs. Rasmussen to set up more "Learning Centers" in other schools and the program has been welcomed by students and teachers alike.

At the same time, Dr. Marie Hughes[17] was attempting to change the deadening school experience of Mexican-American children in Arizona. Her program was a concerted effort to improve the self image of these children with concentration on communicating specific skills and abilities which would ensure their intellectual success. This success would feed back positive images from the school experience, further enhancing their self images. Dr. Hughes felt the basic structure of the classroom must be changed in order to achieve these goals. Teachers had to provide many opportunities for children to talk freely to each other and to the teacher. They also had to provide opportunities for students to be successful in their activities within the classroom, no matter on what level the child was functioning. The result of initial planning was a program in which half of the day was spent in free activities and social interaction and the other half was spent in highly structured learning situations specifically designed to achieve the intellectual goals Dr. Hughes felt were so important for success. This dual approach yielded quick rewards and the program began to spread. Teachers were trained directly by Dr. Hughes and they were not selected for any specific qualities or interest in the program. The program since has spread to other states and has continued to be successful.

During this same time the integrated day of the English primary school, especially that of Leisterschire, was becoming known in this country. Groups of educators and teachers who were seeking directions in which to expand and improve current elementary school education felt encouraged and inspired by the English innovations. My own experiments with open classroom techniques began in 1965, in conjunction with a program sponsored by Educational Services, Inc. My attempts were bolstered by the learning and new techniques being developed at Leisterschire and in other English schools.

Developments in this country and in England convinced

creative pioneers like Mrs. Lillian Weber[18] to draw some of the new educational reforms into teacher training programs. She realized that student teachers would be unlikely to adopt new techniques if they were trained in traditional classrooms. In an attempt to create a better learning situation for student teachers, Mrs. Weber began slowly with an "open corridor" program in a New York City Harlem school. With the cooperation of the teachers along one corridor, she set up activity areas in the corridor itself and at certain times during the day children from the adjoining classrooms were allowed to have free time in the corridor, choosing their own activities. Gradually, as in Dr. Rasmussen's program, individual teachers became aware of the positive kind of learning which was occurring and they enthusiastically began duplicating and extending some of the experiences and opportunities within the classrooms. Parents also became interested in the program, and a group from a Westside racially mixed New York public school invited Mrs. Weber to introduce her program in their school. She did so with great success.

The largest formal program to officially endorse the informal or open classroom has begun in North Dakota.[19] They are currently attempting to convert elementary classrooms into informal classrooms on a statewide basis. As the result of a statewide study of the elementary schools in 1965, state officials recognized the need to overhaul their schools and particularly the preparation of their teachers, who ranked 50th among the states in training. They had to consider that most of their schools were small, rural ones which contained a few children of varying ages. In addition, they also had to consider large urban schools. Because of this diversity and special need to deal with the small one-room schools, they searched at some length for an approach which seemed suitable to their needs, rather than rushing into a quick teacher training program which would improve the status of their teachers but do little to solve the educational problems of the state's children. They decided that the approach of the English primary schools was the most suitable to their needs and they began retraining their teachers at the New School of Behavioral Studies in Education at the University of North Dakota. Instruction is based on the premise that teachers will teach students in the same ways in which they have been taught as teachers. For this reason, teacher trainees are given informal experiences and individualized instruction to prepare them for the open classrooms they will develop. As teachers become available, the elementary schools of North Dakota are gradually being converted to open classrooms.

All of these innovators share a deep respect for the individuality of children and for the right of the student to take responsibility·for the direction of his learning. Each of the programs described is different and preparation was motivated by unique factors.

There can never be one model for an open classroom because each class or group of students is unique and must be dealt with in a special manner. We are only beginning to build a repertoire of educational practices which can be used to implement the open classroom concept. Teachers in individual classes all over the country will provide the laboratories in which new techniques are created and tested. In this book I will share with you some of the things I have learned from my experience as a teacher of the open classroom and as a helper for student teachers in their attempts to develop their own techniques.

NOTES - CHAPTER 1

1. John Holt, *How Children Fail* (New York: Pitman, 1964).
2. Jonathan Kozol, *Death at an Early Age* (Boston: Houghton Mifflin, 1967).
3. Philip W. Jackson, *Life in Classrooms* (New York: Holt, Rinehart and Winston, 1968).
4. Jules Henry, *Culture Against Man* (New York: Random House, Inc., 1963), pp. 283–321.
5. Charles E. Silberman, *Crisis in the Classroom* (New York: Random House, Inc., 1970).
6. For further discussion, see Charles H. Rathbone, "The Implicit Rationale of the Open Education Classroom," in *Open Education*, Charles H. Rathbone, ed. (New York: Citation Press, 1971), pp. 99–115.
7. Vincent R. Rogers, *Teaching in the British Primary School* (Toronto: The Macmillan Co., 1970), p. v.
8. Maria Montessori, *The Montessori Method* (New York: Schocken Books, 1964).
9. For detailed discussion, see Lawrence A. Cremin, *The Transformation of the School* (New York: Teachers College Press, 1967).
10. Susan Isaacs, *Intellectual Growth in Young Children* (New York: Schocken Books, 1966).
11. For a brief summary of Piaget's theories, see *Six Psychological Studies* (New York: Vintage Books, 1967).
12. Ira J. Gordon, "Learning and Development," in *Behavioral Science Contributions to Psychiatry* (Boston: Little, Brown, 1965).
13. John Blackie, *Inside the Primary School* (New York: Schocken Books, 1971), p. 10.
14. *Ibid.*, pp. 1–14.
15. John Blackie, *Inside the Primary School,* and Lillian Weber, *The English Infant School and Informal Education* (Englewood Cliffs, N.J.: Prentice-Hall, 1971).
16. Charles E. Silberman, *Crisis in the Classroom* (New York: Random House, 1970), pp. 307–311.

17. *Ibid.*, pp. 311–318.

18. Walter Schneir, and Miriam Schneir, "The Joy of Learning —in the Open Corridor," *New York Times Magazine*, April 4, 1971.

19. Charles E. Silberman, *op. cit.*, p. 284–296.

Barbara Blitz

the open classroom
making it work

An outstanding work presenting innovative ideas and
techniques for teaching an open classroom!

CHAPTER 2.
RECOGNIZING
PROBLEMS

2.

RECOGNIZING ATTITUDES THAT INTERFERE WITH TEACHING AN OPEN CLASSROOM

Perhaps the most important prerequisite for your success in running an open classroom is a careful and honest examination of your attitudes and values. In my own teaching and in helping beginning teachers, I have found that often we are intellectually attracted to certain values and ideas, but that previous emotional and social conditioning may interfere with our attempts to put more recently acquired values into practice. As one student teacher put it, "I have to have spelling bees when I teach. I know they can be awful because of the competition and the whole idea of testing, but I loved them when I was a child. I always won and I have to have them."

Often, values you learned as a child from parents and teachers are dormant in your mind until a situation which demands action calls them into play. The mere fact of being around children every day encourages you to recall your childhood experiences and occasionally to relive childhood emotional reactions within the context of the teaching situation. One common manifestation of this reliving experience is the tendency of teachers to identify with students, usually a particular student who is "just like I was at that age." You may be aware of this kind of reaction, but often, many feelings and old behavior patterns will emerge within the teaching situation of which you will have little awareness. These feelings can be a powerful influence on your behavior and may cause you to communicate things to students of which you are totally unaware. During my first year of teaching I had five very disruptive children. I had been a mischievous child, and I enjoyed seeing the antics of these five first graders. Although I punished and reprimanded them when necessary, my unconscious enjoyment of their behavior reinforced it. This made their school life confusing and destructive because they developed patterns of disruptive behavior which their next teacher might not find so enjoyable; thus, they were on the way to becoming failures in school and I was aiding them by my inconsistent messages—sometimes punishment and sometimes reward for the same behavior.

Another factor in the teaching situation which encourages the emergence of old behavior patterns is the necessity of making spontaneous decisions constantly, and of acting upon these decisions immediately. This quality of the unexpected and the demanding makes teaching an exciting and everchanging experience, but this same quality also forces you to act without having time to consider alternative behaviors. Your spontaneous choice is frequently based on teaching techniques you have learned or witnessed in college. If these fail, or if you have never had learning experiences dealing with specific situations, your basis for decision making often reverts back to earlier habits you learned as a child or to personal experiences you have had with parents and teachers. For example, if a child soils himself in the classroom and you have never had the experience of seeing a competent teacher handle a situation like this, or have never read about any way to handle the situation in a school setting, you may react as your mother did to your early accidents during toilet training. Or you may react as you have seen your teachers or friends react in similar situations when you were a child. In either case, the reaction is likely to be one of disgust or ridicule, both common reactions in this society. These reactions embarrass and humiliate a child who is already painfully aware of the seriousness of his accident. If you have been trained to handle this situation professionally, or if you have had unusually thoughtful training as a child, you would try to handle the cleanup in a quick and matter-of-fact way, making it clear to the child and to the other students that accidents are a part of life and should be accepted as such.

For another instance, we all accept the fact that children's motor development is intermittently progressive and that they learn to manipulate objects gradually as their coordination matures. Often they attempt to do things which are beyond their physical capabilities. Imagine yourself in the classroom when a new jar of tempera paint is dropped by a well-meaning child. It spills and splashes all over the room and possibly on other children. How will you react? Will you calmly set about helping the child to clean up, seeking volunteer helpers while reassuring the child and suggesting that perhaps the jar was too heavy? Or will you become angry and tell the child how clumsy he is, and forbid him to paint for the rest of the week? Even though you may suppress harsh words if you feel angry, your facial expressions may reveal your feelings to the child. What will those feelings be? Are they what you would like them to be? Unfortunately, much of our early training conflicts with what we know children do and need. Children are not spontaneously neat, while we have been carefully trained to regard such actions as dropping things, messiness and spills as being bad. These actions usually result from errors in judgment by immature personalities and have little to do with being good or bad actions by good or bad children.

AREAS OF COMMON DIFFICULTY
IN THE OPEN CLASSROOM

A conflict between your new and old values may result in inconsistent and contradictory behavior on your part. This kind of behavior confuses and unsettles children. If you want to have a classroom where children move about freely to get materials, sharpen pencils, talk with other students, etc., you will probably encourage the children to do so. If, however, you find that you become tense when too many children are out of their seats at the same time, the children will feel your tenseness. If you continue to feel uncomfortable in this situation and you do not do anything to make it less worrisome for yourself, you can begin to have a difficult problem on your hands. The children will sense your uneasiness but will be unsure of its origin. This will make them feel uneasy and they will begin testing you to find out what it is that makes you unhappy about their behavior. This testing can continue until they force you to establish behavioral limits. Only then will they know exactly what is expected of them and how you will deal with various situations which occur in the classroom in connection with moving around the room. If the students' behavior becomes too disruptive, you may react by becoming tense, tightening discipline and increasing punitive measures. This further confuses the children and makes them test more. Soon you can be participating in a circular pattern of testing and tightening of controls until you and your students are lost in confusion, frustration and anger. You may be forced to use the strictest authoritarian methods to restore any kind of order in the class-room. Obviously, little learning can occur during this kind of struggle. If this situation develops in an open classroom, it is a short step to blaming the situation on the form of the open class-room itself rather than on your own conflicting values and lack of consistency. When it occurs in a more traditional classroom, it is usually blamed on bad children or on an inexperienced teacher.

CHANGING YOUR TEACHING BEHAVIOR

Assuming that you would react in a different way from the way you might wish to react, what can you do about it? With some careful thought and gradual self-training of your responses to problem situations which recur frequently, it is possible for you to gain conscious control over undesirable attitudes and be-havior. With effort it is possible to retrain yourself to control the undesirable behavior and replace it with new behavior which better accomplishes your desired aims. Such changes are rein-forced by the immediate responses you will receive from children and the resulting change in your relationship to them. The grate-ful expression on the face of a child you have reassured about spilling paint and the new way the students relate to you after the incident are more than enough to make you try to control feelings which might hurt this relationship.

During the first weeks in which I was trying open classroom techniques, a child wrote on the blackboard with white crayon instead of chalk, seemingly by mistake. The children reacted very harshly and I myself felt annoyed about the mess I would have to wash off the blackboard. But the fearful look on the child's face helped me control the annoyance I felt. I suggested that the little girl had made a mistake and that perhaps we should look at a piece of chalk and a white crayon to see if we could tell them apart easily. I immediately got pieces of chalk and white crayon for everyone. As the children compared the appearance of chalk and crayon, I began to question them about the differences be-tween the two. The children began experimenting with them, using different papers and textures. They spontaneously verbal-ized their observations excitedly to me and to each other. Every-one felt the texture of both, traded papers and other materials to write upon, and discussed at length the differences between the two. For many children these activities continued in some form throughout the week because they had become so involved in the things they were doing. They began testing pencils, pens, charcoal and also paint. The whole experience was interesting and fun. They did many things spontaneously, experienced extensive sensory stimulation, and through discussion and testing of ideas they learned a great deal. It was an ideal learning experience for almost every child.

Both the children and I learned another kind of lesson. We learned the vital lesson that mistakes can be springboards for learning rather than situations which provoke punishment or ridicule. Communicating this to children will significantly change the way they relate to you intellectually and emotionally. You will become an ally in their attempts to master the confusing world around them rather than another adult who rewards predefined success and punishes predefined failure. True success is learning to understand the world around you. Success in school means complying with the wishes and demands of the teachers, whether you understand what is going on or not. In this perspective most students fail. The open classroom provides an atmosphere in which children can truly learn and be successful.

TRANSLATING EDUCATIONAL VALUES INTO CLASSROOM PRACTICE

No one can anticipate all the varied situations which will occur in the classroom or be psychologically and educationally prepared for them. However, it is possible for you to give some serious thought to your values in education, to imagine how they will be expressed in classroom practices, and to anticipate how you will feel about some of the possible behavioral results which will appear in the children. This will also give you a firm basis for planning basic classroom procedures. As you think about your values and how they can best be translated into action, you make the best preparation anyone can for conducting an open classroom. Awareness of values and priorities allows you to put them into operation more efficiently and consciously, as well as to control those values that interfere with your educational goals.

In developing an open classroom, there are some areas which seem to present major problems for most teachers. Many of these areas involve values which are being debated in the general society. Whatever your personal feelings about these issues, you must realize that your feelings about them will be communicated to your students. Your own honesty and ability to visualize yourself in real life situations will help you to begin to clarify your personal viewpoints and to find ways of translating these values into constructive teaching methods. The areas I have found to be most troublesome are discussed below.

ACHIEVEMENT

Achievement is a broad concept which can be applied to any facet of life. In education it is generally associated with academic accomplishment and success. The emphasis you will place on the achievement of your students in various areas will be intimately connected to your own feelings about achievement and your previous experiences with it. The fact that you are a teacher is evidence that you have been a successful achiever in the school system and probably derive pleasure from achieving. Your experiences during your own efforts to achieve will shape many of the things you do with students and many of the expectations you have for their achievement and success.

Your basic needs to achieve were determined by your relationship to your parents during the first years of your life.[1] Obviously you cannot remember much, if anything, of what happened then. But you can recall your successes and failures in school and how you felt about them, as well as how the significant people in your life felt about them. Were test scores or report cards actually tests of your worth as a person or were they more realistically a part of a complex record you were making in the world? How did your parents feel about your achievements? Your teachers? And you? Was report card time a time for fear or for reward? Was achievement something you had to do in order to be accepted at home or was it something you did as quickly as possible so you could get the rewards and also have more time for things which seemed more important or more interesting to you? How did you feel before taking a test? How did you feel if you got a low score on a test or if you failed? Whatever your associations and values regarding achievement are, you will be bringing these values into the classroom, where they will be a potent influence on your relationships with children and on children's feelings about themselves.

Your classroom practices will also be influenced by professional and social pressures which exist in education today to make children achieve. Most teachers want children to achieve their full potential in all areas. How to go about implementing this is one of the hotly debated issues in educational circles. Though traditional teaching methods continue to be dominant in the schools, they are failing to be effective with large numbers of children. In the last decade there has been increasing pressure on teachers to somehow make children achieve, particularly in urban ghetto schools. Many community leaders and educators have raised the question of teacher responsibility in relation to pupil achievement. Because of the complexity of the learning situation, this correlation is a false one. Certainly teachers have the responsibility to help children learn in every way they can. The difficulty is that we know so little about how children learn and we know even less about the factors which are involved in the complex relationship between teacher and student. How then can we hold teachers accountable for something we know so little about?

As the values in society change, the levels of achievement in various content areas become of greater or lesser importance than they were formerly. We are often confused about which areas are most important and we are anxious about our formal methodological failures. Some of our constructive feelings about achievement become distorted and entwined with the less constructive social pressures exerted upon teachers.

Current questions and pressures regarding achievement focus primarily on reading and secondarily on mathematics. Social studies, science, visual and performing arts, athletics and health are given passing mention, but most people feel little genuine concern for achievement in these areas. Reading and mathematics stand out as the most important subjects for success in our schools and in our technologically oriented society. Achievement in these areas is so important to some teachers that they compete with their colleagues in subtle or obvious ways to produce the most proficient students.

Achievement Tests

Reading-test scores are often interpreted as comparisons of the competency of different teachers rather than as information to compare to the classroom performance of the individual child. There frequently is little consideration of the factors contributing to the child's reading level. How would you feel if your class had the lowest reading scores of all five classes on your grade level? How would you explain this to the administration or to the parents? Where would you look to find the reasons for the low scores? Would you immediately assume that critics of the open classroom system might be right in assuming that it does not prepare children to read adequately? Would you look at the overall ability and maturity of each child to ascertain whether scores were appropriately low? Would you examine the type of errors your students made to analyze more fully their reading assets and liabilities as well as areas where you may have been negligent in guiding their learning? Would you simply blame the children, or yourself, as being inadequate? What will these test scores mean to you?

Achievement tests do measure some specific aspects of learning and they are valuable comparative instruments. You should be aware of what skills the test is measuring and compare the test results with other achievements of the child, not with other children's test scores. In this country, because of our heavy reliance upon tests, we tend to accept the scores as final truths about a child's overall ability. In reality, test scores are merely rough indications of the development of specific abilities. A nine-year-old who has an overall reading achievement score of 3.5 grade level would be considered to be doing well for his age. However, if his word analysis score was 5.2 and his comprehension was 1.9 (all internal scores averaging out to one final score), then there would be something grossly wrong in his reading progress. The most meaningful part of a test is the examination of the achievement of a child in each of the specific areas measured by the test. Unfortunately, teachers usually attend only to the total score, which has little value in helping a child to learn the things he needs to learn at a particular stage in his development.

If you ever have the opportunity to watch an individual child take a test, it can be very revealing in terms of the validity of the test score. I once gave a reading readiness test to about five first graders. I had the chance to observe their behavior closely during the test. Freddie, a very bright and very hyperactive boy, went over each page and marked every item correctly. There was a time limit on this test which required that all the children turn the pages at the same time. Freddie chose the correct answers so quickly that he had lots of time to spare. His inability to be inactive caused him to go back to the only permissible activity in the test. He quickly colored over all the answers for each question, negating his original correct responses. If we could watch each child taking the test, I am sure we could tell stories similar to this one about each child. For this reason we must begin to put achievement tests into proper perspective in relation to a child's ability.

There are multiple factors which influence the level of achievement in reading in the open classroom situation. At the present time, indications are that children in open classrooms read either on equal or slightly lower levels as compared to those given traditionally oriented reading experiences. In my own experience, the open classroom approach does not significantly change reading achievement or test scores. An aspect of the open classroom which can make reading test scores deceptively low is that children may not have been trained to take tests. Students who are trained to give the stereotyped cultural responses to tests will have higher scores than students who have been encouraged to seek more creative or more realistic responses. For instance, the child who immediately responds to questions on a test about going on a picnic with answers indicating that picnics are fun (a stereotyped response in this country) will probably do better than a child who realizes all the possible feelings which can be elicited by a picnic. The ability to choose the stereotyped cultural response from many possibilities indicates that a child has become skilled in this activity and is less egocentric than less mature fellows. However, as well as being an aspect of a child's development, this skill is also one which is learned. If it has not been emphasized by a teacher or parent as being important, then there is no reason for the child taking a test to give the stereotyped responses any more importance than he does equally valid interpretations of the question. Open classroom teachers do not usually seek stereotyped responses or reward them.

Most achievement tests in reading will measure what we consider basic decoding skills and low-level comprehension. They usually do not measure a child's ability to make judgments concerning the quality, style and point of view of what he is reading. They do not measure how well a child can scan material or how he decides what to scan if he has that skill. They do not measure his ability to savor interesting or fine writing for pleasure or to do his own creative writing. These are other important skills to consider in evaluating reading ability.

Even though you may recognize the importance of all these aspects of reading ability, it is easy to say "I don't care about reading tests or achievement test scores; I want children to do their own thing and then they will learn spontaneously all they need or want to know." Many teachers assume that if children are allowed to choose their own activities they will spontaneously learn more than they do with teacher-selected activities. Others assume that they will learn nothing of any value if left to their own devices. The important element here is not so much whether a child is given freedom to choose his own activities, but rather whether a child comes in contact with whatever it is he is expected to learn, and what kind of contact he has with the material.

It is really up to you to utilize the open classroom to teach children reading (or whatever you feel they will need to know to get along in the world) in a better and more enjoyable way than it is taught in regular classrooms. Without exposing children to ideas and things in interesting ways, and without allowing them to learn on their own level of ability and interest, they will not learn. The child who never comes in contact with exciting mystery stories will never know one of the exciting aspects of literature. The child who is constantly presented with material beyond his ability to comprehend will never be able to absorb the material and will probably develop a deep dislike of it.

Standard Grade Levels

Another aspect of reading achievement which is usually ignored is the real significance of the reading grade level.[2] Grade levels are established by testing hundreds of children in many randomly selected classes on each grade level all across the country. From these scores the norms for children in an average class are established. These norms are mathematical computations which represent a composite of children, not any individual child. In such an average class 30 percent of the students should be reading below grade level, about 40 percent approximately on grade level and 30 percent above grade level, conforming to the bell-shaped distribution curve. There are probably no classes so randomly and heterogeneously grouped that the above figures would hold true.

In the case of slow classes or the lowest class on the grade level, all the students probably will be reading quite appropriately below grade level. If you have the top class on the grade, then these children logically should be reading above grade level (this rarely happens). In both these cases the evaluation by grade level would elicit appropriate scores according to statistical expectations. It is normal for 30 percent of a randomly selected group of children of the same chronological age to be reading below the standardized grade levels. However, in actual practice, any child who is not reading on the grade level for his chronological age is considered backward or deficient in some way.

The only reliable way to evaluate a child's reading performance is to compare it with other areas of performance of that *same child*. Do his reading skills match similar skills in math, science and general ability? If Jimmy is able to hear the softest murmur of another child speaking across the room but cannot distinguish the sounds of different letters, then there is a discrepancy between his general auditory ability and his reading auditory ability. This is evidence that he is having special difficulty in reading. If Dolores continually fails to distinguish word endings but can locate a pin on the floor when someone drops it, she may be having special visual difficulties in reading. But if Michael's reading ability seems to be consistent with his general abilities in other areas, he is probably reading as well as you can expect him to, no matter what his reading grade level may be. Comparison of a child to himself in the only fair and reliable measure of his ability. To compare children of the same chronological age to one another, or to compare your class to a set of thirty other real or statistical children, is a fruitless way of evaluating individuals.

Teacher Effort and Student Achievement

Another misconception regarding children's achievement can arise when teachers equate it with the effort they expend in the teaching process. Beginning teachers often fall into this dilemma, unrealistically expecting that the harder they work, the more the children will learn. It does not take long to find out that this is not true. No matter how hard you work at teaching children, if your efforts have been inappropriate they cannot bear fruit. The frustration and anger you may feel in such a situation is easily translated into calling children stupid, dumb or lazy. Or it can mean leaving the teaching field because you feel like a failure when in fact it was the methods you learned which were the true failures. After all, aren't we the stupid ones when we fail to adequately assess a child's current abilities and knowledge, expose him to what experts dictate as the right program for every child of his age, and then expect him to achieve an arbitrary amount of memorized facts or skills? Perhaps we are the stupid ones when we tell a child he could do better if he would just work harder, try harder, not give up. We know that children are only able to do as much as their current developmental and experiential level allows them to do. No matter how hard a six-month-old baby works at walking, it is unlikely that he will be able to do so.

Different Paths to Learning

Another important aspect of children's achievement centers on your ability to observe children and your sensitivity to what you observe. Unless you are specifically trained to recognize many types of learning which may not look like the stereotyped and standard forms which we see in traditional classrooms, it may take you some time to reeducate yourself to understand what children are learning in play and in sometimes apparently directionless activities. You will have to spend many hours in observing and analyzing what your observations mean in terms of children's learning. Most children learn in very individualistic and personal ways. They may choose one activity or many to further their learning. After days and sometimes weeks of appearingly aimless activities, integration and learning may become suddenly apparent. To recognize this kind of learning you must develop your observational skills and sensitivity to many different forms of learning. These skills must be coupled with a basic trust that children truly want to master their environment. If you believe that children will do nothing and learn nothing which is not forced upon them in subtle or gross ways, then you will not be successful in running an open classroom.

Consider how difficult and confusing the world and other people seem to us as adults. Then imagine how much more confusing it must be to children whose intellect is not fully developed and whose experiences are limited. In addition, children bear the added pressure of having to conform to the desires of many different adults while they try to make some sense of what goes on about them. As a teacher, you are in a very special position to become a vital force in the lives of many children. You can help them to master the world and their relationships to others in successful and meaningful ways. If you become just another adult who makes confusing demands on them without helping them to understand things, then you will hinder their progress.

Lock-step Promotion

As you become more sensitive to how children learn and to assessing what they already know, you will be faced with another difficult problem. Since children are advanced from one grade to the next without having sufficient comprehension of all the subject matter in each grade, you will find you have a class of students with widely varying amounts and kinds of knowledge. Even by the second grade the variations in knowledge and ability within one homogeneously grouped class is staggering. You are immediately placed in a dilemma, because the administration has prescribed certain topics and skills which you should teach to all the students on your particular grade level. Thus you may find that you are trying to teach mathematics for grade 3 and you have students who have not learned mathematics for grades 1 and 2. It will be impossible for you to help them achieve in this situation if you do not first teach them the mathematics they must have to assimilate the content for grade 3.

The pressures for achievement are so strong for most teachers that they simply press on with whatever curriculum guides suggest and follow a rigid time schedule in order to fit everything in. They may recognize the inherent illogic of this in terms of the needs of their students, but feel helpless to fight the system to meet the needs of students. Such is the power of institutional pressure on teachers. The learning deficits for most children by the time they reach fifth or sixth grade are tremendous. These learning deficits do not decrease as a child goes on to junior high and high school. They usually increase. *Elementary education is literally an elementary foundation of conceptual development which must serve as the basis for all future education and learning.*

I once taught a first grade class composed of children drawn from five other overcrowded first grades. Since none of the teachers had chosen their brightest or best behaved students, I had a class of unique children with broad ability ranges and even broader emotional development. I used a modified version of the open classroom because the school was a very traditionally oriented one and I did not want to get into fights with the administration. I was still licking my wounds from previous battles of this kind. After seven months with these children, we were still concentrating on the manipulation of numbers one through five. One day the mathematics coordinator came to visit and was dismayed that the children were not learning about the teens and twenties. She wondered how I could waste valuable time by staying with the lower numbers. I tried to explain to her that the children were not yet ready to go on even to the numbers from five to ten. They needed more concrete experiences with manipulating objects, and more activities centered on the first five numbers. She left my room quite annoyed, but I knew I was right. Whenever I had tried to extend their activities beyond the concept of five, they were unable to respond or to use the materials meaningfully. About four weeks after the coordinator's visit, a few of the children spontaneously began counting up to twenty. Soon the whole class was moving into the numbers above five and rapidly going from ten to twenty with a sound understanding of what they were doing. Had I moved them according to schedule (my schedule, not theirs), I doubt that they could have moved ahead with such ease and understanding. Furthermore, since the base of their knowledge would have been uncertain, they could only grow increasingly uncertain as they attempted to build a superstructure upon an inadequate foundation.

EMOTIONAL ACHIEVEMENT

As we try to help children learn, it does not take long to realize that a child's emotional state is an integral part of the rest of his functioning. Many teachers are confused by the emotions they see in the classroom and they feel inadequate to handle them. Others completely reject the role of helping children to handle their feelings. They insist that this is the responsibility of parents or therapists, not teachers. It would make life simpler if we could avoid this confusing area of human development; however, in order to help children to learn well, it is essential that we deal with their emotional development. Exactly how to help them achieve emotionally in a positive way remains a challenging question.

Expression of Emotion in the Open Classroom

In the open classroom where children are encouraged to express themselves in all areas with relative freedom, their feelings and problems become more apparent because they are being expressed more directly than they might be in a traditional classroom with its many built-in behavioral controls. Many opponents of the open classroom believe that it is primarily a therapeutic experience, and one which is inappropriate to the basic educational experience. They feel that intellectual development rather than emotional development should receive emphasis in the child's school experience. However, it is not as easy as some people seem to believe it is to separate these two aspects of the learning process.

When choosing their own activities, children are often able to choose materials or play situations which allow them to express and to experiment with feelings or areas of conflict in their lives which are of paramount interest and importance to them. Sometimes just the involvement in these play activities and situations will be enough to work out the problem.

A boy named John was transferred into my second grade class shortly after the middle of the year. He was adequate in academic work, was quiet and very well behaved, and was probably a little dismayed by the difference between my class and the ones he had known previously. He did not seem interested in doing anything or in making friends with the other students or with me. He sat quietly most of the time watching everyone with interest and good humor. After four days he painted a picture of a house. The feeling of his painting was very stiff and awkward. He proceeded to paint pictures of houses for an entire week, doing one or two a day. He chose other activities intermittently, but obviously the most meaningful thing for him was his painting. Each of his paintings was of the same house. Successive paintings became less stiff and awkward. Each one evinced more feeling than the last. As I saw what was happening in his paintings, I speculated that John was working out his feelings about his recent move from Philadelphia to New York. There was no way to be sure of this, but his deep concentration while painting and his obvious drive to keep painting the same picture over and over made me sure that something very important was happening to John. I did not want to interfere. Even if I was mistaken about the reason for his paintings, it was important that he continue to work out his preoccupation. After a week he produced an exquisite painting of a house. It was full of movement and harmony. Every detail was perfect. He removed the picture from the easel with a feeling of finality. He immediately joined a group of children doing some math activities and for the first time became involved with others in a meaningful learning activity. It is easy to say that there was a connection between the finished painting and his sudden interest in taking part in a class activity with others. This cannot be proven, but the closeness in time of the two events and the obvious importance of the painting make it likely that he used the painting to resolve something that was very important to him.

This is a common occurrence in the open classroom, in my experience. The details of what John was resolving are not important, although it would be intellectually satisfying to know what they were. The important thing is that he was able to resolve something vitally important to him within the school setting through the use of available materials, time and a receptive atmosphere. He was involved in a crucial learning experience. Its resolution opened other areas to him which previously had been closed. I feel very strongly that this is the real meaning of education. Without the opportunity to resolve this problem, John might have been crippled intellectually and emotionally, his mind preoccupied by personal conflicts. John, like other children, needed a place where he could work out his problems and feelings and clear his mind to receive what we have to teach him to help him get along better in the world.

Teacher Reactions to Student Emotions

If you accept the idea that intellectual and emotional experiences of children are intimately connected and complexly interrelated, then you will want to do everything to promote emotional growth and learning. If this can be accomplished, intellectual growth and learning will follow in a normal, healthy way. Imagine yourself in some of these situations where children are working out feelings or emotional conflicts in play activities. Would you be willing to let a child play in the doll corner at some reenactment of family life which seemed very important to him? Or would you be willing to let a child make a clay sculpture for a week without doing anything else? Would it be necessary for you to compromise the feelings of the child and the expression of these feelings in order *to reassure yourself* that the child was doing some "work" as *you* might define it? Do you recognize the expression of feelings or the resolution of conflicts as work for a child? Do you see the successful resolution of a problem as achievement?

On the other hand, would you allow a child to wallow in his feelings without attempting to help him find some means of working them out constructively? Children are even more overwhelmed by their feelings than we are and often need a strong support to help them realize that their feelings can be felt and expressed in constructive and satisfying ways.

Are there areas of expression and feeling which you cannot tolerate? Do you tend to deny the expression of feelings concerning family relationships, sex, sibling jealousy, bodily functions, angry feelings toward authority figures, anger in general? Are you able to express your own feelings in constructive ways? The patterns of your own feelings, their means of expression and your ability to tolerate your own and others' feelings will provide a model for the psychological development of your students. Although basic personality patterns are undoubtedly formed during the early years of life, all close relationships in our lives modify our behavior to some extent. If you have a positive relationship with students, some of them will certainly use you as a model for their behavior. The closer your relationship with them the more likely they will be to adopt many of your behaviors, intellectual and social ones as well as emotional ones. For this reason, awareness of yourself is a crucial factor in organizing the kind of classroom situation you want.

There is also a negative side to the concern for children's emotional expression and development. This concern can sometimes become overinvolvement with children's verbalizations and their feelings. When this happens, you fail to use the emotional content the child reveals for any constructive purpose. Most children are aware of the things that bother them and endless recounting of these things does little to change the situation or the child's feelings about it. You must use your teaching ability as well as your interest and sensitivity to help children in these situations.

Emotional Learning

In the open classroom you must become accustomed to hearing things which are emotionally important. You will experience the expression of strong feelings of all kinds, such as joy, anger, dismay, loneliness and fear. Even if you do nothing to encourage the free expression of feelings, the general freedom in all areas will encourage such expression. It is impossible to separate the intellectual and emotional functioning of children. This is true whether they function in constricted ways or in open, uninhibited ways. The emotionally constricted child will also be intellectually constricted in terms of his intellectual potential. It is very common in the open classroom to see a child relax and become more comfortable with his feelings. As this occurs, there is always a heightening of intellectual development, increased curiosity, lengthening of concentration span and better integration of the facts and experiences in the child's life.

The expression of feelings is only the first step in emotional learning and achievement. Just as in the cognitive learning situation, the expression of interest or curiosity about something is often the first step. The next step in both the emotional and the intellectual areas is to help children find constructive ways of directing and handling their feelings or curiosity. A child may need practice in learning a skill, or varied experiences with the same concept, or trial and error experiences in order to solve an intellectual problem. The same experiences may be needed to solve emotional problems. A child who cannot relate to other children in any sustained fashion may have to try a variety of approaches to find some means of relating to others which is satisfactory for his psychological organization. This may mean that several days or weeks will be spent in alternately fighting and provoking children or giving in to them totally. In the traditional classroom we usually deny children the experiences needed to further their emotional growth. We replace them with culturally acceptable behavioral codes to which children are expected to conform rather passively. If they do not conform we can simply label them problem children and try to effect stronger controls to bring them into line. This is not the type of learning experience which will train children for anything but passivity and conformity or, on the other extreme, open rebellion against a meaningless power structure.

Often as children's feelings begin to flow in the open classroom, you may feel overwhelmed by them. Initially children will experiment with the mere expression of feelings, whether they are important to them or not. This is probably due to the overall tendency to suppress real feelings. Sometimes dramatic personality reversals will occur in these initial weeks which can frighten you and the children if you do not realize what is happening (see Chapter 5). Often teachers feel compelled to give children answers and solutions to all the emotional questions they may raise. It is not necessary to do this. You can avoid this pitfall by providing helpful learning situations and suitable materials to encourage the children to experiment with their feelings and problems, just as you would do with an intellectual problem. If you think about it, there are many feelings and problems for which there is no solution or easy answer. Your personal need to supply an answer will not help a child if there is no answer to his problem.

A teacher I was working with was horrified when a boy in his class told him that his parents had said many times, "You were a mistake." The fact that the boy could tell this to his teacher indicated that he had a strong, warm relationship with him. Unfortunately, the teacher responded by trying to compensate for the child's rejection. He showered him with attention and affection during class time. The teacher's first activity should have been to find out what the word "mistake" meant to this boy and how the boy felt about his parents saying this. The teacher assumed that the boy felt unloved and rejected. This may or may not have been true. It is unfair to project our own feelings onto others. Each person reacts differently to the same situation. Each of us has a unique, complex psychological organization which we use to deal with the world. Consequently, it is grossly unfair to judge the reactions of others by our own reactions.

Had this teacher first determined what feelings had been evoked in the boy, he could then have proceeded to deal with those real feelings rather than with the imaginary ones which he immediately attributed to the boy. Perhaps help would mean assisting the boy to find ways of living with the knowledge that his parents did not want him. As children grow older and are less socially dependent upon their parents or immediate family, it is often possible to help them find many areas of satisfaction outside of the home. In this particular case, it may have turned out that the child did not feel at all rejected by his parents. We will never know. This teacher chose to project his own feelings and then to compound the error by his own need to give the boy *too much* attention and privilege in the school situation.

Every teacher is at some time in her career horrified by a student's relationship with his parents. Granted, some are unwholesome and destructive to the children involved. However, often our feelings stem from our limited concepts and values. The child may not in fact be experiencing what *we feel* he is experiencing. This kind of projection of our own value system usually adds to a child's problems because we do not treat these problems in a realistic way. To help children achieve emotionally, you must be ready to understand what their problems and feelings *mean to them* in relation to their particular style of living. Their thinking and feelings may be very different from yours.

COMPETITION

The degree and direction of your competitive strivings have been moulded largely by your parents. The feelings you associate with competitive situations are determined by your experiences during childhood.[3] Some people have had more intensely competitive situations with brothers and sisters than others have had. If you have brothers and/or sisters you certainly experienced competition on a very crucial emotional level. Your birth position in your family and your feelings about it will be an important determinant in your present attitudes toward competitive situations. Those who need to achieve often repeatedly place themselves in competitive situations. Those who for some reason are fearful of achieving, may avoid competitive situations whenever they can. Few of us can treat such situations objectively.

These basic competitive drives can be stimulated by the school situation, which is inherently competitive no matter how individualized it may be. Any situation which involves more than one person performing the same activity is a naturally competitive situation. There is a spontaneous comparison of who did the most and/or the best. There is always a winner, a loser and many positions in between.

Age Does Not Determine Ability

When we think about the effect of competition on children, there are additional elements to keep in mind. Children are in a constant but variable state of growth. Chronological age is a very rough indication of current development. Our lack of adequate instruments to measure differences in growth levels in most intellectual areas makes it hard to attempt to match children for similar abilities. Besides our limitations in matching, we continue to group together as equals children of the same chronological age. We then give them the same tasks and we judge their performance by those of their peers despite our knowledge that there is a great variation in individual development among children of the same age. This puts children in competitive situations which are unfair, misleading and often destructive. Do you remember taking tests in which you worked very hard and got a very low score? Do you recall taking tests with a minimum of effort and receiving very high grades? The only important factor in the test situation is the extent to which it furthers your knowledge about a child and his own knowledge about himself.

If we examine what happens when children begin to read, we have an excellent example of our inept cruelty in placing children in an inherently unfair competitive situation. We expect thirty children who have different abilities and different growth levels to begin reading the same size print at the same time with relatively equal comprehension. We have no instruments to measure accurately how a child is able to focus his eyes, what size print he is best able to distinguish, or what past experiences will influence his comprehension. To complicate things further, we make it clear that those who are able to succeed in the task of reading are the ones who will receive our greatest praise and get good report cards to show to parents. We leave the child who is *unable* to do the work in an untenable position—unable to do what we require. He will subsequently be relegated to a secondary (or worse) status in the class. Those children who do proceed to our satisfaction receive little substantial help from us in their learning. Despite their differing abilities and interests in reading, we give them all the same books and often the same instruction at the same time. How many dull, wasted, time-consuming hours we make them endure! Not because it is unavoidable, but because we are often misinformed and unimaginative.

One of the most difficult questions I have had to answer has been from eager first graders who want to know why they cannot all read. The most meaningful answer I could give them was to compare reading to the emergence of permanent teeth, to height and to strength. We know there are six- and seven-year-olds who are unable to focus their eyes well enough to recognize the repetition of a word. To convince such a child that he will be able to read if he will only try harder or do more work is a very dishonest and dangerous thing to do. Why can't this child be told the truth? Are we so afraid that children will not work hard if we tell them the truth? The child who is not physically or psychologically ready for reading will, if he does try harder, only learn that you lied to him. If he is less secure and less perceptive, he may begin to think there is something wrong with him because he cannot do what you are so sure he can do. He may begin to develop compensatory behavior to hide or deny the imagined deficiencies.

This kind of problem can be prevented in the open classroom where children work on self-chosen projects and materials. Each child tends to chose things which are near his ability or close enough to it so that his interest is challenged and his motivation sustained. This means that he gets a sense of achievement, that he is not penalized in any way for his progress or lack of it, that he learns what is meaningful to him, and that he sees that each child is different. The children proceed when their bodies and minds are ready, not when our arbitrary or statistically formed schedules say they are ready. Occasionally there are children who constantly choose things to do which are considerably above their ability, but this is the exception and indicative of personality problems, with which you can deal. The open classroom doesn't allow you to place children in impossible situations where they have no chance of succeeding at the tasks you set for them. The fact that nearly everyone is doing something different cuts down the competitive aspect of the classroom. Competition is always maximally present in the traditional classroom, where the majority of the children are engaged in the same or similar activities at the same time.

Competition for Motivation

Another frequent relationalization for competition is that it gives children (the winners) a sense of achievement and spurs on all children to want to become winners. Competition is often used in traditional classrooms to heighten motivation for tasks which are not spontaneously interesting, such as spelling. This kind of motivation or interest is transitory and, unless you handle it very skillfully, its yield is quite poor. No one is truly happy but the winner; however, in the next test he may be the one who is inadequate and fails. In actual fact, this type of teaching probably only convinces the majority of children that they never will be winners. They see that they have no outstanding ability or personality characteristics which will allow them to enter into the magical world of the winners. Thus, we teach all but the winning minority that they are not successful. These experiences may lead them to conclude that they never will be successful. Because school comprises almost 50 percent of a child's life, this is a dangerous and deadly lesson to teach. This type of competition and its results can severely hamper the development of a sense of individuality and self-worth.[4] Everyone should win or lose in terms of his own level of development at a certain point in time. There simply is no other rational way to evaluate a child's performance. If children are to learn, we must provide them with a basically positive picture of themselves. We can do this with honest evaluations of their ability.

Your personal feelings about competition will enter importantly into how you run your class and how you evaluate students. If you enjoy competition, you will probably encourage it in your students and accept the results with little question. If you enjoy competition but realize its limitations for evaluative purposes, you will probably do little harm to students. If you are a person who always needs to be first in competitions, you may compete with your students in subtle ways, or you may encourage destructive competitive situations between them. Whatever your feelings and attitudes, you must be alert to their influence on your teaching.

INDIVIDUALITY

Nearly everyone in this country ardently professes to respect the individual and his right to live as he chooses, provided he does not interfere with the rights of others. I am sure few teachers would claim to be against the concept of the individual or the individual's unique personality and development. Coexisting with this reverence for the individual are great pressures to conform in all areas of life. As an institutional representative of the society, the teacher is often caught between these two poles.

Child development research tells us that each child comes into the world different from all his fellows and that the complexity of his experiences only furthers his own uniqueness and individuality. Because of this, the open classroom is a more valid method of teaching children. It allows us to teach them more efficiently while we preserve, respect and develop their natural individuality. In a traditional classroom, a child must put aside his uniqueness somehow and conform to the behavioral and intellectual demands of the teacher in charge. Although it is difficult to rid ourselves of the feeling that what happens in a traditional classroom is what should happen in school, we must shake off this concept and recognize that traditional classrooms are often breeding grounds for the development of conformity and passivity.

It may be revealing for you to look at your own feelings about conformity, especially if you can think of conformity as the opposite pole from individuality. Perhaps you can measure your own need to conform, and see it as the inverse of your concept of yourself as a unique person. If you can express your feelings easily even when they run counter to popular opinions, you will probably find it easier to encourage diversity of thought and action in your students. If you have difficulty expressing such feelings, or seldom have them, you may have great need to conform. As a result, you will find it more difficult to encourage individuality of thought in your students. If you have always resented your need to conform, you may unintentionally communicate this to students. They may begin to act out your resentment by refusing to conform within the classroom. Your needs and personality will set the standards for your students. They will determine the way students value their own individuality and the respect they learn for the individuality of others.

An important consequence of your feelings will be the way you assign work to children and the kind of learning facilities you make available to them. Obviously, the same work or materials are not appropriate for all students. Since each differs in ability and interests, it may mean that no one will or should follow the same path to achieve their goals. Some children may be able to go from one reading level to another by reading one book instead of the two or three which are recommended. Would you feel ready to accept this or would you feel the child who had not read the required three books was missing something or cheating in some way? Acting upon the concept of individuality means accepting the fact that children's abilities are quite different and consequently will not develop in a uniform way. It means accepting Tom as a top notch reader and a poor singer, Jane as an excellent writer but a mediocre mathematician.

Individual Differences in Behavior

Individual differences in personality and behavior are more difficult to accept than those in achievement and ability. We tend to view differences in achievement as reflective of different genetic endowments. Differences in behavior are usually attributed to poor parental training or faulty school experiences. In reality, there can be many factors involved in individual differences of behavior or achievement. The very complexity of these factors and our difficulty in pinpointing the responsible ones in individual cases often makes us oversimplify the causes. This serves two important purposes: it relieves us of responsibility of further investigation and it relieves us of the guilt associated with not being able to help children who do not fit into our standard molds.

The children a teacher likes the most are probably the ones who most nearly achieve her ideal of behavior. Each of us seems to have an idea of the model child in our minds. This idea helps us to formulate general goals for students. It may conform to what we think we were like as children. More often it probably conforms to the model which was passed on to us by our parents and teachers. Perhaps one which we never seemed to match when we were children. This model may be very inappropriate for your students. Their home lives and values might be quite different from those of your parents. Expectations of children's behavior in school has also changed considerably in the last few decades so that your model of a good student may be far from the real qualities which make for a good student today.

Teacher Expectations

A teacher who likes well-behaved students as we think of them in the traditional classroom may have been a well-behaved child herself. A teacher who prefers mischievous students may unconsciously feel that bad children are the best or most interesting ones. Both attitudes ignore the inherent individuality of children and their right to vary in their personality characteristics from day to day. Children are always aware of a teacher's preferences with regard to their behavior. Sometimes they attempt to conform and sometimes they do not, perhaps even openly defying the teacher.

Although a teacher's expectations can hinder a child's development if they are too rigid and inappropriate for the individual child, they are basically healthy and constructive. Another person's expectations of us can often provide a healthy motivation to extend ourselves and grow to meet those expectations. Everyone likes to please people whom they trust and admire. Hopefully your students will feel this way about you and will meet with realistic demands. The teacher who is indifferent to students can be just as detrimental to their development as the one who is too ambitious in her expectations. I once saw a nine year old boy crash his fist through a glass door to get some attention from his teacher. She was not relating to her students on any level. Even his extreme bid for some notice evoked no feeling from her.

The open classroom can help you change your feelings about conformity in behavior and in intellectual activities. The open classroom makes it easier for you to see and to appreciate individuals in a variety of activities and interchanges with others and with the community. You begin to prize each child for his uniqueness rather than for his conformity and each child will have some remarkable quality unlike that of any other child.

By treating children as unique persons and cultivating their qualities and abilities, you demonstrate a basic respect for them. If you were treated with this type of respect as you grew up, you will probably show it spontaneously in relation to your students. If you have not received this respect in your own childhood, it may be necessary for you to train yourself to give it to students. It is a very vital part of helping children to respect themselves and their ability to deal with others and with the world.

THE TEACHER'S ROLE AS AUTHORITY FIGURE

Beginning teachers usually have mixed feelings about assuming the role of an authority figure—the teacher. If you have been a student for the past sixteen years, you may have mixed feelings about suddenly assuming the opposite role of teacher. If you are interested in running an open classroom, you are probably also interested in having a relatively non-authoritarian relationship with your students. However much a teacher may relinquish authority to the children, she is still the person respon-

sible for the physical welfare of the students, for their behavior
and for their learning progress. To deny that you have authority
is to be dishonest with your students and with yourself. They
know you are in charge and so do you. If you fail to use your
authority when necessary, it can be dangerous and damaging to
the children you want to help.

I have heard teachers say, "My students discipline each
other, I don't have to say anything." This often means the students are telling one another when to stop doing things or threatening each other with punishments or tattling. On the surface
this may seem to be self-discipline. In actual fact, it is a dangerous situation in which a few children are too responsible or too
bossy and they take the opportunity to act out their personal
problems when the teacher tarries or ignores what is happening
in the classroom. Taking over the role of a passive or reluctant
teacher can never help students develop self-discipline.[5] It can
only aggravate their existing problems with authority and their
peers.

Reluctance to assume the authority role is often the reason
beginning teachers complain of difficulty in disciplining or controlling their students. In the open classroom, where there are
fewer restrictions than there are in traditional classrooms, discipline is not as much a problem for the teacher. However, there
are rules to be maintained, and many situations occur which require the teacher's taking control. Children are in the process of
developing inner controls and although we must allow them freedom to experiment with these controls, we must also be prepared
to step in when their controls seem ready to fail them.

Students need to exercise their own abilities, to develop and
to learn how to use inner controls. They need experiences with the
authority role themselves to understand the relationship between
themselves and adults. They need the freedom to express as many
things as possible to delineate the comfortable boundaries of their
own personalities. But they also need the security of an adult who
can supply outer controls when their inner ones fail or are too
weak to operate effectively. They need support in protecting
themselves from overstimulation and overextension. This support
can come only from an authority figure who is willing to allow
them extensive freedom but who does not hesitate to step in and
take charge when necessary. Only with this kind of assurance can

children wholeheartedly venture into new and strange areas of learning and behavior.

Your past relations with authority figures—your parents, teachers, employers—will give you some indication of your feelings about those in roles of authority. If you have had difficulty relating comfortably to these people, you will carry these difficulties into the classroom where you will be the authority figure. Because of the complexity of your relationships with parents, teachers and employers, it is difficult to predict how any difficulties you may have had will express themselves. The important thing is to be aware of your feelings and alert to these same feelings or their opposites which may enter into your behavior with your students.

Assuming authority for and taking responsibility for the lives of others is an important and a frightening task. It is important that you consent to assume this role and that you realize it can be exercised in many constructive and creative ways.

PROCESS AND PRODUCT

As adults we are usually interested in the finished product of whatever we attempt. The quality of a painting or the taste of an exotic recipe we have worked on usually mean more to us than the actual painting or cooking experiences. Although children are quite interested in mastering tasks and producing things of which they can be proud, they are far more interested in the actual process or the doing of a task than adults are. While adults may view the process of a task as the boring, time-consuming part, for children it is an exciting time to explore and experiment with their senses and their intellects. If you have ever watched children involved in making something—a drawing, painting, sculpture, costume for a play, poems, a book, etc.—you may have noticed their intense concentration and meticulous attention to every detail. Their involvement is intense and their pleasure just as intense. When they have finished they may seem only casually interested in the result. It is not uncommon to see a young child paint a beautiful picture and then proceed to cover it over with one color paint. Obviously, the experience of manipulating the brush and seeing the effect of paint on paper and other paint is more interesting to this child than the finished painting is.

Sacrificing Understanding for Efficiency

Because we are so interested in the product itself, we tend to teach children shortcuts to make the process a speedier, less time-consuming experience. There is nothing wrong with developing speed and facility in dealing with materials or problems. Unfortunately, we often sacrifice understanding and enjoyment of the process of a task for speed and facility in obtaining answers. This is wrong. An example of this is our tendency to teach children various crafts rather than giving them the basic art materials from which to make things and with which to experiment creatively. I once worked with a teacher who used to insist that first graders trace their pictures on newsprint with a pencil and then fill in the outlines with poster paint. It was very important *to her* that the children produce good paintings. Actually, a child who is trained to do this will probably never produce a really good painting in an artistic sense. Ideally, children should have both experiences, experimenting with materials freely and learning how to use the materials in more structured ways. Many teachers feel too pressured to allow children to make satisfactory productions, so they cut this process short and teach only the end manipulations of materials which will ensure presentable results.

This cutting short of the process is also present in all the academic areas. Our main purpose in teaching should be to help children achieve and develop abilities in various subject areas, according to each child's interest and potential. In order to do this we often mistakenly teach them as many shortcuts and tricks as we can. This then leaves them with a lack of fundamental understanding of the subject they are studying. It may also give them a permanent dislike of anything related to the subject. This type of teaching is readily apparent in mathematics. We frequently teach children to memorize multiplication tables and to perform the mechanical operations of adding or multiplying fractions. Instead of doing this, we should be helping them to understand the basic relationships between numbers. With a basic understanding of mathematical concepts, students can then go on to experiment with the mechanical operations and perhaps discover shortcuts of their own.

Some of the programs in modern mathematics attempt to help children to grasp basic concepts and to enjoy working with them. But teachers still seem to be attracted to the shortcut techniques which facilitate working problems, but do not always further understanding of the meaning of the problems. This may produce high grades on tests, but it does great disservice to the student and to the discipline it distorts and makes unintelligible.

It often seems easier and faster to demonstrate short cuts and provide verbal, vicarious learning situations for students. Many teachers believe there is not sufficient time to provide any other kind of learning experience. But for most children below the age of 10 years, our verbal explanations are relatively meaningless if they are not connected rather directly to the child's own experience. Often it is necessary to provide this concrete experience or some variation of it in the classroom itself. Children's final understanding of what they are studying will be much clearer and richer if they have the chance to learn through exploring and experiencing in some depth. This certainly makes any extra time or trouble it takes worthwhile.

There can be no quick results or shortcuts in helping children learn. It is easy to teach them to verbalize ideas and facts and to tell ourselves this is learning. This is only a small part of learning and perhaps an even smaller part of understanding. In the open classroom where you spend less time teaching children to memorize, it is not as easy to fool yourself about how much they are learning. When you see them in action, their knowledge or lack of knowledge becomes very apparent.

If you are usually more interested in the end result of what you do than you are with the actual doing of it, you may have some difficulty encouraging children to fully participate in the process and experience of learning. If you are a perfectionist in the things you do and if you feel that time is wasted if projects do not turn out just right, you may also have some difficulty letting children explore and discover things without any definite end in mind. For those who are fond of shortcuts and instant results, there will be problems in trying to teach children on a deeper conceptual level. Since most of us are products of a shortcut type of elementary education, it is especially difficult for us to reverse our patterns of behavior and emphasize the process of learning.

If you have been able to imagine yourself in the situations discussed in these pages, you should have a clearer picture of some of your attitudes and values. As you plan your open classroom, keep these attitudes and values in mind and modify your class plans to fit your personality and your needs, as well as those of your students. None of us is the perfect person we would like to be in all areas, but awareness and planning in the areas which dissatisfy us can help to create the kind of classroom we want to have. With this kind of planning and retraining of our behavior, our dreams can become reality.

NOTES - CHAPTER 2

1. Kenneth Soddy, *Clinical Child Psychiatry* (London: Bailliere, Tindall and Cox, 1960), pp. 267–285.

2. Check the teacher's manual for the set of basal readers you use to clarify the publisher's definition of "grade level."

3. Soddy, *op. cit.,* pp. 13–21.

4. William Glasser, *Schools Without Failure* (New York: Harper and Row, 1967), pp. 59–75.

5. Jules Henry, *Culture Against Man*, pp. 313–319.

BIBLIOGRAPHY - CHAPTER 2

Books discussing teachers' attitudes, feelings and expectations:

Jersild, A. T., *In Search of Self*. New York: Teachers College, Columbia University Press, 1952.

Rokeach, M., *The Open and Closed Mind*. New York: Basic Books, 1960.

Rosenthal, Robert and Lenore Jacobson, *Pygmalion in the Classroom: Teacher Expectation and Pupils' Intellectual Development*. New York: Holt, Rinehart and Winston, Inc., 1968.

Ryans, D., *Characteristics of Teachers*. Washington, D.C.: American Council on Education, 1960.

Books discussing present traditional and experimental classrooms:

Gross, Ronald and Beatrice Gross, eds., *Radical School Reform*. New York: Simon and Schuster, Inc., 1969.

Turner, Joseph, *Making New Schools*. New York: David McKay Co., Inc., 1971.

Books discussing misconceptions about intelligence testing:

Lyman, Howard B., *Test Scores and What They Mean*. Englewood Cliffs, N.J.: Prentice Hall, Inc., 1963.

Sigel, I. E., "How Intelligence Tests Limit Understanding of Intelligence." *Merrill-Palmer Quarterly* (1963), *9*:39–56.

CHAPTER 3.

HELPING CHILDREN LEARN

3.

THE TEACHER'S ROLE IN THE CLASSROOM

The development of an open classroom is an attempt to meet the unique needs of each child within the learning situation. Curriculum, materials, classroom organization and teacher's expectations for each child's achievement are tailored to the needs of the individual child, rather than the child's being molded to the needs of the educational organizations, the school, the classroom and the teacher. An important element of the open classroom is freedom. Freedom means that we give each child the chance to choose his own areas of learning, depending upon his interests, his experiences, and his development. He is free to progress at his own developmental rate without having to feel a constant push to keep up with the statistical averages. You do not direct the child's attention and activity to teacher-selected activities. Instead, you encourage each child to learn things he chooses in ways which are meaningful to him. You respect the need of each child to progress according to his developmental state and his past experiences, without trying to turn him into the average mold for his particular age level. You must take your teaching cues from the behavior of each child and then attempt to further his progress in ways possibly quite different from those you use with his peers.

In many traditional classrooms across the country, this pattern is reversed. The teacher does not proceed from the child's level of maturation, experience and interest; she proceeds from the basis of the rigidly structured school system. She expects the child to relate to the content of a predetermined curriculum, and to pace himself according to a fixed rate. The fixed rate is determined by the teacher, and in a broader way by society. The teacher expects the child to develop an absorbing interest in all the things she presents to him. To accomplish this remarkable task, teachers learn to use a variety of tricks and stratagems in order to motivate students and generate interest in otherwise uninteresting topics which curriculum experts view as comprising vitally important information for children to have at particular stages in their development.

Some teachers become gifted in entertaining children and can make them attend to situations and content which might otherwise be uninteresting to them. It is easier and usually more successful to teach the sound of a letter by using a puppet than it is to do it in a straightforward way. By using the puppet, those children who already know the sound are entertained by the show, and so are those who are not yet ready to learn the sounds of letters. Those who are intermediate in relation to these two groups will make a pleasant association to the sound and perhaps have a better memory for it. The orientation of the teacher here is really to entertain the children into learning something which is not directly related to the interests and activities of most of them. This type of teaching robs the child of the opportunity to learn something just for the sake of knowing that thing—because it is interesting or useful to him. This type of teaching also conditions children to expect to be entertained most of the time while they passively absorb and/or judge the performance. When a child learns that letters represent sounds and he wants to learn to read (and most children start out wanting to learn to read), he can learn the sounds of letters with enthusiasm and without tricks. He will often tell you the moment when he is ready by simply asking "What sound does this letter make?"

Other teachers using traditional methods develop very effective means of controlling children in a friendly yet authoritarian manner, and they use this control as a way of forcing children to apply themselves to the recommended curriculum at teacher-directed times. At the very least, this system insures that children will be quiet while the teacher instructs, so that any child willing to learn will be able to hear the teacher's verbal instructions and the information she directs to the learners. The type of relationship the teacher develops with the children can range from one of extreme fondness and affection to one of harsh disciplinarian and authoritarian qualities. Whatever the quality of the relationship, the essential element required to make the entire class attend to the same materials at the same time is control. Thus, the teacher develops a form of friendly or not so friendly coercion to "help" children learn. This type of teaching ignores the fact that children do want to learn and will eagerly seek a teacher's help if the teacher only listens and takes her cues from them instead of adopting a rigid teaching schedule laid out by a curriculum guide or an administrative staff.

The intrinsic value of these traditional modes of teaching are being questioned today as children "tune out" school and the educational system even in their earliest years. Authoritarian controls in the school are gradually being replaced by the encouragement of self-direction and spontaneous interest in learning. We do not want our children to be products of highly controlled learning assembly lines. To change the rigid and authoritarian atmosphere of the classroom, teachers must move into new roles, create new techniques for helping children to learn, and gain more knowledge about how children learn. They must learn to be diagnosticians of learning to be helpful, alert human coordinators in the child's attempts to learn, rather than to remain disciplinarians and administrators supervising and controlling the child's learning situation.

In order to change your role and the actual operations of your classroom, it is vital that you have a very definite idea of what kinds of things you want to encourage in the learning situation. Otherwise you will work aimlessly with an unclear direction to your teaching efforts. Your objectives should determine the teaching techniques you employ. A discussion of some differences between the open classroom and more traditional classrooms may help you to clarify your own expectations and objectives. This in turn will help you to choose appropriate methods by which to achieve your aims.

COMPARISON OF TRADITIONAL CLASSROOMS AND OPEN CLASSROOMS

The most distinctive attribute of the open classroom is its atmosphere of freedom. An examination of the kinds of freedom accorded to students in the open classroom can help to clarify your aims in teaching. We can think of freedom in terms of 1. intellectual pursuits, 2. emotional expression, 3. physical movement, and 4. social interaction. Many persons undoubtedly would insist that elementary school children in traditional classrooms have these freedoms now, but the concept of freedom in all of these areas is a complex network of interacting variables and the traditional classroom may not be as free as many would like to think it is.

INTELLECTUAL FREEDOM

In most traditional classes, the children must learn the specific content the teacher recommends in order to be successful in the school situation. Personal interests are seldom encouraged; and if they are, it is usually in connection with the planned curriculum. In most of our school systems the most valued mental process is memory. The child who can memorize what he must know in order to do well on tests and to respond to questions in class is the child who will be successful in the school system. Although memory is an important mental process in many aspects of life, it certainly is not the only important facet of the human mind. Often the schools neglect equally or more important abilities such as recognizing problems, analyzing problems, convergent and divergent thinking,[1] perceiving and analyzing relationships, and developing awareness of one's own mental functioning.

Children in traditional classes are required to follow and to think in the patterns laid down by their teachers, their textbooks, their workbooks and tests. Thinking outside these lines becomes wasteful and frivolous when a child realizes that these are the learning patterns which he must follow to achieve any kind of recognition or success. Even if a child does not seek success in school, he must adopt these patterns in order to be left alone by demanding adults.[2] If the learning patterns encouraged by the school system and the teacher are either very different from those of a child's family, or from those of an unusually talented child, then that child is faced with learning to subordinate his innate or family-given thinking patterns to those of a regimented school system or a rigid teacher.

If the thought patterns of the school system and of the teacher are very different from those of the child's home environment, as they often are in the ghetto school in the inner city,[3] the child is faced with learning to exist in two different environments instead of being able to concentrate his energy and efforts toward understanding how to be successful and happy in one environment. Since the pulls of home and neighborhood are very strong during the early years, many children reserve their best efforts for this more meaningful world and spend little time trying to achieve in the world of school.

When a teacher holds discussions and encourages children to express their thoughts and feelings, more often than not she expects the children to read her mind and to verbalize what she is thinking (and what she wants them to think). Often children must follow the lines of the teacher's thought rather than exploring all possible alternatives they can conceive of from their own experiences. Their primary learning becomes the ability to anticipate the teacher's thinking patterns. This may be true of the most liberal and humane teachers. A discussion about the evils of war can be just as predetermined and dogmatic as can one about the glory of our flag and the necessity for being patriotic no matter what this country does.

Very often the teacher who is described as skillful and successful is the one who can give enough subtle clues to children to keep the discussion or answer period going in exactly the direction she intends it to go. By picking one child instead of another, by subtle facial expressions as the children express thoughts, and by a variety of obvious and subtle clues, the teacher can surely and carefully guide children to the conclusions she wants them to have. At the end of such a free and open discussion, she can then say that the children volunteered all the answers and that she certainly did not bias the discussion in any way.

Let us examine such a discussion:

Bobby: My uncle lives in Ireland and they are fighting there. They make bombs and have big explosions.

Teacher: They are fighting in Ireland, Bobby. Does anyone know why?

Alice: I saw that on T.V. There were lots of soldiers and fires everywhere.

Jim: Why is there fire everywhere?

Andy: Bombs! Bombs!

Henry: It is really bad to fight. Anybody who fights should be punished.

Teacher: Yes, Henry, it is bad to fight. No one should fight.

Bobby: My uncle must be bad because he is fighting. Sometimes I fight and I get punished. But I still fight.

Teacher: It is better to discuss your difficulties and settle them that way than it is to fight. Fighting is always bad and the Irish and the English should discuss their problems and fight no more.

Although this teacher would feel that she had just held an open discussion with her students, she had in fact predetermined that discussion by very quickly commenting that fighting is bad, thus setting the tone of the discussion with the intrusion of her own value judgment. She did not give the children an opportunity to discuss their views freely and then begin to analyze some of their ideas. The teacher concluded the discussion by settling the entire matter—the English and the Irish should discuss their differences. This spontaneous discussion could have been the beginning of several weeks of investigation and discussion by the children and could have helped them to understand the complexity of relationships between countries and between people of different religious orientations. Instead, it was a brief discussion which concluded simplistically with the idea that fighting is bad. Now most children fight at some time or another, and so do most countries. Does this mean that most children and most countries are bad, or that they rely on fighting as one method of settling disputes? The children who participated in the above discussion may never know or be stimulated enough to find out.

This type of discussion leads students to the conclusion that there is a simple or easy answer for every problem. Obviously there are not answers for every problem, certainly not for problems between people and nations. Such oversimplification does not enhance the intellectual development of students.

True freedom in a class discussion would mean that a child could verbalize his thoughts and experiences and not have them branded right or wrong according to his teacher's thinking patterns and attitudes. There are usually many aspects of any problem or topic, and except for some arithmetical problems, it is very difficult to get the one unquestionable answer. Usually every child has something he can contribute to a discussion based upon his unique experiences. When a teacher narrows her thinking so that only one or two answers will suit her question, she is severely limiting the thinking and attitudes of the students in her charge. Intellectual freedom means allowing and encouraging different views of the same subject. Students can often provide each other with a variety of outlooks on the same situation more adequately than can a single teacher. This supposes a premise that children's experiences and ideas are valuable. To suppress the expression of their thoughts and experiences is to teach them that their ideas are worthless and not acceptable; that the important thing in life (school life) is to figure out the expected answer.

A freer version of the above discussion might go as follows:

Bobby: My uncle lives in Ireland and they are fighting there. They make bombs and have big explosions.

Teacher: They are fighting in Ireland, Bobby. Does anyone know why?

Alice: I saw that on T.V. There were lots of soldiers and fires everywhere.

Jim: Why is there fire everywhere?

Andy: Bombs, bombs!

Linda: I'm Irish but I don't fight.

Teacher: Let's talk about why the Irish are fighting.

John: Nobody should fight, it's bad to fight. I hit my brother and that was bad.

Teacher: Why did you hit him?

John: He took my new racing car away from me.

Joan: John was angry so he hit his brother.

Helen: Maybe the Irish are angry about something.

Bobby: Then my uncle would be angry too because he is Irish.

Alice: Is that what makes people fight all the time, because they are angry?

Teacher: Well, let's try to find out why the Irish are fighting. Then we can see why some other fights have occurred. We can watch the news on T.V. tonight and look in the newspaper to try to get some information. Maybe some of you will try to remember some fights you have had and what started them.

This time the teacher has opened up an intellectual pursuit which has personal and social interest for the students. She has not closed a complex issue by letting her own thinking patterns or moral values intrude upon the thinking of the children before they have had a chance to consider the question at hand.

In the open classroom children are encouraged and expected to express their thoughts. They are also given the opportunity to pursue interesting topics, since they are not expected to rigidly adhere to curriculum schedules. Although free discussions of this type can occur in traditional classrooms with a good teacher, the stress in the open classroom upon freedom, openness and honesty makes such a discussion more possible and more likely to occur. The controlled, teacher directed traditional classroom in general does not encourage children to bring up questions or to speak freely about topics unless the teacher specifically grants permission to do so.

Student Selected Curriculum

As well as honest expression of thoughts and experiences, intellectual freedom also includes the freedom to choose one's own activities and to follow one's own interests. Most children become deeply interested in a wide gamut of subjects and experiences within the environment if they are given the chance. Young children are much more under the influence of their perceptions and sensations than are adults,[4] so that involvement with objects and actions is natural and more intense for them than it may be for older children or for adults.

Many critics of the open classroom do not feel that a young child can be trusted to select learning areas which will be profitable. I think there are two important things to consider in this regard. First, most curriculum guides have been compiled by assessing the natural interests of children of particular ages and pairing these with the expected developmental skills and abilities for that age group. Thus, a 6-year-old is not only supposed to learn about the family, pets and neighborhood helpers in social studies, he is genuinely interested in these topics because the curriculum guides are based upon his experiences and needs. So even without purposely following curriculum guides, we may find that children are spontaneously interested in the topics covered by them (perhaps not in the same sequential order as listed in the guides). Secondly, the total organization of the class and the materials available within it gives control over how children spend their time and what they learn. If you have a magnificently equipped woodworking table in your classroom but only a few math materials, it will not be surprising if more of your students excel in woodworking than in math. Therefore, even giving great freedom to students to choose what they will learn and when, we still maintain controls inherent in the school situation. When we add the interpersonal relationship between teacher and student, even more subtle controls begin to enter the picture so that the student is never really left entirely free to pursue his own interests.

Advocates of the open classroom believe that children have a natural curiosity and drive to explore and master their environment. Because of this, great trust is placed in a child's ability to choose personally significant learning materials. There is no way to validate the reliability of the appropriateness of a child's choice. This can be done only after careful comparison of children given free choice with those given teacher-controlled learning situations. However, the combination of a child's curiosity, the built-in controls of the classroom situation, and the opportunities for the teacher to act as guide and stimulus in many areas, can combine to give the child a well-rounded exposure to a variety of subject matter.

It is important to remember that the controlled curriculum presented by a teacher in a traditional classroom may not be effective. There is no way to control what or how much each child is learning. Any honest teacher would admit that few of her students completely learn the content she presents to them. For many of their students, teachers have only vague ideas of what they have been able to communicate and to teach them. Thus, controlling children's actions in the classroom may give the teacher a sense of achievement and order, but it is a superficial sense at best. Lesson plans may be tidy and comprehensive, but what goes into each student's mind remains a mystery.

It is precisely to counteract this situation containing so many unknown factors that teachers of open classrooms usually choose to allow students to select their own activities and areas of learning. By encouraging students to select their own learning situations, teachers are able to find out what information students already possess, when they need help and how they utilize knowledge and skills in a variety of situations. Although we lose some control over what we present to children and how we allocate their time, we gain substantial knowledge about how and what they are learning.

In a traditional classroom, we only see children using their knowledge and abilities in a few types of situations, and primarily in the test situation. This gives a distorted picture of a child's ability and development. The teacher of the open classroom has more information about each child available to her from observations of the child at work, and she also has more diverse opportunities in which to further a child's learning.

While the open classroom is designed to encourage children to involve themselves deeply and for long periods of time with materials and topics, the more traditional classroom expects something different from the child. Often following rigid time schedules for studying the different subject areas, the teacher of a traditional class gives every student a set time, perhaps 45 minutes, in which to absorb a certain amount of material on one topic. These time periods are decided upon in order to include all subjects and are arranged to fit the six hour school day, as well as any peculiarity in the class schedule such as going to a music or art specialist. They are not arranged to meet the needs of children. In a typical period of math in a traditional class, many students must sit patiently through a repetition of material they already know. Other students just become involved in the lesson when it is time to stop, and many children never understand what is going on although they sit quietly and open and close their books at the proper times. This type of structure does not allow for individual differences in learning needs. Some students require more or less time to learn a task. Some need repetition while others need very little or none. Some benefit from orderly, sequentially arranged material, while others thrive on disorderly situations which they must order for themselves. By allowing students freedom of choice in their learning, the open classroom can accommodate all these individual differences in learning needs within the same classroom organization.

Integration of Content Areas

Freedom of choice in learning activities also tends to dim distinctions between subject areas. Young children do not tend to think of things in terms of math, reading, science, social studies, art, etc. They gradually learn these divisions and classifications from the teacher as they progress in the school system. Since most of their activities in the open classroom are lengthy (in comparison to the short lessons given in a traditional classroom) students tend to use elements from all the disciplines in most of these activities. This is the kind of program which has led to the naming of the English primary school programs as "the integrated day."[5] We used to plan for this kind of multidisciplinary activity with projects—in which all the disciplines were included in some manner under the general pursuit of one topic such as "Housing." In the open classroom, this kind of multidisciplinary usage occurs spontaneously. When a teacher feels that the student's activities are deficient in any area, she can always suggest some activities which might interest the child in that area or lead the child into the activities she has in mind as a natural outgrowth of his self-chosen activity.

Individual Approaches to Learning

An important aspect of intellectual freedom in the classroom requires that the teacher does not bind children's minds by her own limitations in intellectual interests and abilities. Each of us has a relatively stable approach to learning and to dealing with the environment. As we attempt to teach children, we impose upon them our own perceptions and patterns of relating to the outside world as being the right, the smart, or the easy way to do things. Actually, they are only one person's way to do things and thus may not be suitably applied to thirty children, or even to one. To allow children to develop unhampered by our patterns of thinking and behaving, we must observe students carefully, analyze their individual means of dealing with the environment, and attempt to respect their methods while also helping them to learn additional strategies.

A child comes into the world with certain behavioral characteristics. He also learns specific approaches to the environment from his parents.[6] These approaches remain a basic part of his makeup throughout life, and a teacher can add to or modify this repertoire of reactions. Each significant transaction with the environment influences the structure of a child's intellectual development and his potential for expanding his modes of dealing with the environment. To help children truly enlarge their learning potentials and to expand their ability to deal with the world, it is necessary for the teacher to use children's existing patterns as a foundation and try to build upon them, enlarging the child's store of learning tactics. In traditionally run classrooms, the child sees his pre-existing methods of dealing with the world constantly tested and retested in a variety of situations. If his patterns and techniques are successful in terms of his teacher's judgment and of his school's intellectual demands, then he will do well in this class and school. If his learning patterns conflict with those generated by his teacher, he probably will fail in his scholastic efforts. More intelligent and flexible children are often able to discern the necessary standards and learning patterns of their teachers and will adjust and relearn to meet the demands of the teacher if these demands do not conflict greatly with their pre-existing patterns. In this case, the child will be able to adopt these learning patterns and to use them in order to be successful in the school and other similarly oriented situations. For the child whose learning and behavior patterns are unacceptable to the teacher and who is unable to make a successful adjustment, school becomes a place of failure and degradation. It is clear that most schooling engenders a pattern of making children adjust to the school situations and to the teacher's learning and thinking biases in order to succeed. This is hardly intellectual freedom. It might more appropriately be called intellectual tyranny.

Ideally, the teacher should be evaluating and analyzing the children's learning styles and then adjusting her teaching to aid, enhance and extend those styles. In most traditional classrooms such analyses do not occur; the child simply adjusts to the teacher or becomes a school failure. A conflict develops between the teacher who knows what she wants the children to learn and do and the students who cannot or will not change their basic thinking and living styles to satisfy the teacher's demands. This kind of conflict is portrayed very clearly in many inner city schools, where middle-class teachers attempt to teach lower-socio-economic-class children. The different ways of thinking of these two groups lead to misunderstandings on every level and make it almost certain that the students will not do well in school.

An example of this would be a second grade teacher introducing a unit on "Pets." The most popular middle-class pet is a dog and the teacher may begin the unit with "Dogs, Man's Best Friend," or some similar title. In many inner city communities today very large dogs are kept by some residents for protection against criminals, and in some cases against city welfare agency personnel. Other dogs in the ghetto communities are often strays which may harbor diseases, and children have been warned not to touch or go near them. Very poor children may have seen dogs on T.V. commercials eating more than they do themselves. Such children will not provide a very receptive audience for "Dogs, Man's Best Friend." In order to give children intellectual freedom, we must be able to hold our own learning styles and values in abeyance while we analyze those of our students. By respecting the child's individual approaches to problems and the way he uses his mind, it will then become possible for us to enhance and extend his abilities where necessary, rather than simply to judge him as poor, satisfactory, or good.

Even in a classroom where the background of the students and the teacher are similar and the values held by both are fairly consistent, there are constant conflicts between the natural learning style of each student and that of the teacher. An obvious example of this is the student who needs to explore things fully, take them apart if possible, and view them from every possible perspective. In most traditional classrooms, the teacher is interested in communicating facts and having them memorized. Such exploration is unnecessary and time-wasting in terms of her teaching goals. If, in addition, she is a person who likes to grasp things as quickly as possible without extensive investigation, she will find this student lacking in the criteria she has established for success. Unfortunately, teachers give little attention to individual learning styles in most classrooms, so that many teachers would not even be aware of differences between their personal styles and that of a student. This means that their final judgment of the child would be based only on partially objective evaluations.

The enhancement of individual differences within the open classroom setting encourages children to act spontaneously, in their natural style of learning and behaving, rather than in an assumed style which they think will please the teacher. This play of individual differences gives the teacher vital information about children's learning styles and allows the teacher to spot areas of difficulty as well as of assets. Each child can be a success on his own terms and can learn on his own level and in his own way. This respect for individual style and development generates student awareness of their own and others' patterns of behavior. This, in turn, encourages them to try other ways of doing things as they become cognizant of different styles, all of which are acceptable. This helps them to enlarge their own repertoire of behavior, and this self-awareness helps them to realize their strong points and use them to advantage. It may also correct distortions of a child's self-image.

Freedom to explore without censorship or criticism soon gives students the confidence to explore unknown areas without fear of ridicule. Curiosity and interest double and triple when there is no fear of being ridiculed or condemned by a teacher or by peers.

EMOTIONAL FREEDOM

When children are encouraged to have intellectual freedom, they seem spontaneously to exhibit emotional freedom as well. We do not generally encourage children to express their feelings honestly in the classroom or elsewhere; usually we encourage them to express what we as adults think are appropriate feelings for specific situations. School generally teaches children how to have the stereotyped emotions which are acceptable by the general populace. One is supposed to feel happy about going to a party, although there may be many other ways to feel. One should feel sad when a friend goes away. In fact, there are a variety of emotions one can feel, and none of them are so simple as sad or happy.

To encourage children to express their emotions means that we as teachers must relate to these more complex emotions which are not the cultural stereotypes. This is often difficult and painful to do because many of these emotions will not be happy or joyful ones. It is much easier to relate to the stereotyped emotional expressions than it is to relate to the complex variety of emotions which may be evoked in an individual by a particular situation. For this reason, many teachers never deal with emotions. It is easier not to encourage freedom of emotional expression. Often this is because they see their role in a global sense: they must be able to give an answer or solution when a student expresses any feelings or conflicts about what he does and should feel.

If a child tells you that his father does not love him, you might immediately react by accepting the statement as true and giving the child a generalization such as, "All fathers love their sons," to deal with the situation. If you say this with a certain finality, the child would probably understand the clue that he is not to mention anything more about it, that he should accept your culturally approved statement. However, if you were attempting to encourage emotional freedom you might not accept this surface statement as true or as indicative of the entire story. If you questioned the child about his reason for thinking his father did not love him, you might find that he felt the loss of his father's love because he broke his father's pipe yesterday; or because there are no girls in the family and his father desperately wanted him to be ˙a girl. Any of these things might have prompted the child to make the initial comment and any of them might be true.

To truly encourage emotional freedom and expression you must seek the facts which stimulated the expression, and explore the meaning those facts have for the child. Sometimes children simply try to get a reaction from you when they need attention for some reason. In other instances, the child's intellectual capacity at a specific age may not be developed enough for him to distinguish minor incidents, such as breaking his father's pipe, from more serious family problems, such as being rejected because he is not a girl. However upsetting a child's verbalization of his feelings may be to you, it is essential that you explore a little and find out what the child is really saying and what the feelings mean to him. A friend of mine was very upset when a second grader told her that his family told him he was retarded. When my friend gained control of her own feelings and was able to pursue the subject with the child, she found that the boy did not know what this word meant and was seeking some information from his teacher in order to understand what was happening in his home. A first grader in my class came to me before lunch to tell me that she was going to commit suicide when she went home. She had been a very depressed child in the beginning of the year and had only recently begun to be more cheerful and to relate to me and to her fellow students. When she told me she was going to commit suicide, I could not help but do an inner doubletake. I attempted to control my feelings and, as calmly as possible, I inquired why she was going to do so. She replied that her mother made her wear her brother's hat this morning and that she was a girl and not a boy, and she would rather kill herself than wear a boy's hat. I agreed that it was most unfair. She skipped off to lunch happily. She had simply wanted someone to share her feelings and commiserate with her over her bad luck.

Immature Emotional Reactions in Students

Children may make emotionally charged statements which have different meanings for them than they do for you. Remember that they are immature in all aspects of their development, including emotional development and awareness. Just as their statements about things they are learning reveal an egocentric and immature point of view, so do their statements about their own feelings. You must not read into these statements your own feelings, which are those of a mature adult.

In order to ascertain the meaning and significance of such a statement, you must explore it further with questions as to the child's specific meaning and understanding of the situation. This will help you evaluate the authenticity of the child's feelings and the seriousness of the situation. In most cases the situation can be dealt with easily within the classroom situation. In instances where there is a more serious problem, you may have to discuss it with the parents or the school guidance counselor to further explore the meaning of what the child tells you. Sometimes a child may be upset because of his inability to assess a situation, and you can improve his ability to interpret reality situations by clearing up the situation with parents or whomever is involved. In the case of more serious family problems it may be necessary to talk with parents and perhaps refer them to the school guidance counselor.

Very often children's thinking and emotions become distorted because of their limited intellectual capacity to understand the world and the people around them. Their egocentricity makes them think they are responsible for many things and does not allow them to perceive the intricate relationships and causalities which may exist about them.[7] Part of a good teacher's job is to correct as many of these distortions as possible before they become emotionally and intellectually crippling ones. The functioning of a child in these two areas is interdependent and we cannot deal with only the intellectual aspect of a child's development. In the open classroom you will have many more opportunities to learn what children think and feel as they become comfortable in revealing their thoughts and feelings to you. The honesty and directness with which children are treated in the open classroom enables them to use honesty and directness in their thinking and feelings.

Sometimes you find a child who is confronted with serious family problems and his parents are uninterested or uncooperative; perhaps the best thing you can do in such a case is to help him to cope with his private problems as well as possible. It is often painful to do this when we would like the child's home life to be ideal, but it is better to help a child in this way than it is to try to deny the problem and cut off communication between yourself and the child. This may be the only communication with an understanding adult which the child has experienced. Like the girl who was going to commit suicide, there are many children who just need someone to recognize the pain and difficulty of their situations. They do not expect you to do anything about these situations, no matter how serious they may be.

Handling Emotions in the Open Classroom

In traditionally run classrooms students seldom reveal their real feelings because the atmosphere is generally restrictive and controlled. Teachers do not have the time to observe or relate to individual children long enough to get this type of information. They are too busy maintaining group discipline or conducting formal lessons to spend any amount of time listening to individual children. In an open classroom, however, you are free to spend more time talking with and observing students so that you are ultimately in a better position to help them learn. You can begin to know them as unique people with all the complexities and problems that each of us must deal with. The general freedom in the open classroom will encourage each child to be free in expressing feelings as well as ideas. As they see evidence of your interest in such feelings and your concern for each child as a valued person, the students will express more and more important feelings to you.

Students also become aware of the times you are able to talk intimately with them. I once had an 8-year-old black boy named Harry who had a very poor self-image. One day he began beating up one of the black dolls in the housekeeping corner; obviously the doll represented himself. I grabbed the doll away from him and told him I loved it and would not let him hurt it. We had a hectic chase around the room, but I succeeded in protecting the doll from his attack and showing Harry symbolically that I cared about him even if he did not care about himself. As his self-image slowly improved in the following weeks, we would have periodic chases to save the doll, which reassured him of my continuing concern for him when he was feeling low. One day when we were involved with this ritual chase some visitors came into the room and wanted to talk with me about how the class operated. I wondered what would happen, but simply told Harry that I could not go on with this chase for the moment and that we would have to continue it later. He accepted this as easily as if I had suggested he stop coloring a picture and do some math. He was well behaved while the visitors were in the room and later in the day I suggested we continue our chase to save the little black doll and we did. Harry's ability to delay his emotional needs taught me that children will usually be able to wait for you if they feel you are concerned about them and sincere in your intention to help them.

The Teacher's Emotional State

It may be the case that a teacher is so out of touch with her own feelings that she cannot tolerate the feelings of others. In this case it will not matter what type of classroom she operates. She will not be able to encourage children to express feelings because it will threaten the defenses which she has built up against feeling anything herself. This is a personal problem which every teacher must face privately and attempt to change if possible. All of us probably suppress children's feelings and interests in some isolated areas or subjects because we are unable to face our own feelings in those areas. It is very common for people who have difficulty expressing their angry feelings to suppress all angry feelings in their students. Although this particular kind of suppression gives the impression of a calm and pleasant classroom atmosphere, it is not very realistic in terms of real feelings and situations which occur. All of us feel anger at some time or another, and to deny it or suppress it can eventually lead to mental defenses which can cripple us in expressing other feelings, such as joy and happiness. It is more constructive to admit to the feelings of anger, attempt to understand their source, and find permissible and constructive ways to handle them or express them.

Generally, teachers have handled emotional expression either by encouraging students to suppress their true feelings, substituting more conventional ones in their place; or by allowing the child so much unchannelled expression of feeling that he is overwhelmed by the intensity of his own feelings and often disliked by others who must bear the brunt of his unchecked emotional expression. The important job that the teacher is in a position to do is not to suppress or to encourage the child's original feelings, but rather to help him find constructive ways and acceptable modes in which to express them. The flexibility and broad range of activities that are possible within the open classroom facilitate this.

Expressing Emotions in the Classroom

When given the chance, children often will find their own ways to express emotions by using various materials or by creating games which in fantasy satisfy their unmet needs or their hitherto unexpressed feelings. A child may pound out some clay to take symbolic revenge on a fellow student with whom he has argued or had a disagreement. A girl who always wants to be first may initiate games in which she leads the action of the other children. Barring this kind of spontaneous selection of substitute behaviors in which feelings can be expressed and resolved, it is always possible to introduce a punching bag in the class for children to express their feelings of anger and frustration in a very direct way. One teacher I know has a soft carpet in the back of her room to accommodate children at times when they feel sad or need some semi-private contemplation of their course in life. The direct expression of happy feelings are always welcomed in an open classroom because they do not interfere with schedules and routines. Less socially acceptable feelings such as anger or jealousy are accepted and channelled into constructive expressions or activities when possible. In this way, the child can discharge the feeling when it occurs and immediately go on to learn and involve himself in more productive learning activities. In a more traditional classroom, where such a flexible scheduling is not practiced, the child may be using all his energy to suppress his feelings and may be unable to concentrate on lessons or learning for the entire day or longer.

There are some feelings which people do not express in a public situation such as a school situation. You can help children recognize this fact if they do not already know it. Young children and sometimes older ones often display sexual interest and feelings in the classroom—sometimes through questions or sometimes more directly in the form of masturbation or intense interest in the opposite sex. Because of social taboos, these sexual concerns and behavior are usually suppressed. You can help children realize that their sexual curiosity and feelings can be channelled into learning about their bodies and feelings in a forthright way. However, you must also help children realize that these are personal and intimate feelings which are pursued in depth with their families or intimate friends.

Frequently, when some teachers begin the open classroom techniques, they are surprised by the amount of children's verbalizations on the subjects of sex and violence. In view of the sex and violence on TV, however, it is easy to grasp why this happens; certainly these two areas pose important problems within our society which are unresolved and of consuming interest to everyone. It is not too surprising that in an honest and free atmosphere children begin to express these societal concerns for which there are no easy answers. They must sense the preoccupation of adults with these matters and yet get little help from parents or teachers in dealing with such matters themselves. After an initial outpouring of questions, the children seem to go on to other areas of interest and learning, so that if you can remain calm during these first days, you will find the talk of sex and violence decreases almost as abruptly as it begins. The verbalization of these matters may be a catharsis for the children, as well as a way for them to test your sincerity in allowing them freedom of expression.

As teachers, we communicate to students the mores and values of the society in which we live. We also have the chance to help them to learn that there is nothing wrong with personal feelings they have which may conflict with general societal expectations. The problem arises when they attempt to express their feelings. We have the opportunity to help each child find the most appropriate means for such expression through using a wide variety of materials and activities within the classroom. If a child gets the idea that his feelings are bad or wrong and must not be expressed or even felt, then he is likely to develop crippling defense mechanisms which will effect every area of his development adversely. If feelings are expressed in such a way that they hurt others, then this type of expression and *not the feeling itself* is wrong and harmful. Thus emotional freedom involves the *freedom to feel* and to accept our feelings as part of ourselves. It does not mean the freedom to express feelings in any manner without regard for what such expression may do to one's self or to others.

PHYSICAL FREEDOM

Although less damaging in some respects than the intellectual and emotional control of children, the control of their physical movements also interferes with healthy growth in every sphere of development. Young children need to move about, not only to strengthen their muscles and to release tension, but also to transact with their environment, and to learn from these transactions. To keep them seated for long periods of time and deprived of sensual contact with their world is a harmful and destructive way to deal with their bodies and their minds. It is impossible to separate physical and intellectual learning from one another. They stimulate and complement each other.

The Role of Physical Activity in Intellectual Development

If you expect a child to learn about the things and the people in his environment, then you must allow and encourage interaction with these things. Adults often utilize verbal interaction as one of their main methods of dealing with things and people. We have somehow lost the sensitivity of touch and movement which children have in their earliest years and would perhaps maintain if we encouraged them to do so. Instead, we attempt to move them into a sensorially deprived world where they deal primarily with abstractions and symbols. By the first grade, children are often expected to sit quietly for long periods during the day with relatively little sensory stimulation (except visual) to involve them in learning.

According to the theory of Piaget,[8] young children often are so dominated by their perceptions of the physical world and their movements within it, that they do not have the ability voluntarily to pull themselves away from such stimulation and involvement. They give themselves over completely and involuntarily to perception and physical sensations. Some children may even need protection from this kind of overstimulation. As children grow older they gradually develop the ability to relate to things in a less personal and less intense way. They are better able to separate themselves from the world about them and to use representations of things and people in their thinking,[9] rather than the real objects themselves. After the age of 10 or 11 years, children are able to begin thinking and reasoning abstractly without any need for using real objects, except in the early stages of learning new things, or for occasional reference.

When children have a limited number of real experiences in which they are sensually stimulated, their concepts will not be as rich and varied, their sense of mastery of their world will not be as great, and their contact with the sensual aspects of life will atrophy. Adults are spending millions of dollars today participating in encounter groups so that they can relearn how to touch and to feel and to move. They are attempting to reacquaint themselves with all the sensory stimuli available, to reorient their senses, their bodies and their minds to deal with these stimuli. Children do these things naturally and it is vital that teachers provide the kind of atmosphere and learning which will keep them actively using their senses. The open classroom provides ample opportunity for children to involve themselves actively with the things around them in a concrete and sensorially stimulating manner. It should also provide ample learning activities with symbolic and abstract situations for those students who are ready to move on to higher levels of thinking. Sometimes, in their eagerness to change from the stuffy, traditional classroom with its abstract and remote intellectual content, teachers go to the opposite extreme of providing only concrete learning activities for students. Obviously this can be just as detrimental to the development of children's minds as the abstractness of the traditional classroom.

Physical Movement as a Diagnostic Tool

Movement and action are vital and important parts of a child's life. His interests, attitudes and knowledge will be expressed in them. There is no quicker way to find out what a child is like than to allow him freedom to move about and interact with others and his surroundings. More and more we are realizing that all actions are indicative of how a person approaches life.[10] When you see a child immediately begin to explore the materials in a classroom, you can be sure that he is straightforward and sure of himself in dealing with things. The child who holds back and cannot become interested in any activity is crippled in some way in dealing with his environment. It may be emotionally if he is very shy, it may be intellectually if he cannot be stimulated or cannot initiate any activity with interesting materials. It may be a physical or chemical disability which keeps him from performing because of poor perception or poor coordination. Whatever the reason, if a young, healthy child can find nothing to interest him when he is shown a variety of materials, then something is wrong.

Physical Activity in the Traditional Classroom

As we change our perspectives on what constitutes important learning and realize that children must not only be stimulated by their environment, but must be able to act upon it simultaneously in order to learn, we also realize the importance of giving children the freedom to involve themselves with the environment when they need to do so. Physically constrictive teaching methods are remote, uninvolving, and ultimately less effective than those which encourage children to move and interact freely with the environment at their own discretion. This type of physical involvement endows their learning with a sense of immediacy and with vivid sensory associations, and seems to make the learning more important and more memorable.

In traditional classes, good teachers have recognized the need for the periodic release of physical tension. They allow children to have these intermittent periods of physical exercise in teacher-controlled situations, allowing such freedoms as jumping next to a desk, doing prescribed exercises, etc. They may allow students to play games or have group activities. These activities also attempt to drain off the accumulated physical tensions which have developed during prolonged periods of sitting quietly and concentrating on teacher-prescribed lessons or tasks, and wrestling with the monotony of boredom, confusion, or repetition. In formally prescribed periods of physical activity, such as recess or gym periods, the teacher often controls the physical activity. Every student may be expected to do the same thing at the same time in exactly the same way. In some classes the students must develop almost military-like precision. Unless they are rehearsing for a performance of some type, it seems unnecessary to be so demanding and restrictive.

Physical Activity in the Open Classroom

In the open classroom, students always have freedom of movement as long as they do not interfere with the activities of others. There is no logical reason to curtail movement when everyone is involved in different activities, and students are unlikely to be seriously distracted from their learning by the movement of another child, as often happens in a traditional classroom. When children are very involved in their activities, they are not easily distracted. In the traditional classroom, where students are not always interested in the material they must study, the slightest movement can distract an entire class. In more formal open classroom group periods of activity involving dancing, movement or games, students are encouraged to show their individual differences by doing the same thing as classmates but doing it in their own way rather than in a regimented way.

SOCIAL FREEDOM

Social freedom in the traditional classroom is usually minimal if it exists at all. Children are placed in seats by the teacher and their interaction is limited, except for group projects, occasional recess periods and perhaps a period of free time sometime during the day. Even at a class party there are usually scheduled events and directed activities which limit the normal amount of social interaction that might occur spontaneously. Most of the meaningful talk within the classroom goes on between pupil and teacher, not between pupil and pupil. Children are usually taught to react to peers in culturally stereotyped ways. Within the classroom, this means that they should interact as seldom as possible with other students so that quiet and order are maintained. This makes classroom life run more smoothly but it does not help children learn how to get along with their peers in many different situations. Considering that the students spend the bulk of their day in a crowded space with about thirty other children, it seems strange that we do so little to help them to learn how to relate to each other except on the most superficial level.

The open classroom usually provides unlimited social interaction at the discretion of the individual child. There are times during the day when children are quiet in order to listen to the teacher or to each other, or to complete work in which they become involved. However, other than at specified or agreed upon times, students can move and interact freely with each other. This provides ample opportunity for them to experiment with many ways of relating to their peers in a controlled situation where a helpful teacher can encourage them to learn from each other and to find new ways of relating to each other.

Children in a traditional classroom behave in certain prescribed, teacher-directed ways rather than in spontaneous ways, and may even develop school personalities which contrast with their usual personalities at home. It is often difficult to imagine what they are like outside the classroom; this is because they have submerged their true personalities to develop the social façade the teacher expects or demands. Because children in the open classroom are directing their own actions and interactions with others, they tend to present a clearer picture of their real selves. Because of this, children's problems in relating to other children and to adults become much more apparent within the open classroom. In the traditional classroom setting, you would not have a chance to see many of these problems because of the many controls and regimented behavior required of students. Since children have little free choice concerning their actions, you would not see how they would appraise situations or people and then how they would act in relation to them.

Evaluating Students' Social Needs

When children are allowed to relate naturally to people and situations, it gives you a chance to evaluate their strengths and their weaknesses in this area, and to help them to find more and better ways of relating to others. In the case of a child who is very unsuccessful in his attempts to relate to his peers, you have an opportunity to help him to find more successful ways of relating, rather than constantly meeting with failure. Children learn how to relate to others from their parents and their experiences with siblings and peers outside of school. Most of these situations happen somewhat randomly and with little direct guidance for the child (except in the case of parental guidance). In the classroom you have an unusual opportunity to observe these patterns of social interaction and to intervene when necessary to help to improve them.

Perhaps the most common problem which occurs in social relationships is that of how to settle arguments. Children who have problems with aggression will tend to start fights in the open classroom setting. They might also do it in a traditional classroom, but with the atmosphere of freedom and experimentation, there is more likelihood that these aggressive feelings will be expressed in a free atmosphere. It would be easy for us as teachers if no one ever attempted to take out his aggressions on others, but obviously this is a part of life and finding some adequate resolution of these feelings should be a part of growing up. Children must learn that they can have aggressive feelings but that they must express them in some way which does not hurt others. I have always felt that I would rather have children start their fights within the classroom where I could prevent someone's being hurt and where I could help the children to channel their aggression into some less dangerous means of expression. Children will argue and fight no matter what we would like them to do. It is better to help them to realize the meaning and the consequences of their fighting than it is simply to suppress it in the classroom and have it flare into possibly dangerous situations on the street or in a situation where no adults are present to intervene.

Perhaps one of our fears of letting children talk and interact freely is that they will be wasting their time instead of spending it in important learning. In the open classroom, the teacher has an opportunity to listen more closely to children's conversations and arguments. She usually will find that some very important matters are being discussed and that often important learning is going on, intellectual as well as social (assuming we can separate the two). You may be surprised at some of the very heated arguments which develop over the results of the children's manipulations of materials or investigations of topics. These arguments all serve to help children to exchange information as well as to formulate social behavior. When there is serious disagreement, students will be very motivated to do research, learning how and where to get information they need to substantiate their ideas. This type of interchange also helps them to learn how to argue constructively and to learn from each other independently of a teacher.

The most important aspect of freedom in social relationships is that it helps to prepare children for a lifetime of relating to others. It prepares them more effectively than a controlled atmosphere in which they do not actively participate in social relationships, but instead learn stereotyped recipes for relating to others. Just as a repertoire of recipes is limiting in the intellectual and emotional sphere, it is also limiting in the social sphere. The child who is perfectly adjusted to the controlled routines of the traditional school experience is not the one who will do well in the real world where people must find ways of relating to each other in a variety of unstructured situations. It is grossly apparent today that the old recipes for getting along with others are not working as society is in the midst of rapid social change. Children need to be equipped with experience and skills in assessing social situations and in finding appropriate and successful solutions for their needs and purposes.

With this comparison between the operations of the traditional classroom and the open classroom, I have tried to give you a better basis for deciding on the focus and aims you wish to incorporate in your own classroom practice. You can encourage almost any type of learning in either classroom setting, but because of its flexibility and its organization based upon the needs of the individual rather than upon those of the group, the open classroom affords many more opportunities to develop a wide variety of learning.

It is clear that the teacher of the open classroom provides a much freer atmosphere for her students in the choice of learning materials, subject matter and opportunities to transact meaningfully with things and people. She allows the child to work at tasks which are comfortable for his developmental level and to advance to more complex tasks when the child is ready and able to do so. Although the goals of the open classroom teacher and those of the traditional classroom teacher may in many instances be the same, it is obvious that they are implementing them in very different ways and communicating different things to students.

The following chapters deal very specifically with how to go about designing your classroom in such a way as to implement your personal goals, whatever they may be. The more certain you are about what your goals are for your students, the easier it will be for you to do the basic planning which will give form and reality to those goals.

NOTES - CHAPTER 3

1. J. P. Guilford, "Basic Conceptual Problems in the Psychology of Thinking," in *Fundamentals of Psychology: The Psychology of Thinking* (Annals of the New York Academy of Sciences, 91, 1960), pp. 9–19.

2. John Holt, *How Children Fail* (New York: Pitman Publishing Corporation, 1964), pp. 3–33.

3. James Herndon, *The Way It Spozed to Be* (New York: Simon and Schuster, 1968).

4. Jean Piaget, *Six Psychological Studies,* pp. 17–38.

5. Vincent R. Rogers, *Teaching in the British Primary School,* pp. 60–61.

6. Robert D. Hess and Virginia C. Shipman, "Maternal Influences Upon Early Learning: The Cognitive Environments of Urban Pre-School Children." In *Early Education,* Robert D. Hess, and Roberta M. Bear, eds. (Chicago: Aldine Publishing Co., 1968), pp. 91–104.

7. Jean Piaget, *Six Psychological Studies,* pp. 17–38.

8. Jean Piaget, *Six Psychological Studies,* pp. 17–38.

9. Jerome Bruner, *The Process of Education* (New York: Vintage Books, 1960), pp. 33–54.

10. Julius Fast, *Body Language* (New York: M. Evans and Co., Inc., distributed in association with J. B. Lippincott Co., 1970).

BIBLIOGRAPHY - CHAPTER 3

Bruner, Jerome, *Toward A Theory of Instruction*. Cambridge: Harvard University Press, 1966.

Kohl, Herbert R., *The Open Classroom*. New York: Vintage Books, 1970.

Lindvall, C. M., ed., *Defining Educational Objectives*. Pittsburgh: University of Pittsburgh Press, 1964.

Minuchin, Patricia, Barbara Biber, Edna Shapiro and Herbert Zimiles, *The Psychological Impact of School Experience*. New York: Basic Books, 1969.

Murrow, Casey and Liza Murrow, *Children Come First*. New York: American Heritage Press, 1971.

Rathbone, Charles H., ed., *Open Education: The Informal Classroom*. New York: Citation Press, 1971.

Spaulding, R. L., "Personality and Social Development, Peer and School Influences." *Review of Educational Research* (1964), *34*: 588–589.

CHAPTER 4.

A BASIC ORGANIZATION

4.

COMMUNICATING WITH STUDENTS THROUGH CLASSROOM ORGANIZATION AND ROUTINES

When you have some idea of what you hope to accomplish with students and what you realistically can attempt, given your personality and attitudes, you are ready to begin planning a basic organization for your open classroom. The spatial arrangements, the materials and the organization of time and routines will all communicate your feelings and intentions to your students. If you seat children alphabetically or according to height, you are telling them that you intend to control their placement in the room by arbitrary details over which they have no control. If you restrict their movements about the room by insisting that they raise their hands to sharpen a pencil, to go to the bathroom or to leave their seats for any reason, you are beginning to accumulate rules which tell children you wish to be in complete control of their physical placement and movement within the classroom.

As you repeat this message in situation after situation, i.e., that you are in control of everything going on in the room, your students are faced with an inevitable conclusion. In order to succeed in your class, they must conform to your need to control them. If, on the other hand, you allow children to choose their own seats and move about the room as necessary, you will indicate to them that this is a class where they themselves are responsible for the control of their placement and movements.

Because of a rigid concept of what school should be, children (and adults) sometimes interpret freedom within the classroom as thoughtlessness or indifference on the part of the teacher. Their interpretations will depend upon prior experiences with teachers and schools. Many of the rules and controls which are standard in traditional classrooms are accepted by students and teachers alike as part of what school should and must be. Although many of these rules may have served valid purposes at some time in the past, a great many of them are today outdated and unnecessary in view of our knowledge about how children grow and learn.

We are beginning to realize that a tightly controlled classroom cannot provide a satisfactory learning environment for young children. Control of children's behavior and anticipation of their needs have been thought to be ways of expressing positive feelings for children. Yet this kind of attention in an educational situation can deprive children of chances to learn how to control themselves and how to care for and to anticipate their own needs. To communicate growth-directed purposes to students, you must follow initial signs of freedom with other signs that communicate your interest in the students' development of personal responsibility and initiative. Soon students will have no doubt about your intentions and they will realize that they have opportunities to grow in many areas, utilizing free choice and self-direction.

Children will be able to learn and grow only in the directions you allow. Most of us probably give a varied pattern of such communications, allowing growth and independence in some areas but not in others. We often are unaware of the messages we give to children through our actions and behavior, and are subsequently surprised at some of the results we see. We may also be surprised at the lack of results when we are expecting to see results. Once, as I observed a first grade class, the teacher called upon individual children to come to the front of the room and hold up paintings they had just completed. The teacher seemed very pleased by one particular painting and she suggested that the class tell her what it looked like to them. She received several imaginative answers. She seemed displeased with all of them, however, and finally stated that *she* thought it looked like an Indian rug. This teacher really was asking the students to guess what she associated with this picture, and she was surprised when the children did not guess the right answer. The scarcity of the children's responses probably was due to the fact that these children already knew when the teacher asked them to be creative or imaginative that she was in reality asking them to guess what was already in her mind. How many of us must do the same thing without realizing it.

With clear ideas of your goals with students, it can be a relatively simple matter for you to plan ways of communicating your intentions to students in a clear, concrete manner. If you are going to achieve your goals, you must live and practice the principles you expect children to learn within the structure of the classroom. Through the many activities and routines which make up the organization of a classroom, you can provide the kind of living experience which will embody the values and goals you feel are important. If you are attempting to change your style of teaching, this organization will also help you. It will support your efforts for change by providing both a different atmosphere and different teaching situations from the ones to which you have been accustomed. This will force you to search for new ways to handle these unexpected situations. If you attempt to change your behavior without changing your surroundings and the kind of activity which goes on in your classroom, it will be much harder for you to achieve any change in your teaching style. It is too easy to slip back into old habits when the surroundings are the same as they have always been.

In this chapter we will survey these routines and organizational considerations which many teachers handle as meaningless details, feeling that they have little importance. You will be a more successful teacher if you plan these details with consistency and continuity. You will be more successful if you do not miss the chance to let students know how you feel about them and what your expectations of their lives in school are. I have tried to discuss as many variations of procedures as I felt would be helpful. They are meant to be thought-provoking and, hopefully, they will be springboards for your own individual and creative variations.

There is no way to learn about the personalities or abilities of your students until the first weeks of school. Even if you read over their records before you meet them, you will have little information of any value. You will have no information about how the students operate together as a group. Because of this surprise element in teaching, there are many things which you cannot plan in advance. You will not be able to anticipate and plan for the many decisions you will have to make and the various situations you may encounter. You will not be able to foresee all the varied interests and needs of your students or the depth or rate of the learning which will occur in your class. However, there are many aspects which must be settled before the students enter the room on that first day. It is possible to plan basic routines which

express your educational philosophy and which will be suitable
for any group of students.

THE CURRICULUM

The most important decision you must make as you begin
planning is how you will deal with the curriculum. This will determine many of your decisions in other organizational details of
running your class. Educators in this country are quite reluctant
to give students complete freedom of choice in the content they
study. They feel that students will not have sufficient exposure to
subjects they should know or to situations which will develop
basic intellectual skills. We have no sure way to determine what
will happen to children left to their own motivations in choosing
learning areas. No controlled studies have been done covering
children taught in this way over a period of time.

Many educators and parents believe that children would
learn more important things and more content if they were given
freedom of choice. They argue that basic skills are involved in all
learning and in all subject matter, and that the child must learn
them as he pursues his interests. They also believe that children
would enjoy this type of learning and would not develop the negative attitudes they often do develop toward the standard curriculum offered in traditional classrooms, and toward learning itself.

To consider this issue fairly, we must think about what children learn when they are presented with a standard curriculum.
If we are honest about the quantity of the curriculum which children absorb and understand in a traditional classroom where it is
routinely and completely presented, we might estimate that one-
third to one-half of the students gain some vague idea of the
content of the teacher's lessons. The remainder of the students
may have no understanding of what the teacher is trying to
communicate. At best they may be able to cite unconnected and
irrelevant facts which have stuck in their memory as isolated
phenomena, occurring without a context. Even among those children who absorb some of the content of lessons, understanding is
often superficial and incomplete. It is deceptive to believe that
children will learn simply because they are presented with a
specific curriculum in a definite sequential order.

The pressure in most of our schools causes teachers to rush through the curriculum in order to fit it all in between assemblies, music classes, art classes and gym. I was once supervising a very capable student-teacher who gave an introductory social studies lesson on Germany. No mention was made of Hitler or the Nazi regime. After the lesson, I expressed my surprise about this. She was also surprised, but had been reluctant to bring the topic into the discussion because she felt she might not be able to handle the strong feelings which might arise. Her attitude itself may have been enough to suppress any mention of the topic. I suggested that I come the following day and that she continue the discussion, this time bringing up Hitler. If she got into difficulty, I could help her with the discussion. She agreed, but later that night called me to say that her cooperating teacher had told her there was no more time for Germany, that the program called for going on to Switzerland the next day and France the day after that. To teach in such a hurried and incomplete manner is a waste of your time and a great disservice to students.

As we rush through the curriculum, we often have only vague ideas of what each child knows in a particular content area. Unfortunately, we usually do not have the time to find out. We do know fairly well what most children know about reading, and in some cases, about math. Because of the emphasis on these two subjects, we tend to spend more time on them and we are more careful of our evaluations in these content areas. We are less careful about making realistic evaluations of children's abilities or development in other areas. Even when we do see indications that a child needs help in developing particular skills or knowledge, there is rarely time to give help because then we would fall too far behind in the scheduled curriculum.

For these reasons, it is not strange that many of us are attempting to use the curriculum in a new way—as a flexible framework for structuring the concepts and the content we choose to emphasize or encourage among the diverse interests of our students. In my experience, students in an open classroom bring up three or four times the amount of material covered by a standard curriculum. Your greatest task soon becomes that of deciding which direction to take with students, what topics to pursue in depth and what ones to limit, based upon student interest and willingness.

If you have a frame of reference in making this type of

decision, rather than emphasizing one thing instead of another from some random or unconscious choice, or from personal interest, your students will integrate their studies more coherently and will begin themselves to make choices which are based on some continuity with previous work. The frame of reference you use can be the curriculum guide of your school system. In most systems the curriculum guides are only *suggested* guides which are meant to provide some continuity and similarity regarding the things children learn. The planning and thinking behind these guides is usually quite sound from the standpoint of what children can learn, and of what they are interested in at various ages. The problem has always been to get a whole classroom of children interested in the same thing at the same time, a truly impossible task. It is possible to give up this fruitless task, but it is not necessary to abandon the sound suggestions contained in curriculum guides.

Let us suppose some boys in your third grade class begin playing cowboy and then become more interested in how cowboys lived (to complete details of their play). They may begin by getting books about the lives of cowboys—by their own choice or by your suggestion. You can easily step in at this point to provide focus to the research they are doing on the lives of cowboys. You might want to direct their attention to the cowboy as an essential person in supplying food. Or you might try to contrast the life of the nomadic cowboy with that of the more settled ranchers or townspeople. All this learning can be incorporated into the play situation itself for more exciting and memorable learning. The particular focus you choose could be a direct result of the suggestions of your curriculum guide. It might also be something which is not in the curriculum guide but which the class seems ready and strongly motivated to pursue. It will be much easier for you if you have some guide for yourself regarding the selection of a focus, otherwise student play such as that described above often disintegrates into rather meaningless activity which does not last long.

State and Local Laws

As a teacher, you are responsible for carrying out state and local laws which are concerned with the amount of time spent teaching particular subjects in the classroom. There is no question that you must be guided by these laws unless you have specific permission from officials to dispense with them. If you do not know what these laws are, find out before you develop your program. In most states the legal requirements are general ones— that certain subjects be taught in certain grades and, in some cases, that a given time period be established for teaching the particular subject. The local school board may also have their own laws or rules. These laws, however, are not usually concerned with how you teach a subject. Because of this, there need be nothing incongruous between these laws and regulations and the development of your open classroom practices. If you are dealing with a requirement that citizenship be taught for two hours weekly, this does not mean that it must be taught for two hours consecutively, or for four consecutive half-hours. General citizenship teaching can be incorporated flexibly into your daily life in the classroom and can in this way easily meet the necessary requirements. This kind of presentation would also make for much more effective teaching than having isolated half-hour lessons which would have little real meaning in the lives of the students.

If you feel there are laws or regulations which would severely hamper your open classroom plans, it may be possible for you to develop some alternative plan and present it to your principal for approval. This might comprise an experimental program to improve the teaching of certain material by presenting it in a different way. Or you might be able to get permission to run an experimental program of some sort, after agreeing upon the details with administrators, in which the laws or regulations you feel would hamper you can be suspended or modified. It is becoming easier to do this kind of thing, since the open classroom concept has become very popular in this country due to publicity about the English primary schools. Many schools are attempting to institute at least one or two open classrooms, if only to enhance their prestige or to please parents.

Variations of the Open Classroom

If you work in a system which is rigid about the timing of lessons and about uniformity in the teaching of subject matter, you may have to modify the open classroom concept. Or you may feel that you are not personally ready to devote the entire day to individualized free choice. This does not mean that you cannot have some version of an open classroom. It is possible to teach all the required curriculum in the morning and leave afternoons open for free activities. It is also possible to teach group lessons in such a way that all children participate in the general lesson, but each one is encouraged to pursue his individual interest and skills within the broad scope of the lesson. Usually after the presentation of a lesson, each student is free to take some aspect of the topic to pursue in any way which interests him. This allows for individual differences in development as well as in motivation. This certainly encourages the development of intellectual freedom and independence in learning, although it may not embody other aspects of the open classroom concept.

You can work on a contract system with students. Contracts consisting of an agreement to cover a certain amount of work in a certain time are planned and agreed upon by student and teacher prior to the initiation of the work. Contracts can be used in combination with group lessons and/or free choice individualized work. You may also incorporate individual interests into contracts which are set up in addition to the required curricular ones. This procedure allows children to receive the maximum benefit from the curriculum by working in it individually, and also allows them to pursue their individual interests.

The Open Classroom and the Curriculum

If you use a complete open classroom plan in that students choose their own activities and subject matter at all times, then there are many ways to integrate the suggested curriculum. You will be using it as a broad framework to provide ideas for extending individual interests, for bringing in new stimulation to the students, and for selecting materials and subject matter for group lessons. If you teach children of the same age, they will tend to be interested in approximately the same things. They share many common experiences and concerns about themselves and life. They see similar television shows, celebrate the same holidays and hear about the same occurrences in the neighborhood. These things provide a common core of experience you can use in order to extend students' knowledge and interest into the curriculum areas. The things children are supposed to learn are not always too far removed from what they would like to know. The means of connecting what we feel they need to know and what they would like to know is always the crucial factor in skillful teaching.

It is not against the principles of the open classroom concept to stimulate children with new ideas or topics. Your main concern should be not to force children to do things which do not interest them, especially when they may be involved in other things of vital interest to them. If you run a class with no group lessons where everyone chooses his own activities, there are times when children will need some stimulation or fresh ideas and topics to pursue. Some students are always interested and eager to have new ideas and stimulation. You serve as the input for these fresh ideas. Other sources of stimulation are the things that children bring to class with them, current events and community happenings. When you sense interest is lagging and new ideas are needed, that is the time you must move in to extend the children's interests in whatever way you can. A trip somewhere or an animal skull borrowed from the science room can do a lot to generate new enthusiasm and extend interests and learning.

You will be the mediator between children and the curriculum planned for them. The best way you can help them to learn is to observe their personal interests and abilities and utilize the established curriculum to embellish and extend the interests and abilities of each child. To do this you must have a sound knowledge and understanding of the planned curriculum at your fingertips. In this way, you will be ready immediately to comment on the work a child is doing, ask a question or suggest other materials or directions to help a child move on in his work. Without the background knowledge of possibilities for learning, and some knowledge of what children are capable of learning at specific ages, you will have a less stimulating and effective classroom. If you are unable to provide an effective learning situation, then students might as well be learning completely by themselves.

As soon as you know what grade you will be teaching for the coming year, make a list of the skills and concepts which are generally taught in that grade for each subject area. Include the ones for the grade preceding and following yours. This will give you a good idea of the types of things you will be expected to teach your students and will also prepare you for the range of abilities you will encounter in a single class. These lists can be made from curriculum guides and/or from teacher's guides for sets of basal readers or textbooks (whether you use them or not). These guides are full of useful information about things children can and want to learn. As you go through them jot down ideas for lessons which interest you. Some of the suggestions may help you create your own supplies for activity centers, and others may give you ideas for group lessons.

When you have the range of skills and of content you are supposed to teach firmly in your mind, you will be ready to translate such skills and content into individualized learning situations for children. You will use the interests of the students as starting points for developing curriculum areas or topics.

If you plan to ignore the curriculum entirely, you will still have a sound idea of skills which can be taught for your grade, whatever subject matter or content the students may choose. In this case it is usually a good idea to keep a record (almost a reverse lesson plan) of the areas covered by students so that you get some feeling of continuity or lack of it over the year. Without doing this, it becomes difficult to know when students are wandering and difficult to pull the class together when this happens. To help children learn in any depth it is essential that the class have some focus and direction. This can grow out of individual or collective interests if you are alert enough to use them constructively.

USING SPACE FOR LEARNING

Most rooms are supplied with individual desks and seats for students, a desk and a chair for you, and occasionally some spare tables or desks which someone has neglected to take to the storeroom. There may be built-in or portable shelves, cabinets and coat closets. How you arrange this furniture within the room is as important as what you intend to do within the room. Your arrangement of the furniture communicates your expectations for behavior and learning to the students, and it also controls the possibility for movement within the room.

Because of our own school experiences, our concept of a classroom is a place with desks arranged in an orderly, symmetrical fashion; the teacher's desk is somewhere in the front of the room, and students' desks and chairs are evenly spaced (often bolted to the floor) in a square or rectangular formation (see Figure 1). Students in this type of room are expected to spend the bulk of their school day seated at their own desks, isolated from their fellows so that they can concentrate on the work before them. For millions of school children in this country this type of room represents "school." They know a certain type of behavior is expected in this room and that certain types of learning activities will occur. Generally, the lessons will emanate from the teacher's desk or the blackboard at the front of the class. If you want a traditional type of class, then the standard arrangement of desks will be satisfactory. If you want another type of learning to occur, then you must seek other ways of arranging the environment in the class by manipulating the available space and furniture to accommodate your specific aims. The environment will structure the type of learning and student interaction which occurs.

Do not be discouraged if you are not in a new building with creatively designed learning areas. Few teachers are, and some of them who are in unusually constructed buildings face more difficult problems than teachers in the old, self-contained classroom set-up. Many new buildings were designed with certain set ideas about how they would be used. Unfortunately, when they are occupied by teachers and students, the predesigned purposes are often incompatible with the needs of the teachers and the students. At least in a self-contained classroom you have a certain amount of space which is yours to use and change as you wish; you are not part of a complex of rooms which must be used in one or two specific ways.

Any space can be turned into an open classroom. Keep in mind that *you are in control of the room* and the furniture. *It is not in control of you* or your teaching methods. No matter how drab or awkward the room is, there are many things you can do to give it the atmosphere you want. A room full of happy, busy children is a beautifully alive place, no matter how drab the walls may be. The most depressing school building I have ever seen was a very old one in the Oceanhill-Brownsville section of Brooklyn. The hallways were disfigured by gaping holes which had been chewed by rats. The dull green and yellow paint created a terrible feeling of emptiness. The classrooms were in the same miserable state as the hallways. The children's faces reflected a feeling of gloomy despair. When the university officials came to the school for a meeting, they were so overwhelmed by its poor appearance that they immediately offered money to the student-teachers for the purpose of obtaining supplies to brighten up the rooms. As I met the teachers and began visiting in many of the rooms, I came upon the room of a first grade teacher who was operating an open classroom, and this room was remarkably different from the others. It was covered from ceiling to floor with beautiful, gay paintings and art work the students had made. The teacher had spent no money to change the basic appearance of the room or to supplement the available supplies. She had created a happy, active atmosphere in which children could work and she had used the children's work to gradually change the physical appearance of the room.

If you feel doubtful that such transformations can occur, try stringing one or two lines diagonally across the top of your room. Hang some brightly colored paper mobiles on the lines (high enough so that they clear the children's heads). The mobiles will twist and sway with each movement of air in the room and create a fascinating, moving ceiling. Watch the effect this has on your students. In a week's time they probably will be much gayer, more relaxed and happy than you have ever seen them. If you are wondering whether the mobiles won't distract students from serious work, you are right, they will. That is just the point. We are so busy stuffing little children full of serious things that we seldom take time to create situations which are purely enjoyable. If you must be reassured that the mobiles serve some learning purpose, they will elicit a great many questions about movement, air currents, patterns, shadows and the like.

Room Arrangement

There are some basic principles to remember as you determine how you will utilize your room space. Any type of symmetrical arrangement suggests balance and order, not only in the use of space, but also in the behavior which is expected within that space. The range of symmetry can vary from a rigid arrangement, with fixed dimensions between desks, to a casual one where the basic layout may or may not be symmetrical, but the internal dimensions are variable (see Figure 4). In the latter case you create a feeling of balance despite the uneven placement of your furniture. Symmetry represents the known, the easily assimilated; it follows a familiar pattern. To create an asymmetrical arrangement immediately alerts students to the idea that something different and unusual is occurring. It may take them some time to adjust to an unexpected arrangement and to find out what behavior is possible and acceptable in this environment.

Think of your own reactions upon entering a strange home. If the living room has the accepted arrangement of a couch with a coffee table and several casual chairs placed around the room, you probably feel at home almost immediately. If you enter a living room which contains no furniture, but instead has huge cushions scattered haphazardly about the floor and one large, low table in the middle of the room, you feel much less comfortable than in the previous situation. You probably begin to speculate on the possible uses of the room. You might begin to examine things in great detail, experimenting with their uses. Similarly, a student who sees a differently arranged classroom reacts in much the same manner as you react to the unorthodox living room.

It is always *easier* to relate to the familiar. This does not mean that it is *better* to do so. It is usually more stimulating and thought provoking to be faced with the unfamiliar. Keeping these facts in mind, you must make a decision about how much of a shock and challenge your students (and you) can absorb. If you are teaching older elementary school children who have had experiences only with traditional classrooms, you may find it easier to begin your class with a modified version of the room you would eventually like to have. This will make the transition easier for them and you may spare yourself unnecessary confusion and difficulty in the opening weeks of school. You can always move things to conform to your original plans when the children have adjusted to the modified setting.

When deciding on the arrangement which might best suit your purposes, consider where you expect most of the children's activity to take place. If it will be at their desks (as in more traditional classrooms) then it is important that the desks be placed in such a way that the children will have optimal working conditions. If you want the main working areas in activity centers, then the activity centers should have prominence and take up as much of the space in the room as possible (see Figure 7). The latter situation is usually more typical of the open classroom.

Be as creative as you can in arranging the furniture within your room and in changing the appearance of the space. Remember, there is always a lot of wasted space over our heads. Use lines strung across the ceiling or painted cardboard boxes piled as high as possible to break up the normal appearance of this overhead space. If you can manage wood and nails, have a local lumberyard cut wood to your specifications and build a climbing square or a house on stilts (with student help, of course). If your ideas do not work for some situations, then try different arrangements until you find some that are satisfactory. Let the students make suggestions also, and carry them out. What a wonderful lesson in using space and furniture optimally and functionally. Children spend much of their early years developing their concept of space and their own movements in it. There is no reason why their own classroom should be off limits to them in this pursuit. I have found that *children can often teach us* if we give them the chance. This is not because they know more than we do. It may happen because they have learned fewer cultural inhibitions and so-called correct patterns for dealing with the environment than we have as mature and socially-oriented adults.

The first step in arranging most rooms is the placement of the students' desks. They will take up the bulk of the floor space in the room and their arrangement is an important determinant of the possible interaction between students and of the flow of students to other areas of the room.

Activity Centers

After deciding what to do with the desks and chairs, you will be able to locate areas for specialized work such as manipulation of math materials, science experiments, artwork, a building center, etc. These areas are subsequently referred to in this book as activity centers. In most open classrooms, the activity centers dominate the room to the exclusion of individual desks and chairs. This expresses a basic feeling that children should be learning by working together in active ways rather than by isolated, passive work at their desks. This emphasis on cooperative working centers does not mean than there is no quiet, solitary work going on in the room. There will be at all times, if you establish areas where such work can be done. If you plan to have even half a day given to student-selected activities, then your activity centers should be a major ingredient in the design of your room.

The following figures represent some common arrangements. They may help you to focus your own needs and preferences. Because of limited experimentation with school environments, there are many things we do not know about the results of certain arrangements. It should be an interesting and challenging experience for you to start experimenting with your classroom.

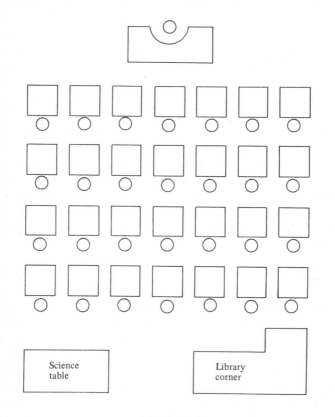

FIGURE 1

Figure 1 shows the traditional, symmetrical room arrangement used in most classrooms across the country. Each seat is isolated from its neighbors by approximately the same distance. This communicates very clearly to students that they are to consider themselves separate from their fellow students and that orderly, non-interactive behavior will be the rule. The teacher's desk is at the front, removed some distance from the students' desks, marking her as a leader who is set apart from the class. If her desk were in the middle of the front of the room, it would put even more emphasis on the teacher's authority status. A child has no question about what is expected in this type of classroom. During the first year I taught, our school received movable desks and chairs to replace old ones which were bolted to the floor. Almost without exception, the teachers arranged the new movable desks in exactly the same positions the old ones had occupied, defeating the entire purpose of the expenditure for movable desks. One teacher went so far as to make chalk marks on the floor to make sure her first grade students kept their desks exactly where they belonged!

The activity areas in this type of class are not meant for extensive use by students. The library corner may be frequented by brighter students who finish their work quickly or by a few students at specific times during the day, usually according to the teacher's direction. The science corner is often for displays to impress visitors and offers little sensory stimulation to the students. Children like to touch and experiment with things. The neater and more attractive the table is, the less likely they will be to touch and use the things on it. Activity centers can be spaced around the walls in this arrangement, but there will be little working space for students. Children will find it difficult to move in or out of their desks in this arrangement because of the limited space around and behind their desks. That is often what a teacher who uses this arrangement intends. Thus the overall impression students get from this arrangement is one of a place for isolated, orderly behavior where movement from desks to activity areas is not encouraged.

Figure 2 is a modification of the arrangement in Figure 1. The desks have been pushed together horizontally to provide more space around the sides of the room for activity centers. This

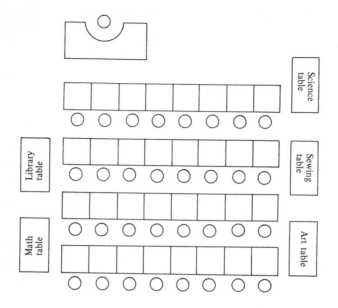

FIGURE 2

arrangement encourages children to have some intimacy with ad-joining neighbors, but they still remain isolated from most of their fellows. Movement to and from desks remains awkward. The placement of the teacher's desk is important here because to center it in the front of the class would be to give a definite feeling of authority and formality. A side placement is less formal. A rear placement would give an even less teacher-centered feeling. The teacher then would be removed from the students' line of vision and their attention would be directed entirely to their work or to fellow students. Activity centers can be placed along the sides of the room in the space gained, by moving the desks together horizontally. As movement is still re-stricted in this arrangement, it suggests periods of group or solitary work done at one's seat combined with other time periods of being away from one's own desk at the activity centers.

There is one problem with this arrangement which may or may not bother you. The long rows of desks seem to move an unusual amount in forward, backward and wave-like configurations. This may be due to individual students' attempts to keep their desks perfectly aligned with their neighbors', so that there is a constant shifting on the part of all the students.

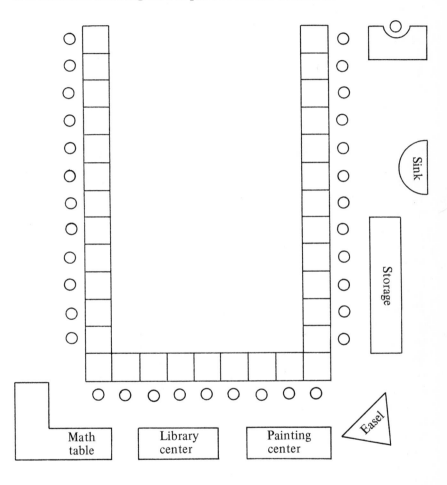

FIGURE 3

In **Figure** 3 the desks are also pushed together, giving greater intimacy to adjoining neighbors and suggesting casual conversation between them. The single desk lineup still isolates students from the bulk of their fellows, as do the two preceding arrangements. However, this arrangement puts all students in visual contact with one another, and encourages greater group feeling. There is easy access to desks, which encourages frequent movement around the room. The large area in the middle of the desks might serve no purpose other than to separate students and could result in a lot of wasted space. Or it might be utilized advantageously for activity centers or small group projects. With this arrangement the teacher's desk can be placed anywhere in the room. A center, symmetrical placement inside the U-shape would suggest an intimate contact with children, but would make the desk somewhat inaccessible. for students and for the teacher. A placement outside the U-shape gives a more distant or casual quality to the relationship between teacher and students. A centered placement outside the students' desks probably would give a feeling of formality to this room. Depending upon the shape of the room, the walls or the center area can be used to set up activity centers. If you anticipate many students using the activity centers at the same time, the space around them could be increased by using only one end of the room and pushing the U-shaped desk arrangement to the other end of the room, as shown in this figure.

Figure 4 is a departure from the previous arrangements. It puts groups of eight to twelve students in close proximity, encouraging them to look at each other, talk and work together. Putting the desks together leaves a great deal of extra space in the room for activity centers and for play activities. The teacher's desk is placed next to a few students' desks. This kind of arrangement can be made when there are students in the class who need to be near the teacher for some reason. It is also suitable when you have a few students who need a lot of structure and external control in order to function within the class. The latter is not unusual in the open classroom (or in traditional ones) because often the freedom which is encouraged and is beneficial for most children can be frightening and overwhelming for a few. These few often benefit from being physically close to you because you are their main source of control and security. If you do not find this kind of placement necessary, the teacher's desk could be placed anywhere in the room or excluded.

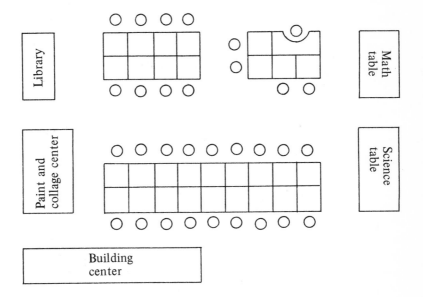

FIGURE 4

This arrangement encourages children to move about the room, since their desks and activity centers are easily accessible to all. Activity centers can be around the walls, in corners, or you can utilize the groups of student desks as large working areas. In the arrangement shown, the grouping to the left of the teacher's desk could be the math area, for instance. Children adjust easily to leaving their desks and letting them serve dual functions, as personal seats and as group activity centers. If you are giving many group lessons where children must watch or copy from a centrally located blackboard, it will be difficult for some students to see with this seating arrangement. They will have to turn their bodies or their desks in order to view the blackboard, or you. However, this is a relatively unimportant aspect, as children are quite flexible and rarely object to turning their chairs or desks in order to see.

Figure 5 also encourages student involvement because of the grouping of the desks. It suggests a more intimate involvement

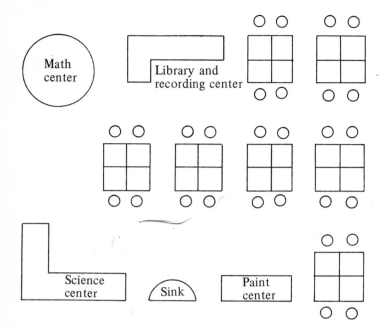

FIGURE 5

than does Figure 4, since there are fewer children in each grouping. The smaller the number of desks in any grouping, the greater the demand you make upon children-members of that group to relate to one another more intimately. As in Figure 4, there is a lot of room space left over for activity centers, and traffic can flow smoothly around the desk groupings. All children have easy access to their seats. Lessons given from a central location or blackboard will necessitate children turning in various ways to see you and the material on the blackboard. For most versions of an open classroom, this grouping seems to work quite well. It encourages intimacy, but at a controllable level so that the noise level and student interaction does not become overwhelming. It also gives you needed activity center space. I have found most teachers prefer this type of arrangement when beginning open classroom techniques.

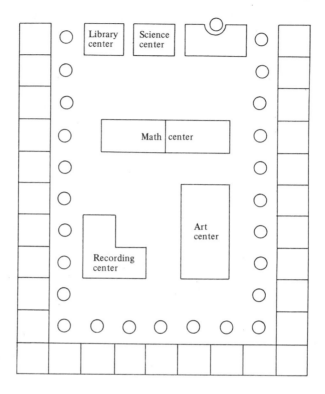

FIGURE 6

Figure 6 appears somewhat stark at first glance. However, it allows communication with adjoining neighbors although it does not encourage a strong group feeling, as children are facing the walls rather than each other (do not forget that they usually face each other's backs so this is not such an unusual arrangement. Solitary work would seem to be the rule in a room like this, since students at their desks would not be distracted by seeing either the teacher or their fellow students. Not seeing the teacher should also encourage more independent work by students. Movement in and out of student desks can flow easily and there is ample room for activity centers at the back of the room and in the large middle area. The center space can be utilized for activity centers or for small groups of children working together on the floor.

This type of room is ideally suited to a class with a mixed contract and individual activity schedule.

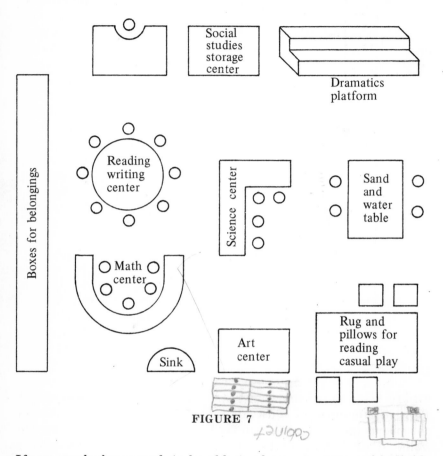

FIGURE 7

If you are lucky enough to be able to clear your room of individual desks and chairs, you will have a major opportunity to be creative and to test new modes of furnishing and using your classroom space, as shown in **Figure 7**. This arrangement assumes that for most of the day children will not need private spaces to work, and that such an arrangement would be very suitable for young children under any learning program as well as for older students who select their own activities most of the day. Quiet working space for writing, reading or research projects can be supplied by some large tables designated for that purpose or a grouping of student desks which can be separated or joined together as needed.

Children usually need some place to store personal belongings; this need calls for some ingenuity when individual desks are removed. In England, some teachers use plastic drawers which can be easily removed by children should they want to transport all their things to one area of the room. Some teachers have felt no need for personal storage space. However, if you do find that children want their private space, you can try several things. All kinds of inexpensive plastic storage boxes and bins are available in the large discount stores. Cardboard boxes are another possibility—boxes of uniform size which children can collect from local merchants. When painted by students (with a cover of varnish or plastic spray by you) and stacked against a wall as high as the children can reach, they make a very attractive wall storage area.

It is important to consider how students will move within the room. Quiet centers for writing or reading should be in parts of the room where there will be minimal traffic. It may be helpful to use screens of some sort to block off the entrance into the room, thus making visitors a less distracting influence. Noise and familiar activities of the room are not the things that will distract students after they get used to the room. It is the unusual interruptions of visitors or messengers entering the room which will create distractions. Your activity centers can be as imaginative and as plentiful as your facilities and your ingenuity allow. Try to make reading areas comfortable and cozy places which call out for someone to stretch out and read a book on an old piece of carpet or an attractive floor pillow. Large, sturdy cardboard boxes can be cut to simulate houses, stores, etc. to create private places for children. Smaller ones can also be painted and varnished and used as large building blocks which children can arrange as walls, barricades, writing tables, etc. If you can hammer nails or have a friend who can do so, you can build all kinds of intriguing structures from plywood. Do not miss any opportunity to build upward. We waste so much space above the first six feet from the floor. Children love to get off the ground. Perhaps because they are always lower than adults, it is a wonderful feeling for them to suddenly be up higher than those giants they must deal with all the time.

It is up to you and your students to experiment in any way you can to make your room assist you in achieving your educational aims.

Placement of Supplies and Activity Centers

After deciding on a basic arrangement for the children's desks and your own, you can then consider the best placement of supplies and activity areas. The placement of supplies will be controlled to some extent by your facilities. If you have storage cabinets reaching from floor to ceiling, your arrangement will differ from one with shelves three or four feet high. In general, you should try to make all the materials which will be in use accessible to the students. If you have hidden or unreachable shelf space, use it for excess materials or infrequently used supplies. If you are teaching very young children, you may with to use these shelves for breakable or dangerous materials. In an open classroom, materials are a primary ingredient of learning and students should be encouraged to select their own materials, rather than to passively wait for teachers or monitors to do so. If they can reach materials easily, they will be more likely to seek and use them independently.

The location of supplies and activity centers should be complementary if possible. Classroom life will be much easier if extra books and reading games are stored near the reading center (if not in it). When a group of student desks is used as a part-time activity center, the materials for the center can be stored in cabinets or shelves adjacent to the desks for quick, easy arrangement of the center at the necessary time. In planning for activity centers, you must decide how the activity centers will be used in your overall plan. If you are planning a totally individualized program where students will select their own activities during the day, then the bulk of their time will be spent at the activity centers, or adjacent to them. In this case the centers should be as large and as varied as you can make them. They will have to encompass a wide variety of learning needs. If you are planning to have teacher-directed work which will be done primarily at the children's desks for the entire morning, or for a large part of the school day, then the activity centers may be of less importance to the learning going on in the room. They can be fewer and less well supplied than in the former case. Some suggestions for a thoroughly planned variety of such activity centers, and possible supplies for each area are given following this part of the chapter. If you do not have room for all the centers you feel are necessary, it is possible to utilize open shelves and other storage space (boxes, cabinets) to house centers which might be used less. It is also possible to alternate centers, such as having a building center alternate with a sculpture center, or the housekeeping center alternate with the spatial relations center or the social study center.

It is important to remain flexible about the centers and their supplies in order to relate to the changing needs of the students. You must remain sensitive to those needs, changing supplies and activity centers as needed. A most important element of the open classroom is to use your materials freely and flexibly. Anything which impedes this is going to limit the learning and growth of the students.

Introducing Materials to Students

After planning the arrangement of your materials, you can place them before the students enter the room for the first time, later giving students a tour of the supply cabinets and activity areas. Another possibility is to leave the placing and spacing of supply areas to the children, thereby making the arrangement a cooperative effort and a learning experience for the students. This also communicates to them that the room is really theirs to order as they choose.

It is very helpful to you to increase your sensitivity to student needs by encouraging them to express any feelings about the centers or the supplies they contain. The amount of decision-making you give to the students in your class regarding the room in general will determine to some extent who is in charge of the room and its supplies. This is probably the fastest way to develop a sense of responsibility in children. If your room is decorated, cared for and used by children, they will also be able to take care of the supplies.

SUGGESTIONS FOR ACTIVITY CENTERS

The centers are listed by subject area, but the materials should be and usually are interchangeable. The materials can be utilized in two ways. Emphasis can be placed on the multiple uses of the materials in different situations as well as on their intrinsic qualities. A paint brush can be used in many situations which call for a brush-like tool. However, there are certain things about a paint brush which make it particularly suited to painting rather than to other tasks. It is important that children learn the general concept of "brush" as well as how to differentiate between different objects which would fall into the same general class.

If your school does not supply enough materials and does not have funds for special materials, then you must look to other sources for them. Before you turn from the school supplies, however, try to get into supply closets, storerooms, etc. Often there is a wealth of material stored away because none of the teachers want to be bothered using it, or assistant principals have some stake in preserving it from teachers and students.

Many of the items listed in this chapter can be obtained from relatives, friends and acquaintances who save things they no longer use. Retail and wholesale stores or factories are another possible source. The children and their parents are usually a valuable source of materials that are in the home. You may also want to buy some of the items yourself, but do not overlook the potential of so-called "junk."

As you teach the open classroom and bring in many things which are not the usual equipment for a classroom, the students will change their concept of school and begin bringing in more materials than you can use. One teacher I knew equipped only one activity center in her room at the beginning of school. She used a variety of gadgets and machines from her kitchen plus materials (food, paper, cardboard, crayons, chalk). After allowing children to work with the equipment, she suggested that they develop other centers by asking their parents for miscellaneous home items which seemed to be unused or unwanted. The students got the idea and in a few weeks they equipped a variety of fascinating centers.

Science Center ✓

The science center must be a place for experimenting, which is often synonymous with spilling and making a general mess. No matter what the age of your students, they need to experiment with things if they are going to learn anything about science. If you do not have plastic or formica coated table surfaces for experiments, then you should buy some plastic by the yard at a local dimestore and staple it in place underneath the table top. Possible supplies include:

Magnets
Magnifying glasses
Small child's microscope
Colored plastic viewers
Scissors
Small dull knife
Tweezers
Nut cracker
Nut pickers
Small hammers
Various sized screw drivers
Pliers
Wire
String and rope
Batteries, wires and bulbs
Light socket and bulb
Old or broken appliances
Pieces of screening
Pieces of wire fencing or mesh
Strainers
Tape

Glue of various kinds
Various sized clips
Rubber bands
Small vises or clamps
Rulers and assorted measuring devices
Clear plastic containers
Bottles and jars
Test tubes and holder
Sponges
Blotters
Cheese cloth
Paper towels
Paper and pencils for recording
Paper cups
Animal cages
Live animals
Supply of sugar, salt, flour, oil, cornstarch, food coloring

Painting Center ✓

This is also a place where "messes" will occur. You will save yourself many hours of work by making table tops and floors easy to clean with plastic sheeting and newspapers. This center should be located away from major traffic areas because of the concentration necessary and the possibility of innocent bypassers being accidentally splashed.

Possible supplies include:

One or more easels
Table for finger and group painting
Brushes of various sizes
Newsprint
Paint containers for easel and table
Washable palettes (tin plates)
Trays
Sponges
Paper for cleaning
Pegs or hangers for smocks
Rope or heavy string for hanging painting to dry
Starch
Sand
Linoleum blocks
Soft wood blocks
Felt and cardboard
Rollers
Spoons
Stirrers, spreaders
Stencil paper
Varnish
Plastic spray
Storage for paint, paper, etc.
Finger paint
Tempera paint
Clothespins for hanging paintings

Social Studies Center

Because of the broadness of this area it is difficult to list all the possible equipment a particular center should have. Much of the equipment and materials will be topical in nature and therefore determined in large part by the interest of your students or by the curriculum being presented to them. However, below are some basic materials and equipment which should be included. Possible supplies include:

Globe
Maps of local areas and world
Graph paper for mapmaking
Newspaper articles of interest
Bulletin board for posting articles
Pictures of different styles of houses from around the world
If you do not have a housekeeping center this is an excellent place for a dress-up center.
Samples of common tools
Samples of common materials
Pictures of people from around the world
Books and magazines of current interest

Housekeeping Center

Although generally thought appropriate only for kindergarten and occasionally for first grade students, this center can be

utilized for all ages, changing equipment and supplies as the students grow older.
Possible supplies include:

Toy sink and refrigerator
Table and chairs to simulate dining
Couch or easy chairs
Carpet to delineate areas
Dishes, cooking utensils
Stock of flour and salt for cooks

Doll carriage and bed
Dolls of both sexes and various races
Newspapers, books
Small items which give home-like atmosphere

Dress-Up Center

Should be placed close to or within housekeeping center. Clothes should be updated according to age of students. Again, this is important for all ages, not just for younger children.
Possible supplies include:

Full length mirror (unbreakable)
Small hand mirrors
Male clothing, hats, accessories
Female clothing, purses, shoes, accessories
Belts, scarves, jewelry
Several strips of cloth two to three yards in length which can be used imaginatively
Several felt or cardboard hat forms which can be used by both sexes for imaginative or dramatic play.
Small stage for plays within class (can consist of carpeting to delineate borders)

Sewing Center

This is important for both sexes and should be thought of as a creative art.
Possible supplies include:

Large plastic needles; assortment of metal ones
Yarn of various thicknesses and colors
Embroidery thread of various kinds and colors
Odd bits of materials, cardboard and plastics

Dixie mesh
Crochet hooks
Knitting needles
Wooden frames for weaving
Small loom or materials for making one
String, rope of all sizes
Macramé board and pins
Tracer's wheel
Carbon paper
Graph paper for scaling designs
Feathers, beads, spangles, etc.

Math Center /

The materials here will depend upon the age of the students, but be sure you have a wide range to allow for students not working on grade level. If you are creative and encourage students to be creative, you can make many supplies and games yourself.
Possible supplies include:

Cuisenaire rods
Montessori sequence boards
Dienes math materials
Large abacus
Small abacus
Counting discs and frames
Miniature adding machines
Miniature computers (class constructed)
Illustrative board for place value
Materials to illustrate relationships of fractions
Variety of materials to sort and classify, such as interesting
    stones, nuts, beads
Pegs and pegboards
Dice
Math games
Paper money (class made)
Measuring devices of all kinds
Graph paper
Heavy construction paper for construction of geometric
    figures
Deck of playing cards
Math games, teacher or student created

Spatial Relations Center

Although these items are often included in a variety of other areas, it is helpful to develop children's awareness of their use of space and their perception of it as a separate area. A vital element in our concept of general intelligence is the perception and utilization of space.
Possible supplies include:

Puzzles
Form boards using shapes that are familiar
Form boards using shapes that are unfamiliar
Nesting boxes, cups, plates, etc. (of greater complexity as students' ability increases)
Large boxes with various sized doorways for children to enter to emphasize perception of one's body in different spatial situations
Materials to encourage development of near-far concept
Pitching games
Cardboard tunnels for crawling through
Any construction which allows children to go up
Dollhouse with furniture and dolls (can be made from cardboard boxes or wood)

Building Center

Children of all ages have desires to build and can learn things by doing so. This center could easily be combined with the spatial relations one.
Possible supplies include:

Blocks—large and small, of as many colors and dimensions as you can find
Pegboard with attachments, and other things such as string, wheels, pulleys, etc., which can be attached to pegboard
Sheets of cardboard, plastic and wood for use in constructing buildings (all can be scraps or clean garbage)
Concrete in dry form
Plaster of Paris in dry form
Sand
Clay
Play dough (homemade)

Glues
Heavy construction paper and oaktag
Collections of used food boxes and cans of all kinds, shapes
   and sizes for constructions
String
Odd widths and lengths of pegboard with nuts and bolts that
   fit pegboard holes
Plastic plumbing pipes and connections
Pipecleaners
Plastic tubing
Rubber tubing or lengths of hose
Hammers, saws, screwdrivers, vises, clamps, hand drills
Screws, nails, nuts and bolts of all sizes
Scrap lumber, wood from orange crates, etc.
Blocks—large and small of as many colors and dimensions as
   you can find
Sandpaper, files
Tinker toys (large ones if possible)
Plastic blocks
Sponge blocks

Sculpture Center

This should be off the beaten track to prevent upsetting work
in progress.
Possible supplies include:

Clay
Plaster
Sand
Soap
Soft wood
Carving tools
Odd-shaped boxes (food, etc.)
Cans of all sizes
Assortment of glues
Trays and bowls to work on

Old cloth for wrapping
Coping saw
Hammer and nails
String, yarn, thread
Wire and screening
Styrofoam shapes
Pieces of scrap metal
Large box of collage materials
Hand drill and screws
Newspaper for papier-mâché

Language Arts Center

My own experience leads me to believe that all phases of
language arts should be grouped together. However, I feel you

should try your own arrangements to find what is best for you and your students. I have listed the following activities as separate centers. You must judge from your own experience how you want to group them or not. If you have students who write constantly but do little reading in the classroom, you may want to give more space and attention to the creative writing area. If most of the class becomes very involved in taping stories or plays and then transcribing the tapes and making books from them, you may wish to devote all the language arts areas to these specific activities for a period of time, converting them when the flurry of activity begins to subside.

Reading Center

This should be a comfortable, inviting place, carpeted if possible, in order to encourage children to stretch out on the floor and read.
Possible supplies include:

> Books—a large variety of subject matter and a broad range in reading difficulty
> Poetry area—a corner or any portion of this area can be devoted to poetry
> Dictionary and/or picture dictionaries

Creative Writing Center

Possible supplies include:

Paper with and without lines
Writing tools appropriate to the age level of students
Stapler, clips, fasteners
Old typewriter, if possible
Set of letters and stamp pad for printing

Drawing paper
Crayons
Magic markers
Dictionary or picture dictionary

Language Arts and Skills Center

Many of the games and drills contained in this area can be self-made.

Possible supplies include:

> Variety of workbooks (of different publishers)
> Reading and spelling games or puzzles
> Drill materials for the development of specific skills (They will vary with age of students)
> Tape recorder
> Overhead projector
> Small area with make-shift stage that can be used for plays when desired. Costumes can be stored with things in dress-up center.
> Phonograph and records related to reading enjoyment or skills

Music and Dance Center

Most children in open classrooms will spontaneously bring music into the classroom. It is helpful to have a special area where they can pursue some of their interests and express their feelings.

Possible supplies include:

> Musical instruments of all kinds, commercial and home-made
> Phonograph with variety of records representing different types of music and music of all countries
> Some interesting light material of 2 or 3 yard lengths which can be used for dancing
> Anything you or the students find which makes interesting sounds

Use of Activity Centers in Beginning Weeks

There are several approaches to setting up activity centers. You can arrange them yourself, anticipating the needs of the students. You can plan them with the students during the first few weeks of school. The latter choice presents the problem of having lengthy discussions during those first days and possibly not enough activities in operation to give students some relief from planning. This situation can be partially avoided by setting up a few very interesting centers yourself and encouraging students to plan others with you. Another approach is to set up activity centers without great thought or planning, perhaps even making some of them purposely inconvenient. After a few days, you can discuss the arrangements with the children, noting their reactions and feelings about possible needed changes. This gives you a good opportunity to see what the students think and perhaps to realize some possibilities for activity centers which might not occur spontaneously to you.

If you plan to include the children in the planning of activity centers in any way, it is important that you act upon their suggestions even if you foresee problems or inconvenience. You know how to make workable plans, but usually children do not. You can give them the *experience* of planning and following through on their plans. The results of their planning will provide a vivid lesson in the importance of preplanning and of thinking of many possible alternatives. It is true that they can learn from listening to you or to someone else telling them how to do something in the most efficient way. However, this is like memorizing recipes for something; it does not develop the child's concept of the situation itself or of problem solving in general. Unless the next problem situation is similar to this one and can be solved by the same recipe, the child will have to learn another recipe to suit the new situation. By giving children the actual experience, you will help them learn a problem solving technique which may be applicable to a variety of situations. Learning by personal experience also seems to leave a more vivid and lasting impression than learning from what you have read or from what someone tells you. You cannot provide children with all kinds of experiences but this is one that is inherent in the classroom situation and should not be missed as a learning opportunity.

Eliminating Difficult Working Conditions

Children are often more keenly aware of the inadequacies of their working conditions than their teacher. They know it would be easier to get to the reading center if they did not have to walk through the block building area. It is difficult to concentrate on math materials while working next to a noisy and distracting science center. The inadequacies will not prevent them from working and learning under difficult conditions; they usually do both. But it is helpful to arrange your room in a way which facilitates learning. Some distractions can be removed by erecting screens of boxes, shelves, etc. It may be possible to let students go out into the halls or into unused classrooms or areas to do work which requires quiet and ideally should be done in a quiet atmosphere. You will have to constantly reassess what is happening within the classroom in order to create the best learning situations for children.

If your room is unusually small you may have to use four to six student desks grouped together as activity centers. I did this one year without difficulty. These grouped desks are treated as one large table or working area for things like math or creative writing. Any center which does not involve work that may spill over into the desks or make a terrible mess to clean up every day is acceptable. The children to whom the desks belong quickly learn to get things from their desks in an unobtrusive manner, not disturbing those using the activity center.

All of us have pictures in our minds about the kind of room or spatial arrangements in which we would like to teach. Reality may never conform to those pictures, but every room and building has hidden assets as well as glaring faults. An awkwardly placed heating pipe or a section of wall can be very attractive and gay if it is colorfully and tastefully decorated and used. As you begin to use the room in different ways, you will begin to see possibilities which had not occurred to you in more traditional rooms.

However well you plan the use of space in your room, it will always have to be altered by the needs of students. You cannot anticipate all their needs and interests in advance, so your initial planning in this area should be thought of as temporary at best. If students feel that the room and its contents are theirs to use and to define, the essential spirit of the open classroom concept is present.

CLASSROOM ROUTINES

Seating

The first routine with which you will be confronted when students enter your class is how you will seat them. If you are running an open classroom with completely individualized and self-chosen activities, you may have eliminated individual seating. In this case you will have no problem. No one will have a specific place to sit or to be in the room at any time. This communicates to students the fact that this is to be a different school experience. They can use the whole room and no longer remain at a solitary desk to learn or to do teacher-prescribed tasks.

If you are dealing with individual seating by choice or by necessity, there are several ways of seating children, each with its own rationale.

One popular method is to seat students by alphabetical order. This helps the teacher to learn children's names faster at the beginning of the year and seems to give many teachers a sense of order and control which they like to have. Another popular method is to seat students by size. The shorter children sit in front of the classroom and the taller ones in the back. This presupposes activity centered upon a blackboard or a teacher standing in the front of the room.

Another way of seating children is to let them choose their own seats. This is not as popular as the other two methods. Many teachers feel that children will inherently choose bad companions or find locations which create problems in controlling students. A variation of this method is to give the majority of the students free choice. Children who have little control or who present a problem can be placed in teacher-selected seats where their behavior can be more easily controlled. Such seats may be in isolated areas of the room or near better controlled children who will not be easily distracted. It is usually better to make these special placements after a few days or weeks of school after you become familiar with the students and can make this type of judgment. A child will usually accept this kind of seating if given an honest and unemotional explanation of your reasons for giving him a special seat.

The seating arrangement is one of your first communications to children. Placing them alphabetically or by height immediately alerts them that you are dealing with superficial aspects of their physical beings rather than with deeper or more meaningful aspects of their personalities. If you want to deal with the personalities of your students, you can communicate this immediately by allowing them to act as responsible *persons* who are capable of choosing their own seats, rather than *things* or *commodities* which need to be dealt with as a set or class. If you feel that students' personal choices do not work well for them or for the other students, you can suggest alternatives. Explain your reasons to the students who are involved in the suggested changes. Children are reasonable when they understand the thinking behind your actions.

A revealing side effect of letting children seat themselves is that you receive immediate information about them. Students who sit near your desk or the front of the room may anticipate your physical presence at these locations. They are students who are eager to please, perhaps eager to learn, have had positive relationships with prior teachers and look forward to one with you. They may also be children who need to be near an adult for support and control. Children who sit in corners, in the back of the room or along walls are often children who are suspicious of adults, children who have not had positive relationships with teachers, and who need to control situations. A few children may move their desks away from others so that they almost have their own private area of the room. Children who seat themselves in the middle of the room will fall in the middle of these two extremes in terms of enthusiasm or caution. You receive less information about them than you do about those on either extreme of the continuum. Any child who seems unsettled by an unusual arrangement of furniture or by the freedoms you allow should be watched. The freedom of the open classroom may be quite stimulating for him, to the point of upsetting his inner equilibrium. You may have to provide more structured and familiar situations for him in order to reassure him that there are some outside controls if his inner ones fail.

Daily Schedules

Chronologically, the next routine (other than actual learning procedures) will be the general time organization of the day. In your planning, think in terms of the total year, not the first weeks of school. These first weeks may need special planning (see Chapter 5, "The Beginning"). Your initial weeks may have to be a modification of your basic plan, depending on the children's prior experiences and yours. However you choose to begin the open classroom, you should have a clear idea of the type of day you eventually want your students to have, and the activities which will be available to them. You may find that after your class is in operation for awhile that you may want to change the organization of the day. That can always be done in a cooperative way with the children, incorporating their suggestions into your plans.

If you intend to allow students to choose their own activities entirely, it is relatively easy to set up your day. The students will be busy with projects from the moment they enter the class until the end of the day.

Clean-up

You will have to make plans for clean-up before lunch and before the end of the day. Pre-lunch clean-up of the room may not be necessary; but the children will have to stop at a certain time to clean themselves before going to eat. Time to stop working can be signaled by a prearranged sign you and students have agreed upon. There should be adequate time for students to stop working, put materials away if necessary and to wash hands and/or face. It may be necessary to experiment with the appropriate length of time your class needs. If you have younger children you can assume they will need more time to leave their activities and to wash themselves. Older children may take less time, but this depends upon the individual class. Sometimes their involvement in their work is very intense and it takes them some time to break away from whatever they are doing.

Children must learn how to care for things and how to create order in their environment. It does seem that children who are constantly pushed to clean and straighten things when it is not really necessary will eventually stop using the materials and may reject habits of orderliness and cleanliness in other areas of life. You must use discretion in the degree of orderliness you demand of students. Remember that order and cleanliness should be functional when you work with children. If there are areas which need cleaning or straightening only once a week or once a month, do not insist that it be done everyday. Some classes handle clean-ups easily, but others present difficulties. If clean-up seems to be unpleasant, try to be less stringent in your requirements. Sometimes simple things like playing a record with a fast tempo or spontaneously starting a song while you help students will be enough to lighten a generally distasteful task. Class discussions about the problem may also be helpful.

Clean-up of Activity Centers

You may want to have monitors to supervise various activity centers. They can be appointed by you at random or can be selected from volunteers. You may also make rules that those who use centers during the day are responsible for their final condition at the end of the day. This becomes unwieldy if there is a lot of movement during the day from center to center. It becomes almost impossible to remember who used each center and in what condition they left it. Often a child who is at a center for a short time can cause more disorder than one who works there half the day. You would probably hold the latter student responsible for a larger portion of the clean-up which would be unfair. In the midst of a busy day it is almost impossible to keep track of where each child is at all times during the day and how much of a mess they made at various centers.

Often the most successful approach to clean-up is to simply ask everyone to pitch in and do whatever he or she would like to do, with the understanding that everyone must do something. Every class seems to have both students who like to clean in a general way and students who like to do meticulous and time-consuming tasks. You can appeal for volunteers for tasks which are left uncompleted, or you can make rotating assignments for them.

By giving such free choice in choosing tasks, you allow children to do things they enjoy doing and give them the opportunity to select tasks which are challenging to them at a particular point in time. Thus you provide another growth-inducing situation. It is impossible for you to know when a certain task will provide a challenge or a learning situation which will further a student's development.

With some thought and supervision you can also provide learning experiences to develop responsible community living. If you want children to develop responsible feelings toward others, you cannot do it by inculcating the idea that everyone is responsible for *his* things, *his* mess, *etc*. A healthy group spirit develops when children feel they are responsible for *our* things, *our* room, *our* mess, *etc.*

There may be students who do not clean-up or who do so quite superficially. It is best not to say anything to them for the first week or so of school. Observe their behavior to see exactly how they spend this time. Usually the isolation from their peers which these children feel after a few days will make them join the others. If you do not find this happening, you might casually suggest that the child help you do some task during clean-up. A few children may not know how to use the freedom you have given them or how to accept the implied responsibility of such a situation. You can show them how to participate in the general responsibility of caring for the room by choosing a task and working with the child. After you do this a few times, you can gradually encourage the child to choose until he finds tasks which he enjoys and he should then be able to proceed by himself with occasional help or encouragement from you.

If you think of children who do not immediately join in to clean as lazy or as malingerers then you will defeat your purpose of helping children to learn. Some children may never have learned in constructive ways how to clean up after themselves or others. You can provide a meaningful opportunity for them to learn in this area if you view the situation as a learning problem and approach it as you would a similar learning need in a content area. If you gave the class a problem in long division and discovered a student who could not work the problem and did not attempt to do so, you would undoubtedly try to help him to do the problem before you labelled him as lazy, dumb or inattentive.

There are many signals you can use to alert students that a clean-up is about to commence or that it is time for lunch or going to a specialist, etc. Among signals commonly used are bells, switching off the lights, raising your voice, raising one hand and holding it up until all children do likewise. Since these are simple mechanical signals, any method you prefer will be adequate. You may prefer that the students assume responsibility for this type of signalling totally or upon occasion. Some children have a very good sense of time and if they are orderly and enjoy helping they might volunteer to do this type of signalling for you.

Developing Group Feeling

One disadvantage to running a class where the activities are entirely self-chosen is that students sometimes become very involved in their individual interests and tend not to share things with fellow students. Because of this you may wish to set aside some time during the day when most of the class meets, in order for class members to discuss and share what they are doing. This can also be a time for suggesting changes in materials or room arrangements.

Another way to develop a strong group feeling in your classroom is to have one or two group lessons a day. This focuses the attention of the majority of the students on one or more content areas and gives them concrete learning situations and interests about which they are usually eager to communicate with one another. Science, social studies, mathematics, language arts or any of the arts are most adaptable for group lessons. All of these areas can tolerate wide individual differences in conceptual development, so that group lessons will be worthwhile and stimulating for almost everyone in the class on some level. You can introduce a concept or experience in any of these areas and let this focus much of the individual work of the students for the next few weeks. Each student can develop the concept in his own way and to the extent of his individual ability. You will have to experiment with your class and with such lessons to find the most efficient number of lessons to give per day or per week. Certainly no more than two a day and no less than one a week will allow you to give some group focus and to keep a feeling of group solidarity in the class. Any students who are busy with activities or projects and do not want to take part in the group lesson should have the option of not participating, as long as they do not disturb those listening to the lesson.

Assigned Work and Group Lessons

At the other extreme, you might feel that you want to run a somewhat modified version of the open classroom concept, such as having a traditional classroom for one half of the day. This type of day is most efficient if the more controlled part of the day occurs in the morning when children are more energetic and able to concentrate on complex work. Then they can do individual work and projects during the afternoon when interest and concentration lag somewhat (although they become amazingly energetic when left to do self-chosen work which is interesting to them). You can develop variations of this type of plan, perhaps working on assigned work from 9 to 10 A.M. or 9 to 10:30 A.M. and having the rest of the day for self-chosen activities. You may wish to have children contract for basic work which everyone must complete and then allow them free time after they complete their contracts with you. It will amaze you how quickly they will be able to finish assignments under this plan. However you work out your plan, basically, assignments or assigned work or group lessons should come before individual activities, as it is destructive to pull children away from self-chosen, meaningful activities and then try to muster their enthusiasm for something which is basically your interest or the schools' requirement. They will be much more receptive to your lessons and assignments before they have become involved in their own chosen activity for the day.

In organizing your class, there are basic things to remember in making plans for the learning schedule. As previously discussed, a plan which calls for a greater part of assigned work will function most easily if the assigned work or group lessons are completed prior to periods of self-chosen activity. You can begin group lessons as a means of drawing children away from individual activities, but remember that this is time consuming and you may not get all the students to begin the lesson at the same time. In this situation, when you have a nucleus of from eight to ten students, you should begin the group lesson. This type of group-lesson procedure usually works best in a class which is oriented largely toward self-chosen activities. The group lessons are infrequent and if you announce the subject or content of the lesson, you will usually get most of the students to participate. Those who are interested in the content of the lesson and who have learned that you present interesting lessons will gradually join the nuclear group. Those students who need or want to finish individual projects should be allowed to do so. Some of them may listen while continuing to work on the individual projects which are important to them. Some students may benefit from dividing their attention between your lesson and some individual activity, since they are unable to concentrate fully on any one thing for a long period of time.

The Significance of Individual Activities

If your main aim is to involve children intensely with materials and subject matter, it is best to encourage these individual activities at times when students come into the classroom, especially in the morning. At these times, they will be preoccupied with meaningful, personal thoughts and feelings which they can channel very directly into their activity choices. When students go to recess, lunch, or classes with specialists, they must turn their attention to relating to people and things outside the protective atmosphere of the classroom. Any difficulties or stimulation which occur during these absences can be translated immediately into a learning situation upon their return to the classroom. They may use materials, play, or some creative repetition of the situation. The child is able to gain control over his feelings and experiences and to fully integrate his experience. Because of the subtlety of this process and our lack of knowledge of why children select various materials or situations to help them integrate experiences or stimulation, we are seldom alert to this type of behavior, and we tend to give it little importance in formal learning.

If we see a child rearranging the sleeping positions of the family in a doll house, we can guess that he has some concern about the sexual relationships in his family. This is revealed by his interest in the intimacy of the sleeping relationships and his attempts to rearrange them. The details of the rearrangement might give us clues as to his specific curiosity or preoccupations. If another child places the baby of the doll-house family into the toilet and "flushes" him down the drain, we have little difficulty realizing that this child is having angry feelings about a young sibling. However, if a child slips while going down the stairs and then returns to his classroom and busies himself with blocks placed in balancing positions, attempting to create precariously balanced structures, most of us would not make a connection between his fall on the steps and his building activity. This child may be working out his feelings and experiences in essentially the same manner as the child who was using the doll family. Both these children are recreating a troublesome real situation in the controlled world of play and they may have to do this many times before coming to some satisfactory resolution of the incident. The child who slipped on the stairs might want to spend one or two hours walking and jumping on blocks, a bouncing mat or some outsize steps in order to increase his balancing skill and to mend his wounded self-image. Even in this very direct attempt to conquer and master his world, few teachers would be willing to allow him the time to do so.

It would be impossible to note each child's every act in a class of twenty to thirty and to try to understand its significance. It is intellectually interesting to notice these connections between the experiences and the subsequent activities of children, but it is not necessary to a child's further development or learning that we notice or understand them. What is important is that we let them happen, allowing the child to seek his own materials and situations for learning when the time is right for him. The less we interfere with this process, the more beneficial it will be for the child. And as we let this type of learning occur spontaneously, we may be able to learn more about it and eventually be more instrumental in its occurrence.

All students will not be engaged in vitally meaningful activities of this sort every moment of the school day. For this reason, and also because children, like adults, become bored and get into a rut in their actions and thinking, they will need some stimulation from you when they are not engaged in personally meaningful activities. This means that group lessons, trips, new materials, or new ideas are absolutely necessary to an adequate educational program for children. It is important not to interrupt the more meaningful learning of the individual children when it occurs. He or she will have other opportunities to learn what is being taught in group lessons, etc. If you do interrupt such activities, you will find that you have very little of the child's attention; his mind will still be preoccupied with his personal interests and needs.

Evaluating and Changing Your Basic Organization

As the school year proceeds, you may have to change the organization of the day many times to meet the changing needs of your students and of the curriculum you want to present. Sometimes children become so engrossed in studying particular subjects or concepts that they will spend a week or even a month so occupied, with the majority of the class doing work in the same area, each in his own way. In a situation like this, you might want to modify a structured day with increased free time. In an unstructured plan (in the sense of not having group lessons), you would not have to change your format, but you might want to have students work in small or large groups at times to facilitate information gathering and exchange.

If you feel uncertain about which organization or method is right for you and your students, it is best to begin with one which seems rather conservative to you. It is always easier to give students more freedom. It is not so easy to tighten controls and take away freedom. After you become comfortable with a more conservative organization, then you can try some experimenting with further modifications of your basic organization and the amount of free time you allow students until you find the kind of organization which seems comfortable for you and for the students.

The more responsibility you give to students, the more independent and capable they will become. They can often help you to find new ways to organize the day or to make lessons more interesting, and sometimes they can give good lessons themselves. Whenever you try new methods in class, discuss the results with the students. Give them your ideas about how the new method worked and ask them for their ideas. Everyone will learn. You will learn what the students are thinking and how they responded to the changes which were made. They will learn that their teacher values their opinions and that there is no one set or right way of doing something. The only way to become a creative teacher is to experiment. When you fail, analyze why you failed so that you can learn from the mistake. When you have a success, try it again and then try variations of it. Try to analyze your successes also and their variations to find out what made them work well. This is more difficult to do because you may be less motivated to find the reasons for your success. It is enough to have a good lesson. When you fail, you will be very eager not to fail again, and therefore you will try harder to analyze the reasons for the failure. Try to pinpoint what was happening when the lesson seemed to go wrong; this may give you a clue as to what the problem might be.

As you analyze the failures and the successes, take into account the feelings and the ideas of students. If you have a ghastly lesson and do not have the slightest idea why, go back to school the next day and tell the students you thought the lesson you gave yesterday was not a good one. Tell them you do not understand why this was so or what went wrong with it. See if they can help you. Undoubtedly, if you are receptive to their comments, they will be able to give you some clues. Again, you will learn more and the children will learn that you are interested in their feelings and ideas. They will soon begin to express their ideas spontaneously, perhaps even in the middle of a bad lesson. Embarrassing? Perhaps, but if everyone is learning more and communicating better a little embarrassment will not seem so bad. As students learn that you are sensitive to their feelings, they will try to be sensitive to yours and will attempt to make their criticisms tactfully. The most important lesson you help the students to learn is that there are many ways of dealing with mistakes or failures. Ideally, failures should be used to change future procedures. Failures need not be denied or ignored. Students will learn that honesty in communicating with others is satisfying and growth-inducing for everyone. It is healthier for the children to direct their energies to this type of failure analysis than it is for them to find ways to excuse, deny or hide their failures.

Moving Students Outside the Classroom

In most schools there are times during the day when students must move from the classroom to other areas of the building; to specialists, to lunch, to assemblies, or home for the day. Your manner of dealing with these situations should reflect as closely as possible your beliefs about children and how much responsibility they should assume for themselves. If you are in a school where children are accorded respect and given independence, then they are probably allowed to leave the building for lunch or for home at the end of the day individually or in small groups. If you are in a more regimented school, which would include most of the schools in this country, then the students are probably required to move out of their classrooms in a quiet, double line. The stringency of the requirements regarding quiet, symmetry and other details will vary from school to school, but essentially the principle is the same; an orderly group of students moves through the hallways in a double or single line, maintaining quiet so as not to disturb others. I personally view this as a very regimented manner of dealing with children, although it is consistent as long as our schools remain regimented in so many other ways. The question here is how to make some adjustment for your students, especially if you are running a completely individualized, nonregimented type of classroom.

Children must constantly deal with inconsistencies in the behavior of the adults around them and the rules by which they are expected to live. Many of our adult-imposed rules do not make much sense to children, though they seem to conform to most of them with a minimum of resistance. If necessary, they will be able to conform to and accept another inconsistent and perhaps meaningless rule—that of walking in a single or double line through hallways. The need for quiet is not difficult to understand, but the particular pattern they must form, and the required symmetry of the lines must have little meaning for them. I suspect it has little meaning for us either. It is simply the way it is done.

No matter how free your classroom may be, you can make it quite clear to students that the rules outside the classroom must be obeyed even if they are different from those within the room. Students usually have no trouble in differentiating between the two places. In my experience, the students from an open classroom are usually more easy to handle outside the room than ones from more controlled, traditional classrooms. The former are not interested in wasting time. Their school time is meaningful and important to them. They also have a more open and honest relationship with you, so they do not need to misbehave or test you in the hallways. They will do it in the classroom, if at all. If your administrators are willing, you may try to move the students in different ways. An informal passage of small groups of students through the halls should not be offensive to anyone. Whatever you can do to change regimented conditions in hallways will be a valuable contribution to your school.

Your main difficulty in moving the class from the room will be to get everyone ready to go at the same time. As students become involved with their chosen activities, it is often difficult to persuade them to stop. For this reason you must try to give an ample amount of time for preparation to leave. After you announce preparation for a departure, you may have to help some students who find it difficult to stop or to clean up. You may even want to alert some of these students ahead of time. The age and disposition of the students you teach will have a great deal to do in deciding the time you must allow. Younger children take longer to clean up and to leave tasks than do older ones. Children who tend to become deeply involved in their work will have more difficulty leaving it than those who seem able to go from one activity to another without difficulty. You may have students who have behavior problems or are severely disturbed in some way. They usually react badly to leaving the room. You may wish to help them get ready a little earlier than the others, giving them some personal attention in order to reassure them and calm whatever anxieties they may have. Sometimes it helps to give them some responsibilities for straightening up materials or doing something else, preferably near you. This gives them a constructive way to work off the physical tension induced by their anxiety about leaving the room. They will be leaving a secure and known place for a less secure and uncertain one. By keeping them near you and letting them know you are available to them at these times, you can also use your relationship with them to help calm their fears.

I once had a second grader who would begin sobbing inconsolably every morning about 11:15. This went on for a few weeks with absolutely no discernible provocation. Suddenly we would hear a soul-catching sob breaking the calm of the room. The children got so used to it they hardly even looked up from their work after the first few times. I finally realized that Irene was afraid to leave the room to go into the noisy, overcrowded lunchroom. She was a very sensitive, creative child and reacted profoundly to her environment. Our lunchroom could ruffle the least sensitive children. Irene also had difficulty controlling her behavior in the hallways and was reported by monitors almost every day for talking or running on the stairs. When I realized what the difficulty was, I began giving her tasks to do before and during lunchtimes to carry over the comforting influence of my relationship with her into the lunch period. I also reminded her daily before she left the room that she would be returning to the room very soon. I had some of the more motherly girls take care of her on the steps and in the hallways when I was not with the class, so that Irene would have some external controls to help her. The conformity and regimentation required in the hallways of this school made life very difficult for her, but somehow she managed with the external props we were able to provide. Hopefully, as teachers are able to change their methods of teaching to more relaxed and natural ones, their attitudes will spread to administrators, and those gruesome hallways will be changed into lively places where children can talk and move freely.

Homework

Another basic routine is homework. In many school systems teachers are required by law to assign a specific amount of homework for grades 1 through 6 for each school day. In others no rules are required and the assignment of homework is left up to the discretion of individual teachers. Even in traditionally run classrooms, homework is a problem because of the wide range of ability and comprehension among the students. Unless you give homework on the lowest level of ability within a single class, there will be students who are unable to understand or to complete the work. This is grossly unfair to the other students. There is really no way to decide how to fairly choose a level of ability for the homework assignment. Wherever you decide that level should be, the majority of the students will probably find the work too hard or too easy. This usually results in careless work or in parents or siblings helping to do assignments, both undesirable results.

To do away with homework because of the individual differences within the class is to deny the benefit of extending learning into the home. Many children love to do homework. Many students who enjoy school like to take home an extension of their school day to make their time at home more enjoyable. This is particularly true of children in well-run open classrooms. They often do not want to leave at the end of the day and therefore are pleased by an assignment which they can do at home.

My most trying time during the week was always on Friday afternoons. The students were unusually disorderly and uncooperative at that time. It took me some weeks to realize why. When I did realize that it was because they did not want to go home for what was to them a long weekend, I interpreted their feelings and things became much calmer. I gave many of them assignments to do over the weekend or suggested things for them to collect to bring to school on Monday. One little boy verbalized the feelings of many of the students when he yelled at me, "We'll be right back on Monday!"

How then can you provide for all these contingencies and still assign justifiable and reasonable homework? One method is to make several suggestions for homework each day growing out of the general activity of the class. Each child may choose one of these suggestions. It will probably be the one which seems most interesting to him. Or it may be the one which is the easiest for him. In either case, he will be doing something constructive which he has chosen and committed himself to doing. Many students do not like to do homework and it certainly is no crime for them to feel that way. If they always choose the easiest assignment, you should not penalize them for this.

Another method for solving the homework problem is to broaden your definition of homework. It can be collecting things to bring to school, thinking up problems instead of working them, reading a book, writing a story, visiting a store, noticing things about the environment which can be used in class activities, etc. Many of these broader definitions of homework, like a general lesson, will allow each student to work on his own level. If these assignments are growing out of work done within the classroom, it will be relatively easy to check on who does the homework as the work will be continuing within the classroom the following day.

The open classroom attempts to create a love of learning and a love of pursuing one's own interests. If it is doing this, then homework will grow naturally from the classroom situation. To help students take responsibility for their own homework assignments, you can begin to suggest that they continue some aspect of work they do in the classroom during the day. After a few suggestions from you, they will begin to assume this responsibility themselves. If you are bound by legal requirements, as previously mentioned, then you will have to make a special effort to have children decide on their own appropriate homework and check to see that they do it. For older children, it is possible to have them keep daily records for you, to have them check off the work they do as well as the work they do not complete. If you find some students who are unable to assume such responsibility, then you yourself can give them direct assignments each day and check their daily work.

BIBLIOGRAPHY - CHAPTER 4

General books on organizing the classroom:

Bruner, Jerome S., *The Process of Education*. New York: Vintage Books, 1960.

Hertzberg, Alvin and Edward F. Stone, *Schools are for Children*. New York: Schocken Books, 1971.

Holt, John, *What Do I Do On Monday?* New York: Dutton, 1970.

Rogers, Vincent R., *Teaching in the British Primary School*. Toronto: The Macmillan Co., 1970.

Hawkins, Frances P., *The Logic of Action*. Boulder, Colo.: University of Colorado, 1969.

Books on materials and specific organization of activity centers:

Barth, Roland S., "On Selecting Materials for the Classroom," *Childhood Education* (1971), *47*, no. 6.

Glasser, Joyce Fern, *The Elementary School Learning Center for Independent Study*. West Nyack, N.Y.: Parker Publishing Co., Inc., 1971.

Hegeler, Stern, *Choosing Toys for Children*. London: Lavistock Publications, 1963.

CHAPTER 5.
THE BEGINNING

5.

This chapter will contain three main sections: factors to consider in beginning the open classroom, beginning the open classroom in a modified way, and beginning the open classroom for the entire day. It is preferable to begin open classroom techniques on the first day of school, if possible, so that students will not have to unlearn routines. But do not feel that you must wait for the next year in order to begin the open classroom. Children can adapt to change if you take some steps to help them.

FACTORS TO CONSIDER IN BEGINNING THE OPEN CLASSROOM

When you plan the beginning weeks of your open classroom, you must take into account several factors: the age of your students, their prior school experience, their personalities and your own personality. By considering all of these factors and their interrelationships, you will be able to plan for the start of your open classroom so that there is a minimum of confusion and uneasiness for both you and the students.

Age of Students

Young children, under the age of seven or eight years, tend to be more flexible than older ones. They usually adjust more quickly and comfortably to new situations regardless of their prior school situations. For this reason you need not hesitate to begin an open classroom with them immediately. After the age of about eight years, most children have internalized sufficient cultural mores so that they have definite expectations of what school should be like. These preconceptions are often in conflict with the reality of the open classroom. You will be presenting the students with a new experience which may make them immediately uncomfortable and unsure of what kinds of behavior are expected of them. It will take time for them to learn the new concept of school you are presenting.

You can ease these uncertainties and anxieties if you start from what students have been accustomed to thinking of as "school" and proceed to something different in a gradual way. This is the same thing you would do if you were trying to change a concept in social science, in math or in any other intellectual area. This gradual change will allow students to assimilate the new routines as you introduce them slowly, rather than being overwhelmed by a whole set of new rules and expectations (or lack of them) which they cannot comprehend or assimilate immediately.

You will have to communicate your wishes to them in many real, concrete situations within the class before they fully comprehend those wishes. To say to students, "Anything goes," is not very helpful. Your definition of "anything" may be quite different from theirs. It is this difference which must be elaborated through your actions in real situations. Only this will enable them to understand your definition of "anything." You may tell students they may choose to learn to read any book they wish and then let them do so and accept their choice. After several weeks, they will understand that you mean what you say. However, if you begin to comment that this book is "too easy," that this one is "too difficult," etc., this will communicate to them that you would like them to guide their "free choices" by some subtle criterion of difficulty which you have predetermined. Thus, the "free choice" is only a new label for teacher-selected books. You can deal with this problem more honestly by truly giving students free choice and encouraging them to learn how to decide which books are too easy or too difficult for them—a valuable lesson in itself, which doesn't take too long to learn. If this makes you uneasy, then it is far better to give students a choice within a selected range of books you have chosen. To say to Tom, "Here is a list of books I think are appropriate for your reading level, choose any of them you like," is still giving a good deal of choice to a student and is a direct and honest procedure. Whichever way you approach the free choice problem, the above methods will make clear your intentions so that students do not have to play the game of "Free Choice" with you, one which in actual practice has little to do with choosing freely.

As you communicate clearly to students what the new structure of their learning situation is, they will understand what you expect of them in actual classroom situations. As they begin feel secure within the new structure, they will be able to begin experimenting with new behavior to find out what is appropriate and rewarding for them in this new milieu. This process takes time.

If you flood the children with a totally different situation all at once, they will be faced with the dual tasks of trying to understand your expectations and simultaneously adjusting their behavior, without sufficient guides for doing so. This usually leads to anxiety and confusion for most students and may set off a variety of destructive behavior for some of them. This kind of behavior is difficult to handle and can be upsetting to you and to the students themselves. In attempting to understand the limits of behavior, students may become destructive with materials in order to find out your reaction to such behavior. If you do not interfere in quarrels, students may suddenly begin actual fights after a few days—again to make you commit yourself more definitely regarding the range of behavior which is acceptable in the classroom.

When I first began the open classroom, I overestimated the strengths of many of my first grade students. I immediately changed the structure of the class from traditional to one in which any child could do whatever he wished to do. For several students, it was like freeing them from prison. They suddenly became busier and more interested in everything, happier and more content than they had ever appeared to be in my traditionally run classroom. Other students went through weeks of attempting to adjust to the new plan, showing little interest in anything except how to decide what was expected of them and testing out situations in many ways. They were constantly watching for my reactions to their behavior. Other students began to act out rather serious behavior problems in the context of a looser external structure and control. For example, Henry spent much of his time in the clothes closet, occasionally emitting Tarzan-like yells. When he emerged from the closet, he would immediately pick a fight with the nearest child. He was acting out inner problems which he was unable to suppress in view of the lack of external controls. Another student, Ronald, became overly excited and boisterous for a week, and then appeared to be severely depressed for several weeks. There were many instances of such disturbing reactions within the class, but essentially there seemed to be three basic responses to the abrupt change in structure:

1. Relief and immediate adjustment by students who probably had healthy personalities, and who were inhibited by the usual traditional classroom
2. disorientation and confusion for students who had previously made successful adjustments to the school situation where they were required to sacrifice their own needs and interests for those of the teacher and the school
3. fear and absorption with preexisting personality problems by students who were not strong enough to function without any external controls.

It may be more comfortable for most pupils if you change things gradually, rather than doing everything all at once. Only you can evaluate this. I am sure I could have saved many of my students and myself needless upset and emotional strain if I had changed over to the open classroom more gradually.

If you prefer an exciting time and have a fairly secure group of students in your class, it is possible to change the routines suddenly and not have too difficult a time. Simply tell the students beforehand what you have in mind and then proceed to do it. Problems which arise can be handled immediately and directly with the students, and changes can be made as needed. Be clear about your expectations, communicate them quickly, and preferably by means of real situations, whenever possible. This will help students to understand the new behavior expectations more quickly and easily and will minimize behavior testing on the part of students.

Prior School Experience of Students

Another factor which is important in your determination of how you begin the open classroom is the prior school experience of your students. The more rigid and traditional it has been, the greater effort you must make to begin the open classroom in a modified form. Slowly lead children into the type of classroom situation you would like them to have, as they become ready to use the freedom and the new learning situation. To open up the classroom from the beginning is inviting them to test behavioral limits and to act out any serious problems they have with authority figures or with past negative school situations. In the hands of a skillful therapist, this procedure can be a beneficial interlude. In the hands of most teachers, it is simply a very trying and often destructive time which can sour even the most ardent follower of the open classroom about the whole concept. The chaotic moments which occur in the opening weeks of the school year in the open classroom are usually due to poor judgment on the teacher's part about how much freedom to give to the class at that particular point in time. By careful planning you should be able to avoid many mistakes and errors in judgment.

For students who have had a moderately open or relaxed kind of classroom in the past, it is certainly feasible to begin immediately with the open classroom in full swing. The contrast between the students' previous experience and this new one will be minimal, and so the adjustment will be easier.

For students who are twelve years or older, I would suggest beginning immediately with the open classroom situation. By this age, students are usually fed up with the traditional school routine and are often mature enough emotionally and intellectually to take immediate advantage of a new, more promising school situation. The difference between your classroom and their prior experiences is in this instance meant to startle them out of their bored state into a new kind of involvement with school. They are immediately shocked out of boredom by the strangeness and freshness of the situation. Before they can classify your classroom as some version of the same old thing, hopefully they will become involved in the exciting new learning situations available to them.

Personalities and Problems of Students

Another important factor in the planning of the opening weeks of your open classroom is the varied personalities of your students. It is true that you cannot know them before you meet and work with them. The kinds of records you receive from the previous teachers are so superficial that they are relatively worthless. However, if you are taking a class which has a special label such as "slow," "difficult," "emotional problems," "temperamental," etc., you had better plan to use a modified version of what you eventually plan for your open classroom. Children in these classes often have been misused by the school system and have gained various names which generally mean that the students do not conform to the official mold of the particular school system. This does not mean that these students do not have problems. Most of them do. But no one has tried to help them live successfully with their problems; they have simply been rejected because of their problems. These students will not feel secure in any school situation. And with good reason! Their feelings of insecurity are based on prior mistreatment they have experienced within the school. They are used to failure and hostility and they will need all the support and structure you can provide in the beginning. After you see what their problems are, you can begin to give them freedom when you feel they can use it constructively. In the case of seriously disturbed students who usually end up in these classes, they may always need a lot of external structure in order to function.

At the other end of the continuum, if you are having a very bright or "good" class, then you might also start out with a modified version of the open classroom. The brighter and better behaved students have so far been quite successful within the school system. As you take away the standard props of the traditional classroom, you will also be taking away the source of their success and achievement. They sometimes find it exceedingly difficult to reorganize their behavior without a great deal of support from you. They frequently are not initially successful in an open classroom situation, where they must direct their own behavior rather than being guided constantly by an adult. They are used to working to please a teacher, not to satisfy their own needs or curiosity.

We can see disturbances like this in all grades, even including university graduate school courses. In some cases the suppression of natural curiosity and interest has made it almost impossible for students to work on their own initiative without the promise of the teacher's approval or a good grade. In some cases the suppression of natural childish feelings, interests and behaviors has occurred to such an extent that the children will become quite destructive and malicious when deprived of external controls and constant supervision. This is not good for them or for you. Frequently when these situations occur, teachers blame it on the open classroom system. Certainly poor judgment in using the open classroom techniques can precipitate such occurrences, but in the long run we have to turn to the home and school environments which have helped build up these feelings within the children and have forced them to repress and control normal feelings to an unreasonable degree. Often children either are forced to control their real feelings entirely or meet with rejection and failure. The controls which a child adopts in these situations may be so crippling that he cannot regain or develop his own natural spontaneity.

Max, a first grader in one of my classes, was a very sweet and well-behaved boy. This was unusual behavior in the black, lower-class neighborhood where I taught. The boys were noticeably not sweet or well-behaved by traditional middle-class standards. After several enjoyable months of the open classroom in an entirely free situation, Max was not disorganized or noticeably changed in any way. One day, he painted a beautiful picture which he described as a "dead clown." That picture represented Max. He had somehow sensed through seeing the other children's happiness and involvement with the activities and with each other, that many of the feelings he saw around him were dead inside him, and he felt they could not be revived.

Unfortunately, if you begin teaching the open classroom, you may find that you have some "dead clowns" in your classes. These children will need a great deal of support from you if they recognize their limitations in a situation which encourages them to express their feelings honestly and to relate to reality rather than to distort it and act in a stereotyped manner.

If you have any students in your class whom you know or suspect are emotionally disturbed, you must be very careful with them. The sudden freedom they will experience in the open classroom is very threatening. These children have comparatively few effective controls over their feelings and few adequate defenses, so that their inner conflicts are close to the surface and easily aroused. When outside controls are removed, their feelings and conflicts can become overwhelming and they may begin to act them out or simply to become panicky or disorganized. It is not impossible to run an open classroom with very disturbed children, but you must take special care to provide some structure and control for them so they do not become overwhelmed by their actions or their feelings. One year I had a second grader who seemed quite secure and intelligent. After two days in my class, he became disorganized in many ways. Typical of his disorganization was the deterioration in his handwriting, which had been meticulous and often neater than my own. It slowly deteriorated until he was only making scratches and scribbles on his paper. It was apparent that he could not concentrate enough to write even one letter. This occurred in the space of one week. Unfortunately, by the time I realized what was happening to him, his mother withdrew him from the class and I was unable to help him regain control by providing external controls to support him. She was not interested in having her child in the open classroom to begin with, and certainly not after she witnessed his meticulous behavior collapsing. I cannot blame her for those feelings or for removing her child. Had I been more sensitive to his needs, I would have been able to prevent such disorganization of his behavior from occurring.

Personality of the Teacher

Another important factor to consider in beginning the open classroom is your personality. If you are a person who is basically in touch with her feelings, who enjoys life and is easy-going in most situations, then you probably can move easily into the open classroom. If you are a controlled person who tends to suppress feelings, you may have some initial difficulty in the open classroom situation. In a sense, the same precautions which hold true in regard to the students also hold true in regard to you. If you are thoroughly used to, and relatively happy with, our present educational system, then you had better venture slowly into the open classroom, if at all. The great lesson we have learned from England and from pioneers in open classroom techniques in this country is that the teachers who are highly motivated to change present learning conditions are the ones who can utilize open classroom techniques most easily and most successfully. If you have felt dissatisfied with the learning situation but have been unable to pinpoint the source of your dissatisfaction or the factors which make you uneasy, then you may move more quickly and easily into the open classroom situation. You may find the increased reactions and interest of the students will fill a lack you felt in a more traditional classroom.

If you have been teaching for many years, it may be difficult for you suddenly to change well-established habits. The older and more experienced we become, the more difficult it is for us to change characteristic behavior. Because this behavior becomes such a habit, we are often unaware of things we do in the classroom, or of the significance they have in communicating things to students. You will need time to relearn and to develop a different perspective and orientation as to how children learn and how you can help them to learn.

Whatever your situation, caution will not harm anyone. It is better to go slowly, in order to spare yourself and the students unnecessary pain and anxiety, than to rush into the open classroom when neither they nor you are prepared for it. The following pages will give some very specific suggestions about beginning to move into the open classroom situation. Try to choose the ones which sound most reasonable to you. The greatest problem I have encountered in helping both students and experienced teachers to develop the open classroom has been with their personalities, their values and their habits. Some of these have severely restricted the teachers from giving their students freedom to learn in a new and more satisfying way. Old habits and training are powerful.

Occasionally when a teacher changes to the open classroom techniques, changes in her own personality are precipitated as well as changes in her students' personalities. If you rush into the open classroom before you are ready emotionally as well as intellectually, you may find yourself feeling confused and bewildered. You then will probably blame your difficulties on the nearest scapegoat—the open classroom concept. Actually, the real culprit will be the change itself. For this reason, give ample thought to your own personality and to the amount of change, newness of experience, disorder and emotional upheaval you can tolerate.

BEGINNING THE OPEN CLASSROOM
IN A MODIFIED FORM

There are many ways to begin. If you are hesitant to start open classroom techniques, you can begin slowly. After seeing how you and the students react, you can increase use of the techniques or the amount of time in which you use them. It is possible to think about beginning either in terms of the time devoted to open classroom techniques or in terms of the way you structure the material students are to learn. You can begin by modifying the structure of assignments you give to students, by allowing students to choose their own assignments in one subject area, or by allocating a period of time for free choice activities.

Each of these paths gives you a different amount and type of control over what goes on during the time you have open classroom activities. You will have most control by structuring your lessons and assignments in such a way that students begin to work individually, within the context of a group assignment which is determined by you. This can be done without changing your seating arrangement, your routines or your general classroom organization. The intent and content of your lessons and your expectations of students will change. You give up intellectual control of the students in this method, and some control of what they learn, although it is questionable whether you ever have much control over this. You will maintain control over most of their behavior. If you are reluctant to allow children free choice in activities and in behavior, then this will be a gradual and very easy way to move into the open classroom techniques and to evaluate their effects on your students. As you see how children blossom intellectually in this learning context, you may be more willing to give up other controls which have seemed important to you for personal or philosophical reasons. Or you may decide that the open classroom techniques are not for you.

Another method which will give you a high degree of control over students' behavior is that of allowing students to choose their own activities and topics of investigation within one content or subject area, such as social studies. They can use any materials or situations which interest them or which will further their learning within the content area you have selected. This will give them a new way to experience learning. They will move away from the more abstract and verbal learning which they are used to, into a more concrete and experiential type of learning. I would not recommend your selecting reading or mathematics as the free subject area if you feel very eager to have children achieve in these areas. Your vested interest in their achievement may interfere with the amount of free choice you will give them.

As in the previous method, this one allows you and the students to behave much as you always have in the majority of classroom situations. In the time set aside for the study of the subject area chosen for free choice activities, it will be necessary to change class routines and materials in order to facilitate individual free choice of learning situations.

The third method is very popular, but gives less control over student behavior at certain times during the day. While you run a traditional classroom in other ways, you release a certain amount of time during the day or during the week in which students are encouraged to pursue their own interests, either within the context of school activities or without any restriction. It has become common practice for teachers to give students one hour a day or perhaps a minimum of two hours a week for free time.

Many teachers allow students to choose any type of activity they wish during this time, encouraging them to bring in things from home or to introduce games not usually allowed in school. This time is considered by teachers and students as non-school time, almost non-learning time. It is a time for fun. Many educators believe that because children learn so much outside the classroom, we should attempt to incorporate this type of spontaneous, extracurricular learning into classroom life. However, I think there are some pitfalls in this position which should be considered.

When you suggest that students bring in games or things from home which interest them, you cannot be sure of what the home situation is like or what the child has experienced as interesting at home. It might be watching television all day, playing baseball, or just waiting for something to happen. You easily can make the assumption that students have engrossing activities at home, and this may not be the case. Most children like to go to school to get away from the dull routine at home, even though they may simply replace it with the dull routine of school. Parents often are too busy to really involve themselves in children's interests or projects in any meaningful way. Therefore, to suggest to students that school may be the same as home may be a destructive action.

There is also an implication here that there are not enough interesting things to do in school. There are many interesting things that can be studied and learned most easily in an open school situation. I do think that to start off a free time period by essentially telling students that they must bring in non-school connected materials is a mistake. If you are beginning an open classroom, even in a modified form, you should have enough interesting materials and activities for students in the classroom. If you do not have them, then you are not ready to begin.

Each of these methods is easy for you to implement with a minimum change of regular routines. You will begin to see the advantages of the open classroom techniques while still feeling secure within the structure of the traditional classroom you and the students are used to and more comfortable with. The students will begin to learn and behave in different ways, and their concept of school and what can occur there will slowly begin to change without any abrupt dislocations in behavior or thinking.

The activities and learning which occur during these newly structured lessons or free time periods will begin to spread spontaneously into other aspects of the classroom if you allow them to. Suddenly the divisions between the free periods or subjects and those which are more traditional will seem false and artificial to you and the students. You will discover with your students that there are better and more satisfying means of learning. You will probably be eager to extend these ways of learning into all areas of learning. Some more detailed examples of these methods will help you to implement the method most suitable for your class.

RESTRUCTURING LESSONS TO ENCOURAGE INTELLECTUAL FREEDOM

Your purpose in using this method is to help children begin to work individually and independently within the subject areas you have selected. You will present all the students with a group lesson to initiate the topic and to focus the learning activities which will subsequently occur. After you present this focusing part of the lesson and have involved most of the students in the topic, you will encourage them to proceed on the level and aspect of the topic which is most appropriate for them. In this way each child will move immediately from the group lesson to pursuing his particular interest within the general subject, and he will be allowed to pursue it with some degree of freedom.

If you want to introduce the concept of three dimensional measurement to your students, you can begin with a group lesson to introduce the concept. You might begin by having students use cube shaped blocks to build three dimensional structures. They can work individually or in small groups; at their desks or grouped around tables or desks. Any lesson in which students use real, manipulable materials will be more interesting. The materials will stimulate their senses and often involve them in the subject despite some initial disinterest.

After some initial activity with the blocks, you can focus their activities by asking that they build some type of building, measure it and record their measurements so that someone else will be able to use them to reconstruct a building that will look exactly like theirs. This assumes that students are familar at least with two dimensional measurement. Have measuring materials of all kinds immediately available in some central location (tape measures, rulers, slide measures, etc.). The children should obtain and select their own tools for measuring. This procedure will communicate to them that they are to seek out their own tools for learning instead of waiting passively for them to be passed out by a teacher or monitors. It is neater, faster and easier to pass out materials, but it also encourages passivity and lack of initiative or responsibility in students.

The first few times you have this type of lesson there may be many questions and misunderstandings as students get used to new ways of working. You can help speed the process of adjustment by verbalizing some of the purposes you have in mind: that each child produce his own unique construction (in this case, block building and measurement), select any tools or aids he needs, be responsible for his own materials and working area, not be concerned about what others are doing, do what he wants to do or is interested in doing. Try to circulate among students to see what they are doing; who progresses alone, who is unable to do anything without help or support from you or other students, who seems to be interpreting the directions correctly, who is not, who cannot tolerate frustration, who can, and on what level individual students are working.

As students ask questions about how to do things, try not to give them direct answers. Sometimes it seems laborious and wasteful of time to watch children work things out for themselves. It would be so easy to give them an answer here, a rule there. But if you do not allow children to question and work things out for themselves you will deprive them of valuable experiences in learning how to formulate questions and pursue topics independently. You may even kill budding interest by supplying an answer too soon, before the uncertainty of what is happening has become interesting enough for the student to pursue the topic in any depth. By allowing a child to pursue questions independently, encouraging him to question why and to seek an answer by using his own resources, you improve his image of himself as a learner and a capable, independent person. You also lead him closer to the joys of self-discovery.

Until you feel sure of yourself in freer learning situations where you have given up control of students' activities, it is not necessary to answer any questions. In fact, it will probably speed up the development of individual initiative and independence if you simply refer the question back to the student. You can always counter questions with comments such as, "Well, what do you think about it?", "I don't know, how do you think we can find out?", or "Let's try . . . maybe that will give us the answer." If you urge students to do something however they can, try to find the answer in some way, and constantly urge them to experiment in order to find an answer, it will speed the process of helping students to become truly independent in their search for knowledge. You must constantly reassure students that there is no one right way to do something, that there usually are many ways and that students do not have to do things the way other students do them. Years of learning to do things the "right" way and learning by imitating others will have to be counteracted within the classroom. This will take some time, but the more you verbalize your feelings on the subject, the more willing students will be to try your way. When you express excitement and happiness over a student's discovery or solution to a problem, you will give the children further incentives to learn independently. Soon, the doors to exciting intellectual learning will be open to all your students.

There may be some problems in the beginning with students who cannot tolerate much frustration. Before they learn new ways of approaching problems and feel secure enough to try many approaches to problems, they may find this new way of learning quite frustrating. In this case you may have to come to their aid with a suggestion now and then, so that they are able to see some progress, and do not simply give up the task completely. It is always helpful to suggest that they put the problem on a simpler level or limit the scope of their investigation in order to find an answer quicker. With these students, you may find it is better to give them suggestions for resources or other materials sooner than you would do with other students. As they learn the thrill of discovery, they should gradually be able to tolerate more frustration. Often, students have learned to be impatient with their learning pace because adults have been impatient with it. When you take a different point of view, it can help students like this to change their attitudes toward themselves rather quickly. For a few students who seem to be constantly frustrated with situations they cannot solve immediately, you may be able to have only a slight effect.

You must also be able to judge during these early lessons how much frustration and ability to concentrate your students as a group are capable of. It may take them a long time in this measuring lesson to simply write down some measurements. If so, end the lesson when they have accomplished this much. Do not worry about students who are unable to do this; they have been exploring different ways to measure. They have not been wasting their time. They have probably learned more than they would have if they were working in a workbook with only a slight idea of what they were doing. Their actions have revealed to you what they do not know, and usually in a very vivid way. If you have been a careful observer, you will know how to help them in the next lesson. You should reassure these students that it is all right that they were unable to finish, that they can continue next time (name a specific time you plan to give the next lesson), and tell them you know they worked hard at solving the problem.

If you feel it is necessary to stop your class after most of them have made their measurements, collect the written ones and then have students clean up their own desks. Ask for volunteers to put the measuring tools away after each student has returned his to the central location. The clean-up should encourage all students to be active and responsible members of the class. This is a new learning situation for the students and you cannot expect all of them to know exactly what to do. There may be confusion and difficulties as students attempt to leave their desks or working areas to return tools. If you do not intervene, students will probably work out these problems for themselves. They will learn to avoid bumping into others and how to share tools and help their neighbors. If you feel you must intervene when there are too many students in one area or when students are colliding with each other as they move about the room, then it is best to take a matter-of-fact attitude and raise a question about how some of the congestion, or whatever the problem is, could be avoided. You will get the quickest and the best results if you try to elicit suggestions from the students and then act upon the ones which seem most promising. Remember that this is another learning situation for students, and the learning will be more significant if you do not supply them with formulas. Let them find out how to think up their own.

Your students may also become frustrated over their mistakes in measuring, and in attempting to follow your instructions. Because your instructions leave many things to the judgment of the students, they may feel uneasy. The more relaxed you appear and the more you are able to laugh good naturedly with the students when they make mistakes or have some failures, the more you will help them to try again. Here again, you must watch carefully for the level of frustration. When it begins to increase, you may have to cut off the lesson and suggest that students may need different kinds of measurements than those with which they are familiar or that there is some way to describe buildings which they have not yet discovered. This will set the stage for your next lesson.

This initial lesson should have provided you with important diagnostic information. You should know which students need help in very basic measuring concepts, which ones are ready to move into more advanced three dimensional measurement, and which ones already know the material you wish to cover. This will help you plan your next lesson. It will have to contain material all the students can understand and work on. If the range of knowledge among your students is very broad, you may have to give students several choices of activities on different levels during the individualized portion of the lesson. This can be accomplished by setting up several working centers, assigning students to them and giving the students at each center a different task.

If you have found that your students are not very knowledgeable in two dimensional measurement, you may have to do some background work in the next lesson to prepare them to move into three dimensional work, Or if they seem competent in two dimensional measurement but confused when they get into three dimensional tasks, your next lesson could be a demonstration lesson in which you give students one way of taking three dimensional measurements. During the individual portion of the lesson, they will attempt to duplicate what you have shown them. After duplicating your method, they should be encouraged to explore and find other ways of doing measuring, using variations of your method or new methods they discover themselves. This will reinforce their learning on a practical level, and will also encourage them to make further discoveries about the concept of measuring, as well as variations in methods of measuring.

It is also possible to reverse the two lessons just discussed: for example, you may give a demonstration lesson with individualized work as the first lesson, in order to introduce the concept and skill, and then give a discovery lesson with freer exploration of the concept and materials as the second lesson. The only drawback to this procedure is that it tends to inhibit the free discoveries of students, since you have already given them a frame of reference or a set from which to work, so that free discovery is less likely to occur. However, in classes in which students seem less secure or are slow to grasp concepts, you may prefer to begin with demonstration lessons. Other classes may function better by having discovery lessons to begin a unit of study. After some use of the open classroom techniques, almost all students will feel secure enough to use discovery methods to begin units of study. This lets them approach learning problems independently and gives you invaluable diagnostic information about their level of prior knowledge and their learning procedures.

In this type of lesson you are controlling the content, but

you are increasing the spectrum of complexity in which students can work within the content you have presented. You are giving them many indications that you expect them to be more independent, self-motivated and responsible for their own learning. You are communicating this in real situations. Ideally, after giving lessons like this in one or more content areas, you would move on to allow children more freedom and responsibility in all the content areas, despite the fact that you are determining the actual topics studied.

PROVIDING INTELLECTUAL FREEDOM IN A CONTENT AREA

In the second method, you can select one content area in which students have complete free choice to determine their learning activities. You will not focus them or assign topics for them to study. You will be controlling the range of things students study by the materials you provide, from which they will choose learning activities. You must have enough interesting materials and things to do which are connected with the content area you have selected.

You might decide to select science as the subject area for free choice. If your room is not set up with activity centers, you can push desks together to form large working areas during the science period. Check your curriculum guides for the grade level you are teaching. List the topics and materials which students on your grade level should be learning about and using. This will give you an idea of the selection of materials you should make available. Most schools have a good supply of science materials. If you do not have many in your room, borrow from other teachers or from the science resource person. You do not need one tool or object for each child. A few of each thing will be enough, and if you can only get one (such as a child's microscope), one is enough. These supplies should cover a broad range of topics—electricity, living things, machines, plants, the surface of the earth, optics, physics, ecology, etc. You will control learning by the materials you supply. The broader range of materials you can have, the more leeway you will encourage in the topics and situations your students can select.

The first few lessons will consist of allowing students to experiment with the materials, perhaps suggesting they find out whatever they can about the various things in the room. You will have to use your judgment in the timing of these lessons. Some classes can use an hour of this type of work while others could only use fifteen minutes or one half hour. The best procedure is to have other lessons planned to follow these free periods and to terminate the free exploration period whenever you feel it is best. There may be a lot of noise and movement during these initial lessons. Until students settle down with something which truly interests them, they will tend to look at all the materials briefly. If you feel this would make you uncomfortable, you can set some limits for the noise and establish signals to tell children when they must be quieter.

As students begin to examine the materials and experiment with them, move among them without becoming too involved with any one student. You do not want to inhibit their exploration of the materials before you have some idea of what they are interested in and what they seem to be capable of. Most important, do not provide easy answers unless there is a problem concerning the operation of equipment or the proper use of some instruments or materials. This is a period for free exploration and discovery. You want the children to discover and explore on their own initiative, not at your prompting or instruction. The sensory stimulation of handling materials will stimulate students to make further observations. Soon they will begin to formulate questions about what is happening. As they begin to ask questions, you can begin to develop their skills in investigation by suggesting further explorations or by directing students to other material or sources of information for more facts on the question they have formulated. If you cut into this process by giving answers before they have fully formulated the question in their minds and developed some curiosity about the answer, you may limit the students' learning and involvement with the materials and the subject matter.

When you have decided that interest is waning for the majority of the students, signal them (with your prearranged signal) that it is time to stop. Then give directions for clean-up. You can use any of the methods suggested in Chapter 4 for clean-up. If the method you have chosen doesn't work very well, discuss the reasons for this with the students, or try a different method. In general, you might start with more controlled methods of straightening the materials and then try moving into freer methods where everyone assumes responsibility for the entire room.

After a few periods, and in some cases in the first one, students will become interested in a particular material or subject. When this happens it is important that you watch closely to see the direction their investigations are taking. Sometimes a comment about what they are doing, a question, or supplying an added implement or material will be enough to spur them on to new learning. For some children, you may have to sit with them and play with them, the materials, or the equipment. As you do so, discuss what is happening if possible, mainly by asking questions, making simple comments, and showing some interest in what the child is interested in. In this way it may be possible to get a better idea of what the child is interested in and capable of understanding at this point in his life. The greater your enthusiasm toward the things children are working with and discovering, the greater will be their interest and their desire to go further with their explorations. They are still interested in pleasing you and in learning what the expectations and limits in this new situation will be. If you are thrilled when a child discovers he can move iron filings over paper, and you do not become excited or angry when the magnet slips and some of the iron filings fall to the floor, you will be communicating the important message that learning is the most important thing that can happen in this classroom. Often in traditional classrooms, we reverse these priorities and are more concerned with behavior and tidiness than we are with real learning and experiencing.

When students seem to be interested in pursuing some topic, get all the materials or resource books for them which you can (if the student is capable of getting the materials himself, encourage him to do so, but be ready to do it yourself if he has difficulty or for some reason does not do it). You must be the model for this new type of learning. You show students how to get what they need and where to find it, so that as time proceeds, they will be able to seek out their own learning aids.

When you are running this kind of free choice period for one subject area, it is a good idea to keep a folder to hold students' work and/or to keep a record of what type of work each child does during the free time. Either you or the student can do this, or both of you. Any written, drawn or constructed work should go into the folder if possible. Often students want to take their work home and they should have that option. In such a case, make a note of the work and put it into the folder as a record. If it is a construction of some sort, the child might make a small drawing of it to be put into the folder. This serves several purposes. It gives you a record of what the child has accomplished and what his interests have been. It gives a tangible record of learning to show to administrators, parents and students when the need arises. After a period of several months, it is very interesting for children to look back over their work. They are almost always impressed by the amount of it and may laugh at the ineptness of some of it (feeling very mature and advanced in their present state). They also may pick up threads of it or begin new aspects of previous projects. If you must grade students, this folder record will provide a good basis on which you can do so.

The kinds of learning which occur in a period like this should be different from what you would encourage or expect in a traditional classroom. Students will be exploring the many aspects of the materials and topics which come under examination. The interests of one child are complemented and enlarged by the interests of all his classmates; there is seldom any need for stimulation from you except in the form of materials. Children should have the chance to explore freely, without prior planning if they choose. This way they will begin to experience some of the joys of learning. You will see that their ability to work hard and for sustained periods of time on one subject will develop gradually as they become truly interested and involved in learning. This activity encourages the kind of interest and eventual hard work which most people expend on things outside the formal learning situation, such as hobbies. Such involvement in a subject, and the ability to follow it in all the twists and turns of doing research or experimenting, promotes the child's learning, and you should recognize this whole process as learning. You will have to respect individual learning styles and modes of investigating problems. Since we often think of learning as the kind of process which occurs in a traditional classroom, it is often difficult to allow such individuality to occur and to flower. It would be nice for us if learning was always neat and orderly. It seems that it seldom is, however, and the unpredictable and uncontrollable quality of learning will become more apparent to you within the open classroom situation. Children will be able to learn in their way rather than in a way imposed by you.

The learning which occurs will tend to be on a more concrete level of thinking. We know that most students do not learn abstractions until about the age of ten or eleven years.[1] In a traditional classroom, teachers tend to encourage students to learn abstract ideas with very little background of concrete experience. It is easy to teach children to verbalize ideas or abstractions. It is not easy to help them to obtain the foundations of experience which will enable them to formulate the abstraction themselves when they are mature enough to do so. Research indicates that no matter how hard we try to speed up the learning of abstractions, it is impossible to do so.[2] The organism cannot make abstract deductions before it is physically ready to do so, and when it is physically ready to do so it must have the experiential background to make valid abstract deductions. As you observe a child working, you will get an impression of his level of development. This will enable you to suggest appropriate materials and resources for each child when the occasion warrants it.

PROVIDING TIME FOR FREE CHOICE OF ACTIVITY

The third method is the one most commonly used by teachers interested in developing open classrooms. It involves giving the students a certain period of free time, usually in the afternoon. Students are allowed to do anything they want to do. Although many teachers encourage the children to bring in things from home, and some teachers bring in games themselves for students to use, I feel this is not a constructive use of this kind of time and does not give a valid picture of the open classroom. It almost seems that the teacher uses this time to communicate her own alienation from the established school routines without providing anything very constructive in their place. She is saying, in effect, that there is nothing very interesting within the school, so students should bring in games, puzzles, etc. from home to use in this free time of the day.

I think we make a big mistake in telling children that school is impoverished. If you want to use open classroom techniques with students, you will only delay the initiation of these techniques by using this free time as a time for games and amusements brought in from outside the school situation. If a child spontaneously wants to bring something to class, you should encourage him to do so. However, if you cannot provide a stimulating atmosphere within the room, then you should not be attempting open classroom techniques. You may still want to give children some free time to work on things from home which have no value as learning tools or materials, but do not call this the sum total of the open classroom concept.

For this type of beginning, you will need a well selected supply of materials for students to work with. You will want to have materials drawn from a variety of subject areas to attract children. Certainly a large array of art materials, math and science materials, varied reading materials and whatever else you can collect will be helpful. After assembling some materials, check them to see that you have a broad enough variety to provide some type of activity for all the students. You should have things for children who like quiet work, for those who must be active and busy, and for those who like to work with others. If you can have a tape recorder, overhead projector, or any other machine available at least during this free time, it will add to the interesting things students may choose to do.

After several days of allowing students to work freely with the materials, you may be able to see trends in their interests, and then you can begin to narrow down the selection of materials more specifically according to the needs of your students. You may want to add some and take away others. At this point, it helps to suggest that students bring in things from home which might facilitate whatever they are currently doing in school. Tools may be needed for some special project, food or kitchen equipment may be necessary for other projects.

As students work, circulate among them and observe them. Watch how they work, what they work with, whom they work with, how long they stay with one activity, how they complete projects or activities, what they do when searching for something to interest them, etc. In the first weeks, try not to watch them too closely or obviously. You do not want to inhibit them in their free choice and explorations. As with the other two methods, it is important to verbalize to them that you want them to try new things with the materials and to do whatever they wish to do. Your enthusiasm about their interests and their discoveries will help them to see that you are truly sincere in your verbalizations.

It is important to make connections between what is done during the traditional class time and the materials available during this free time. This will emphasize the idea that children can learn in new and individual ways, as well as in the group lessons they are used to. It will also provide more complete learning for those students who are interested and are able to carry on their learning from the traditional period of the class into the free period. It will let them repeat some things and discover new things for which there was no time in the group or traditional lesson. For instance, if you are teaching a unit on electricity, using batteries and bulbs, or magnets and iron filings, you should have these materials available during the free choice period. Or if you are doing a unit on clothing, you should have many dress up clothes available for the students in a variety of styles and fabrics (these could probably be obtained from the homes of students).

It will help you to evaluate the amount of work done by each student, the content areas covered, and the interests of each child, if you keep records of how students spend their time. These do not have to be detailed, but should show general trends of activity. This will also help you and perhaps your administrators to decide whether or not to expand the free time period for students.

As you move into the routine of these free periods, students should slowly take over the responsibility of getting materials ready and of cleaning up when the period is finished. This may take some time to accomplish, but move into student responsibility as soon as you feel students are ready to assume it. You may also have to experiment with physical arrangement, trying different ways of arranging desks, tables, etc., to facilitate student activity. If it is necessary to move furniture, this should also become the responsibility of the students (if they are old enough).

Any of these three methods can help you to begin to communicate different things to students. The purpose of all of them is to broaden the spectrum of individual interest and activities within the area you select (topic, subject area, or time space).

The purpose of these methods is the opposite of the purpose of traditional class methods, where all spontaneous student interests and activities are suppressed in the hope of concentrating the students' attention on a teacher-selected lesson. There are flaws and defects in both systems of education. The question is: which system helps children to learn most efficiently and most pleasantly?

The open classroom techniques described here can gradually lead both you and your students into more interesting and more challenging ways of learning. By giving one of these methods a fair chance, you can have enough experience with open classroom techniques to decide whether or not they are for you. A fair chance means trying the method for at least a few weeks and during that time constantly assessing what is happening between you, the students and the materials. As you begin, you are bound to make mistakes and lack skill in guiding students' interests and learning. Do not blame the open classroom for your own inadequacies in these early weeks (see Chapter 8, Evaluation).

If you decide the open classroom is for you, these methods can be gradually expanded as you and the students are ready for increased use of open classroom techniques. These techniques tend to spread into other times and content areas whether you plan for them to or not. Both you and the students will spontaneously begin to use the practices which make learning more interesting and more fun in all areas of learning.

The independent and self-sufficient behavior which is encouraged at certain times will become part of the students' total behavior if you allow it to do so. Intellectual curiosity and honesty also tend to spread into all content areas as a result of your limited encouragement of it. It is an easy step to move into open classroom techniques for the entire day after you have begun with one of these methods.

USING OPEN CLASSROOM TECHNIQUES FOR THE ENTIRE DAY

To facilitate the operation of a traditional classroom, you would arrange your environment in a certain way. Desks would be arranged in such a way that all students could easily view the blackboard and the center position from which you would give lessons. The room would be cheerful, but would have a minimum of distractions, so that students would focus their attention on you when necessary, and on their work at their desks when that would be necessary. It is even more important to arrange the environment of the open classroom, since the environment will play a large part in what goes on within the room, and how children work and learn. A good supply of materials is most important in the beginning days of the open classroom. The selection of materials are especially important in the beginning weeks because children must learn to use them in new ways and in some cases, they must relearn the ability to involve themselves with materials. In later weeks you will find the students become involved in more complex projects which frequently require fewer materials but more thought and planning. They will also begin to bring in things they need themselves as time goes by, easing your job of supplying things somewhat. If children are to find their own areas of interest and to choose their activities than they must have a substantial variety of things from which to choose.

Materials for the Beginning Weeks

There is a list of materials organized under activity centers in Chapter 4. You will probably be able to include as many new and interesting ones as those listed. In the beginning days of school, the quality of the materials is more important than the quantity. You need materials that the children can use easily, without your assistance, and ones which will involve them for a period of time. For instance, magic markers, crayons, colored chalks, and paper will involve most children for a lengthy period of time. It is the rare child who will make only a quick pass at a piece of paper with any such materials and not feel compelled to continue to make some kind of picture. Scissors and paste, with a box of collage material (three dimensional if possible), are also almost irresistible to most students. For those boys who never want to do anything, an assortment of varying lengths and sizes of pegboard and a variety of nuts, bolts and screws will work wonders. Large magnets with iron filings, boxes of paper clips, nails, pins, etc., will also provide interesting hours for some children. Simple looms with weavings already begun can interest others. Many of the Montessori math materials and the Cuisenaire rods are especially useful in the beginning days. They are attractive and have many possibilities for student exploration built into them. A table with clay or homemade play dough will also keep students busy. Few children can resist an invitation to record their voices on a tape recorder.

An attractive library center should contain a few books which you know the students will enjoy, such as sports for nine to eleven year old boys, mystery stories for older girls, and classic favorites for younger children. If your administrators would not object, you can have some good comic books, easy to read newspapers and magazines, etc. If you can get an old rug or piece of carpeting and some throw pillows for the floor, these things make for a much more intriguing reading center in the beginning days. Just the novelty of lying on the floor to read will attract many students. Such an arrangement also tells students that you think reading is fun and not always a formal, life and death matter.

In choosing materials for the first days and the beginning weeks of class, you must realize certain things. For one thing, materials must be inviting and challenging in and of themselves, because in the beginning days the students will be exploring the materials for their intrinsic interest. If you choose materials which have little intrinsic interest for the age group you are teaching, your students will have excess time on their hands with few if any outlets for their energy, particularly in the first few days of the class when you may not be focusing the interest of your students in any particular manner. They will be left only the materials at hand with which to involve themselves. As you emphasize the concept of measurement within the class, scales, tape measures and rulers may become very valuable items and may be used with almost every project or play activity. But until you do this type of general focusing, these items may be relatively useless and uninteresting to students. On the other hand, a wardrobe of clothes, hats, etc., and a full length mirror will be of great interest in the beginning days of class, as children of all ages love to dress up (for older children simply modernize the clothing or have them bring in their own to share). This wardrobe of dress-up clothing may be important later in creative play or in dramatic productions; however, it will be inherently interesting on those beginning days.

An important aspect of materials to consider in these early days is how messy they are. In the first few days of school, before you have had time to establish any rules or systems for cleaning up, messy materials can present a problem. Unless you have help in cleaning and supervising such activities, it is best to avoid them in the first days of school. These activities include painting, fingerpainting, printing, papier-mâché, use of glues or paints which are not water soluble, etc. Materials which require your supervision during use, such as sharp tools, should also be avoided. Equipment which requires detailed and lengthy instructions to operate will be a hindrance to you in the beginning when your attention should be directed to other things.

The placement and appearance of materials within the room is important to the success of the first few days. They should be arranged so that children will be able to see them, and accessible enough for students to immediately begin working with them. Many of the materials you will choose to have in the beginning are colorful and attractive. For those that are not, it is helpful to draw attention to the materials by putting a large area of color close to them, or some attention-getting decor such as a large clown face over the drawing area. Blackboards can have large colorful letters saying, "Write on me!", or something similar to draw students' attention to the activity. The more successful you are in choosing and arranging the materials, the less difficulty you will have on the first days of school.

Room Decoration

When your materials are arranged and furniture is in position according to your plan, you can give some thought to decorating the room. You may wish to decorate it simply, using large areas of bright color to highlight interesting materials and make the room more vibrant and cheerful. Use what we know about color to enhance the various areas of the room. Red, orange and yellow will give a gay, active feeling to areas and would be appropriate for areas such as science and math activity centers. Blues and greens will give a more quiet and subdued feeling, which you will want in the language arts centers where more concentration and isolated work may be required. Black and/or white will provide stark areas suitable for background to sculpture, dress up or dramatic centers. A large red arrow can draw everyone's attention to an interesting display, such as a building center or a live animal which you may want everyone to see.

You may wish to leave the room almost bare, waiting until you can let students decorate and arrange materials. Or you may find that you can add brightness and color with one simple decoration which suggests a room fully ready for students, although, in fact, you may wish to leave most of the decorating and sorting of supplies and materials to students. The most effective decor of this type which I have seen was a room which was bare except for a large, yellow, construction paper sun with a smiling face—about three feet in diameter—and the words, "Let The Sun Shine In," written in bold letters beneath it. Subsequently, the students finished decorating this room, but the bright sun provided a sunny welcome for them on the first days of school.

A SAMPLE DAY

An example of the first day of an open classroom might go as follows:

8:40—Students enter. Introduce yourself and invite students to look around the room and use any materials they find interesting.

9:15—Request students to gather together or to go to individual seats if they have them. Anyone not finished with something may continue working quietly.

The first day always involves many clerical procedures. How you approach these will depend on the age of the students—the older they are the more responsibility they can assume. Reintroduce yourself. Have students introduce themselves (if old enough). This will give you attendance check. Let students make name tags if you plan to use them (or pass them out to young students). They will facilitate learning names quickly, which is difficult when students are allowed free movement during the day. Take care of any other clerical procedures as quickly as possible.

If you noticed any activity or materials which seemed of special interest to the students, you might begin a discussion about the materials in the room by mentioning your observations. Encourage the students to comment about those materials they liked, and answer any questions they might have about them.

Let this discussion lead eventually into some explanation of the things in the room and what the students will be doing in the classroom. If you are using a contract system, half traditional day, half open classroom, etc., this is the time to explain it briefly and clearly. Remember that your actions will be more convincing than your words in dealing with elementary school children, so limit your talk. Finish clerical jobs quickly if you have not already done so and get back to the really important thing—students learning about materials and each other and you.

9:35–9:50—If children have a snack, this is the time for it. If not, go on with a group lesson at this time. If you are not having a snack you must announce to students, or signal them in some way, that you want them to assemble for a lesson. Again, anyone who is in the middle of something and is reluctant to leave it should be allowed to continue quietly. Sometimes if you assemble the materials to be used for the group lesson on tables or desks, you will gather a nucleus of interested students even before you make your announcement.

Try to give a lesson which uses materials that students can use individually during their free time. Your lesson will focus their interest in one conceptual area which they can pursue independently.

During your lesson, each child should have something to handle or manipulate, if possible. In the case of limited materials you can divide the students into groups (preferably let them do it themselves if they are not too reluctant on these opening days). Then let each group work with whatever materials are available, with individuals taking turns.

If you are using Cuisenaire rods or some other materials which eventually will need some direction from you, this is a good time to introduce it. For the first time, let children explore materials freely. Your next lesson can be more structured and you can give specific directions for use of materials. For older students who are familiar with the rods, you might introduce the next math area you think they are ready for, giving some leeway for free exploration to give you information about what they know and how great the spread of knowledge is. This will help you plan subsequent lessons.

Let us use as an example, a science lesson introducing the concepts of solvent and non-solvent. For this lesson, test tubes or small plastic or glass bottles are necessary, one for each student. You will be better off giving this lesson using either several large tables or eight to ten desks grouped together to form a large working area. If your class is already arranged this way, as in Figures 4 or 5, Chapter 4, you are ready to begin. If not, have students move desks together. For each group of tables you will need a container of oil, water, sugar, flour, salt, and liquid soap. Each container should be labelled. You can prepare this yourself or enlist students who seemed uninvolved in exploratory activities during the morning. Older students can label the containers and assemble the materials needed for each table themselves. You will also need several eyedroppers and small spoons for each table. You can have available absorbent paper such as toweling or manila drawing paper on which students can drop the materials. Each group of tables should be supplied with paper towels for spills and clean ups. Food coloring should be available to give to students if you see that they are able to handle the materials well.

Food coloring is messy if it is spilled, so wait to see how students work with colorless materials.

When you are ready to begin the lesson, explain simply and clearly what you expect students to do with the materials. If you want them to explore and see what they can discover about which substances will dissolve and which ones will not, make that clear to them. If you want them simply to find out all they can about the substances on the table, say just that. If you expect answers or discussion of findings at the end of the exploratory period, inform the students so they can keep records or try to remember. After letting them know what you expect, distribute the materials with some help. I always prefer to ask for volunteers from each group and narrow down the selection if there are too many volunteers, telling the others they can help next time. It is important to give out the materials after you tell the students what they will be doing. Otherwise, you will be competing with the stimulation provided by the materials and you will usually lose. Some children may hesitate to explore or experiment with the materials. Some may prefer to watch others and some may only do a few hesitant mixes of materials. In the beginning, it is best to just observe what is happening. Later, when you know the students well, you can try to prod some of them into action or otherwise influence their behavior. While students are working, it is good to verbalize your expectations of them. Keep telling them to try different things. Your encouragement and the stimulation of working with others will encourage most students to work. The whole purpose of gathering children together in a situation like this should be to ensure that they will stimulate and learn from each other. It is not so that you can pass down your words of wisdom to a large audience at one time. A machine can do that if programmed correctly. Don't let yourself be a machine!

When interest seems to be lagging and the students have exhausted their ideas, it is time to stop. Sometimes students become so involved in the work that they will seek out other materials to experiment with. Or you may realize that some other materials would be helpful. If they are within your room, by all means give them to the students when you think of them. If not, you might bring them for the next lesson of this type or for free time exploration. Some students may want to continue working, although the majority are ready to stop. This can be accommodated by allowing them to continue at one table while the rest of the class cleans up and goes on to other things.

It is always difficult to know exactly when to suggest that students stop working. If you notice that most of the students continue to work after you announce clean-up, then your announcement has been premature. In this case, let the students keep working. If some of them begin cleaning up, this is all right; they may be ready to go on to other things. Through trial and error you will gradually become more sensitive about the best times to stop working. Usually there is a certain rise in the noise level in the room which tells you that it is time to stop.

When interest seems exhausted, suggest that students finish up their experiments. While you have their attention, let them immediately know how you expect them to go about cleaning up. For older students, you can post large, previously prepared written instructions. With younger ones, give a few simple directions, including the fact that they may choose their own activity when clean-up is completed. Help to keep everything moving smoothly toward clean-up. Help where you are needed and try to keep a sense of humor about spills, mistakes, etc. This is a learning experience and an important one. Your attitude will determine the attitudes students develop toward cleaning and responsibility. If some students do not participate in these first few days, just note the fact and do not press them until you learn more about them. However, be sure that they do not go on to other activities before the clean-up is completed. When students have done a reasonable amount of work, you can let them move on to other activities on an individual basis, or you can have everyone clean until cleaning is finished and then proceed to activities as a group. It is difficult to make a decision about this until you get to know your class.

10:30–11:00—Free activity period. Attempt to spend time with students, talking to them about what they are doing, noting the materials which seem to have the most staying power and which stimulate the most interest and involvement. If there are things which are especially interesting, try to get more of them or a similar one for the next day's class. You may also get more ideas for materials from seeing the students work with those available.

11:00–11:30—Gather students together for lunchtime by giving a signal (if later than this, extend the previous free period or gather students together with a signal and have a story or record for them to listen to). Have students complete any clean-up which is absolutely necessary at this time. They will be returning to free activities immediately after lunch, so that a minimum of clean-up should be enough. Encourage students to gather around you with chairs for an intimate and friendly discussion. If this is not physically possible, move about individual desks as the discussion proceeds so that you are physically close to the students. This close contact will encourage them to express their thoughts and interests more freely. In a formal situation where there is some distance between you and the students, they are less likely to speak spontaneously. This is the time to discuss any special arrangements which must be made for lunch, doing clerical procedures if necessary, and assigning monitors, leaders for the line, etc. Casually but clearly tell students the procedures you will use for leaving the room, what will happen in the lunchroom and after they finish their lunch. Also tell them that when they return to the room they can immediately resume their activities or begin new ones. Encourage students to express their questions and interests freely. If a topic comes up which you feel needs further group discussion and there is not enough time, set aside a time for the discussion and tell students when it will occur (such as in the afternoon or tomorrow morning). There might be some question about how to select monitors or leaders for the line, etc. If there is time and students seem interesting in talking about the group lesson or any of the work they did in the morning, encourage them to do so. You may want to comment on what occurred during the morning's learning activities. Comment on the clean-up, and try to be honest but positive. Encourage students to make suggestions about how they think it could be improved if there were any problems.

When it is time to leave the room for lunch, try to get out as quickly as possible so that students are not bunched up in front of the door. Bunching up encourages students to talk and jostle others; it should be avoided whenever possible. Leave the room immediately, expecting cooperation and quiet, not talking about it. If you find you have misjudged the time, take students on a small tour of your floor or the important rooms on the way to the lunchroom. Keep them busy and moving so that excess talking, etc., do not become a problem. If you see your friends and colleagues in the hallways, greet them exactly as you would expect your students to greet their friends.

12:30–1:00—When students return to class after lunch, they can return to their free-choice activities immediately. They should have at least forty-five minutes to one hour to work at this. Have the materials from the morning lesson available, in order that students who were involved with the lesson can pursue their individual interests as far as they wish. This is a good time to circulate among students. It is difficult not to express your preferences and feelings as you talk with students, but try to remain as neutral as possible so that students will involve themselves in a spontaneous way. Any indication of your desires or impressions will color their handling of the materials. It is difficult not to express some feelings as you see children working, but try to keep a somewhat neutral and encouraging manner. If you are able to verbalize questions about what students are doing which may lead them into new discoveries and activities, do so. If not, do not feel obliged to make any comments.

1:45–2:00—The time to end the free period must be a matter of your own sensitivity to the restlessness of the majority of the students. If there is a small group which seems restless at this time, you might want to start a casual kind of lesson with them which will not interfere with the other students. If the class is able to work at free activities the entire afternoon, that is fine, and let them do so. However, if you feel the students need some direction, this would be a good time to give out any books or materials which students will have as individuals. You can always gather students together by starting a song or record. As students leave their work, they will join you. When you have a sizable group, it is a good time to talk about the activities of the day, discuss with students the fact that this will be the way they spend their time in school, that their learning will be different from what they have been used to. Try to get any of their reactions to the day, your plans, the materials, etc. Discuss in some detail your plan for the running of each day and their responsibility for their work. If you are keeping folders or student-kept records you might introduce them briefly at this time.

2:30–2:50—Start clean-up. Usually you can allow about 10 minutes for clean-up, but on the first day you will need longer. Before students leave group discussion, mention clean-up for end of the day and be explicit about what you expect students to do. Again, this is a learning experience and you should only be watching to see what students are doing in these first days.

2:50–3:00—Time to prepare for leaving the room. See suggestions for lunchtime departure. You might want to give a general homework assignment, such as having each student bring in something from his mother's kitchen which can be experimented with for its solvency.

Whether you begin the open classroom at the start of the school year or in the middle, it is possible to begin it in the manner demonstrated in this sample day. You may want to have more group lessons in the beginning days, giving students gradual access to free time. Whatever you do, students should have lots to work with and keep them busy whether they work individually or in groups. Children who are bored will not do well in any kind of classroom.

Variations in the day presented might be to have students working on decorating the room, arranging supplies and activity centers, etc. Or if you are using some modified version of the open classroom, you might have the students working during the morning at assigned tasks and then give the afternoon as free time.

In the beginning days and weeks of school, everything that you do is of importance. Each act builds toward a complex edifice of behavior. Students will be observing you and looking for patterns in your behavior which will communicate to them your feelings about them, your expectations of them, and your rules for acceptable classroom behavior. The more consistent you are in your behavior, the sooner the students will feel they know you and the sooner they will relax and begin to work.

The same thing is true of students' behavior. Each task they perform and each action they take within the class gives you more information about their abilities, their personalities and their needs. If you have planned materials and lessons which give you information quickly, this acquaintance process is hastened. This will allow you to know your students more fully in a short period of time and then to begin teaching them what they need to learn in a variety of ways.

If you have taken advantage of this receptive period with students, you have lost no opportunity to tell them what you expect and what behavior is valued in the classroom. By allowing them free choice in their areas of study, you have communicated to them that you respect their interests and their individuality. You are telling them that you want them to express themselves and to take some responsibility for their own learning. By giving them responsibilities for arranging and maintaining the classroom and the materials within it, you have communicated your trust and belief in their good judgment, integrity, and ability to assume and carry out responsibilities.

In most traditional classes, the teacher maintains great control over behavior during the first days of school. This control communicates clearly to students that any freedom or privilege they have within the class comes directly from the authority of the teacher. The open classroom is quite different in that it is undesirable to maintain strong authoritarian controls during the first days of school. If there are enough interesting things for students to do in your classroom, control of behavior should be only a minor problem. It is usually possible to spot trouble situations before they become serious. When you see a student getting restless, or an argument beginning, it is possible to intervene before the minor difficulty becomes a major one.

If you feel uneasy in leaving learning to the discretion of the students' interests, you can give two or three group lessons in the beginning days of the open classroom. Students can be permitted to sit in on lessons or not, as they choose. If they do not take part, they must be quiet so that others can do so. These group lessons should be ones that encourage all students to use materials. This will provide more impetus for students to work with the available materials during free time and it will provide more concrete experiences for the students.

PROBLEMS THAT OCCUR IN BEGINNING THE OPEN CLASSROOM

No matter how well you plan your materials and whatever lessons you give, you may still find you have students who cannot become involved in the materials or in your lessons. They may be withdrawn or they may try to provoke arguments with you or with other students. The newness of the situation may frighten them. Or they may be individuals whose personal problems prevent them from learning. In the absence of outer controls by you, they may be unable to give even superficial attention to the real world. Sometimes it is possible to engage them in activities by working closely with them. You may also be able to have them help you make some project or game for the room which involves simple cutting, lettering, measuring, etc. Sometimes these students respond if you stay physically close to them as they work. Your presence acts as a control for them. These students may need considerable supervision by you and structured learning situations. Do not forget that you must treat the students in the class as individuals. These particular students may require very different treatment from that of the majority of the students.

For students who are disruptive, it may be necessary to watch them during the day and attempt to intervene when they seem about to get themselves into some difficulty. You may choose to allow such a child to act out his problems within the class later on, but in the beginning days it is better to control some of these things. When you have a better feeling of the makeup of the entire group, it will be easier to handle a child with acting out problems. You may have to reeducate such a child as to how they should use materials and work with other students. Often this can be done by showing them how to do things, using your own actions and verbalizations as guides. Gradually you can help the student find acceptable ways of behaving and materials which interest him and provide an outlet for some of his emotions. These students usually respond negatively to being left alone.

They need the control and guidance of a strong figure because they lack their own inner controls. Often, through their disruptive behavior, they are symbolically asking for someone to guide and control them. By showing them that you are willing and able to take on this task, you can calm their initial anxiety in a new and perhaps confusing situation.

If it is impossible to involve a student in the above ways, then you may have to confront him with leaving the room if his behavior is disruptive and disturbing to others. Most children will not push you this far, as they seem to realize they are in a good situation and they do not really want to lose it. They are really looking for reassurance from you that you have the strength to deal with them and control them. A child like this probably would also have great difficulty in a traditional classroom, and would need the help of a physician in order to remain in any school situation.

In these beginning days your main aim should be to get things running smoothly. In order to do this, you must deal quickly with students who present a problem, getting them under superficial control. It is always possible to deal in more depth with their problems after you have the whole class running fairly smoothly.

SOURCES OF PROBLEMS IN THE BEGINNING WEEKS

If you are having trouble as the days go on, you will have to examine carefully what is happening at the times you are having difficulty. There are bound to be misunderstandings and problem areas as you and your students adjust to one another. If there is confusion and disorder during the clean-up period, then you must examine what is going on in a critical manner. Perhaps you are expecting too much in the way of cleaning up from the students— is everything they are doing absolutely necessary? Perhaps you are not allowing enough time, or are allowing too much time, so that students are left with nothing to do when they finish. Are you finding transition periods uncomfortable for you or for the students? How are you handling them—do you expect every child to finish his work at approximately the same time, or are you more realistic and realize that students can be staggered in their attempts to stop working? Do you begin group lessons when you have a nucleus of students or do you wait too long, expecting to begin only when every student is ready? All these things will influence the direction and tone of your class. You must stop to analyze trouble spots in the early stages, correcting them if you can; in this way, certain behavior habits and patterns will not become permanent problems.

If things seem to be going wrong and you do not have any idea why, examine the time when you feel there is a problem. If you know approximately when things begin to go sour, sometimes you then can examine in detail what happens at these times and perhaps come up with an answer to the difficulty. Even if you are unsure of what the problem is, if you know about when it is occurring, you can begin to change some of the ways you do things around these times and perhaps remedy the situation without really knowing what or why there is a problem. You will have to constantly assess what is going on in the class, what is working well and what could be improved. Many of your efforts to make things run smoothly will have to be on the basis of trial and error. Do not be afraid to experiment with new techniques. You are encouraging the students to do so and there is no better way to give them an example and model than to be free enough to do so yourself.

EVALUATING INDIVIDUAL ABILITIES

Traditionally the first few weeks of school are spent in testing and evaluating students' performances in review work. By using reviews and tests, the teacher is slowly able to place each student in a relative ability level. Then if she wishes to group students for reading or math, she is able to do so on the basis of ability, putting students into relatively homogeneous groups.

When you are teaching in the open classroom, knowledge of individual abilities and interests becomes even more important, because you are attempting to make a long range educational plan for each student rather than for the class as a whole. Such plans must be based upon the child's current abilities and past experiences to be most effective. In this way we can help each child to move from his present knowledge and functioning into the next stages of development and learning. Your primary source of information will be your observations of the child in action with materials, with others and with you. Another source will be any work the child does within the context of lessons or individual activities. In both situations, you will be evaluating students on many levels. You will not be looking for right-wrong answers to questions about predetermined content as is done in traditional classrooms. You will be looking for a wide range of abilities and knowledge. The skill in observation which you are able to achieve will have a vital effect on how you evaluate students.

You should try to retrain yourself as soon as possible in observing how students learn. Move about during the free time period after students feel comfortable about choosing their activities. Watch everything you can and try to detail for yourself the type of learning which is going on. Try for awhile to suspend your judgment about how worthwhile such learning may be; simply notice it. See how students can work out problems between themselves in dealing with materials. Notice how a child uses bits and pieces of information he has gathered in the past to approach problems in the present or to act in a situation. Watch what happens when students have time to think within the classroom. Essentially, for a while at least, you must forget about *teaching* as you know it and begin watching learning in progress. When you become skilled at observing spontaneous learning, then you will be ready to begin shaping and influencing it.

NOTES - CHAPTER 5

1. Jean Piaget, *Six Psychological Studies*, pp. 49–60.

2. Lawrence Kohlberg, "Early Education: A Cognitive-Developmental View," *Child Development*, 39:1013–1062, Dec., 1968.

BIBLIOGRAPHY - CHAPTER 5

Thought-provoking books about initial attempts to change the traditional format of classroom life:

Ashton-Warner, Sylvia, *Teacher.* New York: Simon and Schuster, 1963.

Channon, Gloria, *Homework.* New York: Outerbridge and Dienstfrey, 1970.

Dennison, George, *The Lives of Children.* New York: Random House, Inc., 1969.

Hawkins, Frances P., *The Logic of Action.* Boulder, Colo.: University of Colorado, 1969.

Herndon, James, *The Way It Spozed to Be.* New York: Simon and Schuster, 1965.

CHAPTER 6.

LEARNING STYLES

6.

Learning to live and function in a satisfying way in the world and in society is a long and arduous process, and children begin learning from the instant of their birth.[1] We are just beginning to realize to what extent children are able to learn during their first years of life. The learning which occurs in the first three years seems to be crucial to the formation of patterns of learning and behaving in each individual.[2] These learned patterns and genetic ones tend to persist for the rest of the child's life.[3] Each individual develops a unique manner of approaching learning tasks, perceiving the outside world, processing perceptions, integrating new information with prior information and ideas, adapting to new information, and making some decision about how to respond (or not to respond) to new perceptions. This unique manner determines what often is referred to as learning style or life style. Because of the complexity inherent in the life style process, we still know very little about it. However, we do have some information about how individuals operate in many of the activities which comprise the life style, and we can describe and identify characteristic ways of dealing with the environment in almost all of the above activities.

As teachers of elementary school children, we are dealing with students who are still immature in their development and whose learning patterns may be relatively modifiable. Since basic patterns of dealing with the environment and relating to it are probably well formed in the earliest years of life, we cannot make any basic changes in students' intellectual and emotional behavior. However, we can modify their existing patterns by helping them to develop awareness of those patterns they already have, add new ways of dealing with their world, and give up behavior which is destructive to their general functioning. In order to do any of these things, we must be able to assess the level of a child's maturity and the patterns of learning which seem to dominate the behavior of each child. With this knowledge, we can create situations which will lead to modification of the child's behavior through specific experiences and situations. We can personally act as a model and a guide for the student to help him observe and try different ways of dealing with his environment.

In the traditional classroom, however, teachers do not function in this manner. They tend to set up situations in which the student is exposed to materials and predetermined methods of dealing with materials. The child is expected to learn certain facts and given procedures, regardless of his own individual learning patterns. Teachers may attempt to help individual students who have trouble, but often they must act intuitively or in a hit or miss fashion, trying to guess what will be most helpful to a particular student without really diagnosing his unique patterns of approaching the learning process. Eventually, students are judged on their ability to adjust their learning styles to those of the teacher and to obtain the culturally stereotyped answers for which the teacher is looking. This is only one aspect of the learning process, and concentrating on it alone leaves most of the student's important learning to random influences.

Often teachers in traditional classrooms have mentally tracked students according to verbal ability levels and they feel little hope for much change in the student's ability or performance. Often this tracking can severely hamper a child's potential development and performance.[4] Because they concentrate on verbal abilities, they have a limited view of the student's intelligence. And because their teaching efforts are usually directed to further verbal learning, their expectations for a child's progress are often fulfilled since they are dealing with only one area of intellectual functioning.

In the open classroom, teachers are more interested in the long-range development of the student than in short-range answers or scores on tests. They also have more time to observe students' learning behavior in a variety of learning situations. They are able to observe students in action dealing with their environment in direct ways, rather than passively answering questions about it. This gives them a fuller picture of the child's learning style and the range of his abilities and learning needs. The teachers in open classrooms view the student as a unique person with characteristic behaviors and with a potential for continual change and development.

ASSIMILATION AND ACCOMMODATION
OF NEW MATERIAL

If we think of learning in terms of Piaget's formulation of assimilation and accommodation, the teacher's task should be to present materials and situations which can be assimilated by the child. This means that we should present things which are compatible with the child's previous experiences. If material is not compatible, the child may reject the new experience intellectually (denial) or he may distort the reality in order to accommodate the material and make it part of the structure of his intelligence (rather than deny its existence). We cannot know what is compatible with a child's thinking and previous experiences unless we observe that child carefully and try to assess his developmental level and his accumulated knowledge and experience.

Let us imagine that for the first time we give students Cuisenaire rods to experiment with as they like. You might see one child using them for building blocks, another child sorting them by color, and a third child arranging them sequentially by length. From these observations it would be apparent that the third child is ready to begin working with the rods because he has already noted the most significant characteristic of the rods. The second child might also be ready, but you would have to observe him in more situations to be sure. The first child may not be ready at all if he sees the blocks at the level of their simplest attribute, objects to pile. It may be that the first and second children are capable of more advanced thinking and use of the blocks than is evident from this one instance. If they are, you will have many opportunities to observe their ability in the open classroom, where students are encouraged to use their skills and knowledge in a variety of active situations. You cannot always judge what a child does not know because, as in the above situation, he simply may not be using his knowledge. If he does demonstrate some skill or knowledge, you have some definite and concrete indication of it. When you see children repeatedly acting in characteristic ways, you will know what they need to know in order to increase their knowledge or extend their learning tactics.

Structuring Learning Situations to Promote Progress

To help children accommodate new knowledge, we can let them engage in situations which will let them use the new information they have acquired. If we are keen enough, we can structure those sitations to strengthen the student's own accommodation attempts. For instance, a child who has just learned to classify objects on the basis of their function rather than on the basis of their physical appearance (color, shape), should have as many opportunities as possible to use his new knowledge and get it firmly under control in the realm of action. We can facilitate this in two ways: by allowing the child to repeat his new knowledge in real ways and situations within the classroom and by making sure that the necessary materials are available to him. Some students may feel fully confident with their newly acquired knowledge after only a few activities in which they exercise it. Others may need many situations in which to exercise the new ability before they feel it is a part of them and they can go on to other things. Obviously the flexibility and the general organization of the open classroom is ideally suited to this type of aid to learning. When viewed in this way, teaching becomes a process of diagnosing and then aiding and abetting the natural course of learning for each child. Because there are so many unknowns in the area of how children learn, this is a more uncertain and fumbling path for a teacher to pursue. However, even with all the mistakes which occur due to our ignorance of the learning process, this path is usually more successful for the student and more rewarding for the teacher who is willing to take a few chances.

In a traditional classroom, teachers attempt to help children assimilate and accommodate the material by presenting it in an orderly, sequential fashion. There is a major assumption that all children have learned approximately the same things prior to their entrance to school. They are supposed to absorb sequential lessons which are based on this common foundation and which can be an outgrowth of previous learning. However, children are not seriously evaluated at the beginning of the school experience to determine what unique experiences might influence their course in school. Instead, students are given an identical exposure to the same content in the hopes that they will suppress their uniqueness and build up a similarity of school experiences which will provide a foundation for learning the various intellectual and behavioral patterns that teachers feel are desirable and necessary. There is no way to insure that children are learning everything we teachers want them to learn along the way. Unless the school environment is consistent with that of the home and the prior school experiences, students may learn very little.[5] When the school experiences differ greatly from those of the home, the student may have to deny his school experiences in order to maintain his home experiences. Many students fall far behind in conceptual and in operational knowledge. Since there is little time to work with any student who does not fall into the average level of ability and performance, the students who fall behind build up an increasing deficiency of learning.

In the open classroom we have abandoned these unsuccessful practices. In order to get a more accurate picture of the child as a totality of his experience and genetic make-up, we have created an environment in which he is encouraged to seek out learning situations which suit his needs, his experiences and his developmental level. In his seeking out certain learning experiences, he gives us many clues about his abilities and his learning needs. As the teacher receives information about students from their behavior, she is able to construct more efficient situations and materials to help individual children learn more readily and more completely. She is able to use this knowledge and her relationship with a student to help him expand his learning techniques and his store of knowledge when it is appropriate. She is in a better position to know when to apply pressure to a child to work harder at a task and when to suggest that a child leave a task until he has further experiences which will prepare him for it.

GENERAL MODES OF LEARNING

To provide this kind of learning atmosphere, it is essential that teachers understand the language of learning. There are general modes of learning which all children use: they are play or experimentation, imitation and vicarious learning (through books, films, verbal information).[6] If you observe them closely, it seems that they prefer one method or another at various times, but we do not have enough information in this area to make any generalizations about their behavior. It is possible that children are genetically predisposed to favor one kind of learning; or that they simply choose whichever form is most expedient for their immediate needs. Because we know so little about this use of various methods, we should provide all of them for students to choose from. In the open classroom, we do.

Individual Modes of Learning

In addition to these general methods of learning, each child will have learned unique ways of approaching and dealing with learning activities. These individual styles of learning are also acquired through the more general means of play or experimentation, imitation and vicarious learning, but because of the unique experiences and the genetic makeup of each child, each one has acquired a unique learning style made up of selected elements from his genetic background and from his environment. As teachers, we must give attention to both the general and the individual modes of learning. Most of us are familiar with the general means of learning from our own experience as humans and from our professional training. We are less familiar with individual learning styles because they have only recently been given attention and are as yet poorly defined. Some teachers intuitively recognize these individual styles in students. They may not categorize them, but they somehow know that Tom has to learn by handling and working with materials, and that Jim needs constant repetition of content before he can learn and integrate it into his general store of knowledge. Billy has to learn things fast because his frustration tolerance for time consuming tasks is very low. Louise must approach things meticulously and be sure that she has covered every detail of a subject before she can feel satisfied that she has finished with it. Nancy seems constantly preoccupied with other things and can only vaguely give her attention to learning situations. All these things are indicative of individual learning styles. Each child approaches material uniquely, perceives it uniquely, absorbs and processes it uniquely and reacts to it uniquely.

The Teacher's Learning Style

One step leading to the awareness of individual learning styles is to develop some awareness of your own learning style and of the many different ways to learn. Universities all over the country have been giving courses to teachers in which they become students and are allowed to "play" with whatever materials or content they like. This helps teachers to experience the kind of involvement children feel in their work, understand the varied and valuable types of learning which can occur spontaneously, and realize the value and importance of situations which allow free exploration of the environment without predetermined learning goals or tasks. Usually there are one or more skilled instructors to assist when the teacher wants help in various areas. These courses also help teachers to get an impression of their own styles of learning and approaching materials and problems.[7] They are of great value in retraining the teacher to appreciate the activity which will occur in open classrooms and to develop awareness of biases which can influence the teacher in helping children to learn.

If you are not in a location where such classes are available, you might try to gather together a small group of colleagues who are interested in the open classroom and try to help each other in observing the various learning styles in the group. You can all work together on some topic which interests you: a hobby, a new interest, something you have never had time to learn and always wanted to, etc. If this is not possible, do it by yourself. Sometimes it is possible to get some of these experiences with an art or craft class where you work very directly with materials. You will have to be both the student and teacher in observing your learning styles in this situation, but it is possible to get some benefit from it. I recently took a sculpture class for personal pleasure. I found that I learned a lot about my approach to working and dealing with learning situations because of my interest in education, which gave me a frame of reference from which to observe myself. I also found at the end of the course that my visual perception was markedly changed. I began to notice qualities of color and line which I never had seen or else had not been aware of previously.

Working with Materials

Any of these experiences will give you some feeling of what children experience in the classroom when they are allowed to work freely with materials. Obviously your impressions will be different because of your maturity and your mature cultural orientation, but you can get some of the feeling and experience which children have. Enjoy the feeling of the materials you handle, take all the time you want to do simple, directionless tasks. Feel textures, temperatures, hardness, and pliability of your materials. Try to observe your approach and involvement with the materials or learning situation. Are you timid in working with the materials if you do not have a preconceived plan? Do you get so involved with your work that you lose track of time, forget to have lunch, perhaps decide to increase the time you work at this "play"? Do you have difficulty doing anything with the materials? Do your productions turn out to be very stereotyped things you have seen somewhere or do they have some originality (not necessarily talented originality, just originality)? After you feel some pleasure and relaxation with the materials, try to note your methods of working. Do you finish very quickly or take a long time to complete work? Do you find it difficult to complete work at all? How many ideas occur to you as you work? How do you react to them? Do you try to carry some of them out or do you select only one? Do you experiment with alternate solutions to problems or hit upon one and not try to think of others?

All these things will be characteristics which are part of your learning style and which will effect your teaching style. They will also be the things you are trying to observe about how students approach learning tasks. They will use a variety of approaches to things and people. Their techniques of dealing with the work may be different in play situations, structured learning situations, peer directed situations, individual or group situations. I think we must assume that it is better to try to understand what is going on than to dismiss it as inconsequential because we do not understand it.

UNDERSTANDING INDIVIDUAL LEARNING STYLES

A discussion of some of the approaches of scientists to understanding children's learning styles will help you to develop some skill and understanding of the many factors involved in the learning process. Some factors have been isolated from the general process of learning and have been studied with some success in research studies. By becoming familiar with them, you will be able to see how they vary from individual to individual. Many of the factors described can be easily observed as students go about everyday classroom activities, if you know what to look for. In many ways you are in a better position to observe these things than scientists who work with isolated factors under laboratory conditions. You can see children operate more naturally and spontaneously in a normal classroom setting which is not distracting to them. Many tools for studying children can be taken directly from intelligence tests, or can be some variation of the same principles used to construct such tools. You will not be looking for a score or I.Q., but rather for the learning needs and strengths evidenced in the way the child handles a problem presented to him.

Whatever tools or situations you use to get information about students and their individual learning styles, you must remember that you are getting only a partial picture of an immature being. *Such information is not adequate to make any judgment about the child's intellectual potential.* It is adequate to provide clues to you about how you can provide more stimulating and more appropriate learning situations for each child. If you use this information in a judgmental manner to label students in one way or another, you will be defeating the basic intentions of the open classroom concept.

Is Change of Individual Learning Style Necessary?

It is always difficult to decide when it is appropriate or desirable to attempt to modify a child's behavior. If we claim to respect individual differences, then we must be willing to accept them. However, it often becomes clear that students have learned patterns of behavior and learning techniques which are detrimental rather than successful. In some cases, the necessity for change is easily apparent. In others, a child's behavior may not be detrimental but you may feel it would be helpful to increase his repertoire of procedures in a particular situation or area. If this can be done without harming the constructive techniques which the child already uses, then it would seem ethical to try to enlarge the possible approaches and abilities available to the student. Obviously if these techniques are genetically determined predispositions to do things in a certain way, you may not be able to modify them. If they are learned behaviors, it may be possible to make some changes and additions to the behavior the student uses.

In the atmosphere of the open classroom, students are encouraged to explore and experiment in all ways. It is not uncommon for them to begin experimenting with different learning techniques and approaches spontaneously. If this happens, you can encourage them to try a variety of techniques, suggesting some they do not think of spontaneously and helping them to differentiate between more effective and less effective ones. If this direction is suggested gradually and without undue emotional involvement or predetermined intentions on your part, it is unlikely that you will do any harm to the child. If you respect his individuality in general, he is likely to tell you when he does not want to do something or does not feel comfortable doing something in a certain manner. Even if the child does not verbalize this feeling, chances are that he will not do anything he does not feel comfortable with for very long. When students do not have to conform to a teacher's personal idiosyncrasies in order to make their life in school bearable, they usually are quite honest and independent about their feelings and their behavior.

THE LEARNING PROCESS

To give some order to the discussion of learning and the different procedures and techniques of which we are aware, I will present the various intellectual activities in a logically sequential manner. I will do this even though we do not know in what order these activities actually occur. We can conceive of learning as a sequential process proceeding in the following order: approaching the problem or situation, perceiving the details of the situation, processing this information, integrating it with previous information, and responding to the original situation in some fashion. In each of these activities there are many techniques which are observable in classroom activities.

Approaching Learning Materials and Problems

As children approach materials and/or problems, you can observe many individual differences. There are indications that some children are born less eager to approach unknown or new stimuli or people than are others. There are also marked individual differences in alertness and irritability in the neonate and these traits seem more pronounced by two or three months of age. Children who come into the world with these predispositions will experience the same situations differently.

In the classroom we can see evidence that some students are always eager to try new things. Others seem to have an insatiable curiosity. Still others always take a cautious attitude toward anything new. Some students will not try new things until they see others do them first, or see you demonstrate them. Some students can give their attention only briefly to anything, moving from one activity to another without being able to concentrate or attend to a problem. Hyperactive children often present this problem. This will seriously affect the way they are able to approach learning situations. As children are encouraged to react spontaneously in a variety of activities, traits such as these become more apparent.

As you observe differences in the way children approach problems or materials, it is important to note the consistencies and variations within the individual child's manner of approaching them. When you are sure of a pronounced pattern for a student, and you feel that it is detrimental to his learning (such as a very cautious attitude with new things or complete withdrawal when new materials are introduced), you can slowly attempt to modify it. Any attempt to modify behavior must be gradual. In the case of a child who completely withdraws from materials, you might try to show him a new material privately. Demonstrate its use and try to involve him in using it *with you.* If this is successful after several sessions, you can try to give him new materials and let him use them without your assistance. It may be necessary to remain physically close to him while he works so that your presence supports his attempts at independence. As you see changes in his behavior toward a more accepting attitude of new materials and situations, you will know that his behavior is modifiable. Then you can try to move him slowly toward whatever long range goals you may feel are appropriate for him. If your attempts are unsuccessful, try other approaches. As long as you are going slowly, the child will not be damaged and you may gain insights into other aspects of his behavior which will give you more valuable information about the types of modification which will be successful and what methods to use to achieve them.

With students who constantly rush into things without any concern for danger or difficulty, you may want to help them begin to discriminate between things which are safe and those which are not. Within the structured situation of the classroom, you will have an opportunity to introduce materials which require caution when in use, such as tools, equipment which must be run in precise ways, and chemicals which can be dangerous. Once a student trusts you enough to attempt some change in his basic approach to situations you can suggest or present to him, he will usually continue to try new behavior, sometimes self-initiated. Once this happens, you should encourage him to experiment freely on his own, if possible. You can still make suggestions when needed or requested by the student. Eventually he will choose the most comfortable techniques for him. If you still feel he is capable of further growth, you can attempt more changes after allowing him fully to accommodate to his new behavior, trying it out in many situations.

PERCEPTION

When it comes to perception, it is more difficult to know what children are actually perceiving when they attend to an object or situation. Even in a structured test situation where students give verbal or written answers, you cannot be certain what they are perceiving because you can only see their response and must deduce their perceptions indirectly from it. There are many factors which influence perception. They are so complexly interrelated that it is impossible to know which ones are operating or not operating at any given time. Perception can be influenced by organic, emotional, and cultural factors.[8]

Organically, perception can be influenced by mechanical factors which impair the normal operation of the nervous system. A child who is near-sighted will have a different perception of a giraffe which is far away from that of a child who has normal vision. In other instances, there may be some abnormality in the chemical composition of the cells in a sense organ or in the central nervous system which will distort perception. An illness or exposure to some toxic substance can alter perception temporarily. Metabolic factors are also important, as is fatigue resulting from inadequate nutrition.

Emotional factors can markedly influence perception. When a child is intensely interested in one subject, he will tend to notice everything that is relevant to that subject and perhaps disregard or not see many other things. This process is referred to as selective inhibition. Probably all of us have at times been engrossed in working or reading and have not heard or noticed another's attempts to get our attention. All of us must learn to inhibit the conscious perception of a noise and/or movement within the classroom to attend to things with any depth of concentration. People who are depressed or very pessimistic tend to notice the gloomier aspects of their environment, while those who are unusually happy or optimistic will tend to notice the happier aspects of their environment, disregarding the less happy ones. Our perception of time can be markedly influenced by our absorption in our work. When we are busy and happy time seems to fly by. Conversely, when we are doing something we dislike, time seems to drag on endlessly. One's self-image will influence perception to a great extent. A child who feels he is a failure and unintelligent will have difficulty perceiving any successes in his life even when they occur.

Perception is also influenced by one's life experiences. Urban and rural children differ in their perceptions of the same things, as do children from the North and South, mountain and valley, seaboard and plains.[9] In a similar way our perceptions are influenced by symbolic or vicarious events. Things we read or hear about from others can have as much influence on our perceptions as real experiences. Our perceptions are constantly influenced by previous, less complex perceptions which have been differentiated from the environment. For instance, a child cannot perceive the concept of multiplication until he has previously perceived the concept and mechanics of addition.

Cultural training will influence our perceptions in many subtle ways. From infancy we are trained to attend to certain aspects of the environment and to ignore others. In general, people will tend to perceive things which affirm their beliefs and biases and to ignore those things which bring them into question. This is true of our cultural beliefs and attitudes also. Society encourages the perception of situations which confirm its mores while it tries to play down or ignore those which are contrary to its beliefs and customs.

In the classroom you may notice indications of perceptual problems in visual or auditory skills. If you think a child has such a problem, there are simple tests[10] you can use within the classroom to confirm your observations in the visual field. If your suspicions are confirmed, you should refer the child for further testing and professional evaluation. If you suspect auditory problems, you can request auditory testing from the school health service.

If you have valid evidence of organic problems in perception, you may have to help a child learn to work around them as best he can, recognizing his deficits and learning to live with them. A child who has problems in visual perception can be encouraged to seek out auditory information whenever possible to increase the correctness of his perceptions.

You may notice that some students seem to perceive the overall picture of a problem or situation, but often miss significant details. Other students may do the reverse, noting many small details and missing the general or overall picture. Others will fall into categories in between these extremes. This aspect of perception is closely associated to phenomena commonly referred to as field independence and field dependence.[11] In a complexly detailed picture, a child who is field independent will be able to find a detail such as a small bird in the picture quickly, apparently able to focus only on this task, ignoring the rest of the picture or field. A field dependent child will have great difficulty finding the bird, seeming to be dominated by the many figures simultaneously available to his vision, unable to focus on one detail or to scan the picture in such a way that he finds the bird quickly or easily with little attention wasted on irrelevant details. It is not uncommon for workbooks in language arts to contain several pages using this type of exercise.

If you find students who show definite trends in the way they perceive things, it may be possible to give them extensive exercises to encourage them to expand their abilities in this area. For instance, someone who is field dependent might benefit from training in finding one object within a visually complex field, starting with less complex pictures and building up the complexity as the child progresses. Little controlled or systematic training has been attempted in this area so we have little idea of what can be accomplished.

INFORMATION PROCESSING

What a child does with his perceptions is of great importance to subsequent intelligent behavior. Being able to process information received from the environment in such a way that we give it some order or some significance is a crucial operation in intelligent behavior and living. This area of intellectual function has been given a great deal of attention by scientists. Some of the major areas of their study are classification activity and the ability to discriminate patterns in the environment. The way the individual orders the information he receives will influence all subsequent steps in the learning process.

Classifying and Ordering the Environment

Classification and ordering activities are essential to all aspects of learning and living. Generally, skill in this activity proceeds according to developmental sequence.[12] From being able to sort by concrete, physical attributes (color, then shape), the child proceeds to sorting by related function. An example of the latter would be associating a mitten with a hand or a dog with a doghouse. The next developmental step is to classify in a more abstract manner. Classification takes place on the basis of an abstract quality such as function (tool, clothing), or an inferred quality (intelligence, socioeconomic class). This ability to classify using abstract criteria usually does not appear until late in the elementary school experience.

You can supply many materials within the classroom which lend themselves to sorting and classifying. You can introduce lessons on sorting things according to various elements or attributes, to find out where each child is in his ability to classify according to cultural expectations. It is often very helpful to verbalize your thoughts about sorting or to encourage children to verbalize theirs. You will provide them with language tools to facilitate their learning and they will provide you with valuable diagnostic information which you can use to correct errors or distortions in thinking which may hinder the child's effective development of this skill. You must be careful here not to push students who are functioning on a primarily concrete level of thinking into situations too difficult for them, such as those requiring abstract thought. When they are ready to make this jump they will do so on their own, and then you can pick up on their spontaneous behavior and help them to gain control over more abstract thinking processes.

Closely associated to the ability to classify objects within the environment is the perception of classes of similar objects which are given a common name, despite some variation in appearance. This is concept learning. An advanced form of learning concepts is principle-learning,[13] which is the combining of concepts into entities referred to as ideas, rules and facts.

The open classroom is a fertile place for the development of concepts and for principle learning. The more you can provide a concrete experience demonstrating a concept, the more likely a child will be to learn the concept and to integrate it into his existing knowledge. Usually it helps to present several examples of the concept with only slight variation in the common attribute which forms the basis of the concept. For instance, in presenting the concept of "alive," you can confront students with plants, pets and some totally inanimate objects until the students are thoroughly familiar with the concept. After you feel confident that the student has grasped the essential element, you can present a variety of situations in which this element becomes harder and harder for the child to discern. In the case of the concept of living things, you can begin by introducing things like food, fruit and vegetables. Numerous questions about degrees of aliveness and how we can define "alive" and "dead" will lead students to more subtle aspects of the general concept. In principle-learning, you can do essentially the same thing, but you must be sure that the child is knowledgeable regarding all the concepts contained within the principle, otherwise you will be teaching him to parrot words, not to learn principles. Also remember that elementary school children usually are not able to think abstractly until the later years of elementary school, or after age nine or ten. Teaching children to memorize verbal rules or principles is not helping them to gain knowledge which is useful to them. It only gives them a chance to parrot back things which please adults, convince them that learning is occurring, and convince students that school learning is a rather meaningless thing.

Discriminating Patterns

The ability to discriminate patterns in one's experience is essential to learning and living. If a child cannot discriminate patterns, he certainly will be unable to speak, to read, to comprehend math or to make much sense of anything which occurs in his world. This can be one of the most fruitful areas of learning you can encourage in your classroom. Children often benefit from very direct teaching in this area. Often we present material to them without making the inherent patterns apparent. We expect them to deduce from the material presented that certain patterns exist. Some children do not discern them and will never do so without some direct help from you. When you begin teaching the discrimination of patterns, students' performance in all subjects usually improves.

When you teach children place value in mathematics, you are teaching them how to understand a pattern and how to use it effectively. The world and the classroom are full of patterns. Once you decide to help children understand their world instead of judging their current functioning within it, you will find you have unlimited resources in the world and in the classroom. After you focus students' attention on a concept, they will usually try to discern many patterns even you had not noticed. I have found work in this area to be particularly helpful with poor readers. No matter in what area they choose to seek out patterns, it seems to improve their overall reading performance, perhaps because of a transfer of learning. A very helpful activity associated with test questions is to help students to pick out the patterns of knowledge sought in the test questions, and then reproduce those patterns with questions of their own. Students usually love to do this and they become very successful in taking tests. If your class is receptive to working with patterns, you may want to have them try some introspection and see if they can discern patterns within the classroom or within their own behavior or in their homes. There are truly limitless possibilities in helping children to learn and advance in this area.

Recognizing redundancies in one's experiences is an important part of discriminating patterns. The most commonly known use of this intellectual ability is the forming of a set[14] or a frame of reference. This means that we recognize similar characteristics in situations, associate them to previous situations of the same type, and react as we have been trained to react to the previous situation, or in a way which has brought us success. More intelligent people seem to form sets more quickly, perhaps because they are more skilled at discerning the similarities in different situations. Set can also work against us. When we take a test which consists of the same type of questions and a dissimilar question is thrown in, one for which we must reorganize our thinking, the test is more difficult to do because we will continue to operate out of the set we have established for the previous problems on the test. The set influences our perception of the problem by limiting the aspects of the situation which we perceive as significant. It also limits our response because we try to use previously successful responses instead of seeking new ones.

It is usually not necessary to teach children to form sets. This ability seems to develop naturally for most people. However, it is helpful to try to make students aware of them on some level so that they can understand what happens to them in problem solving situations.

INTEGRATION

After information has been processed in some way, theoretically it will be incorporated or integrated with existing knowledge or structures within the brain. This will modify or change the structure of the brain. How this happens remains a mystery. It is probably a chemical and/or electrical process.

When this integration of new knowledge or information with previously acquired material is accomplished, the individual is then ready to make some decision about acting upon the new information or situation, if necessary. In a traditional classroom there is often no necessity to act in any way upon learned information. Students may have to recall the information at a later time. They may have to make inferences from the new material, or answer some type of written question concerning the material they have just been exposed to, but usually they are simply expected to store it for later recall. In the open classroom, students are consistently called upon to complete the learning process by acting upon their environment in some way. They must utilize the new knowledge in order to perform effective transactions with the environment. Thus, the structure of the open classroom situation forces them to complete the learning and thinking process in some way.

When it comes to the integration of knowledge, you can try to determine whether or not a child has difficulty in this area. If he seems never to have a very accurate picture of how things work or occur and cannot connect new information with previous experiences, then he is probably having difficulty with integration. It may help this type of child if you try to simplify new information for him, presenting it in very concrete or experiential terms. It also should help this kind of student if you verbalize what is happening while it happens. Show him through direct demonstration, when possible, how these new things are connected to specific, pleasant, past experiences the child has had in your classroom. Sometimes you may be able to make simple connections for students which can serve as a model for them in learning how to make these connections themselves. Sometimes experiences are too abstract or too complex for students to absorb. You can be the mediator and model for the child in this task. There is always the possibility in a situation such as this that there is some central nervous system damage or dysfunction. In this case, it is unlikely that the student will improve. However, it is worth a lot of experimentation on your part before giving up. The reward of successful assistance can be very great.

RESPONDING

All the factors effecting perception again come into play to effect reactions to situations. The organic, emotional and cultural makeup of each child will vitally influence how he is able to respond to his environment. Any decision will be affected by all these factors simultaneously.

One aspect of response has been well defined by Guilford.[15] He has defined two discernible types of responses which occur as a result of the thinking process: divergent thinking, in which there is a production of multiple responses to the same question (what can you use a stick for?), and convergent thinking, in which the individual focuses on the most acceptable or probable answer (a stick is to throw for a dog). Both types of thinking can occur in the same individual or there can be a preference for one kind of response over the other. Divergent thinking is often associated with creativity and certainly is one aspect of it. Convergent thinking is essential for successful test-taking and for any situation where a single action must be decided upon and/or taken.

In responding to the learning process or to new situations, students will vary widely, depending upon their basic emotional makeup and their learning styles. There are some general things you can do to provide an atmosphere in which all students will grow. You should encourage students to experiment freely, to try a variety of solutions, and not to be discouraged if they do not get a satisfactory answer immediately. As you abandon the idea of the one right answer in your class, students will spontaneously feel a little freer to do things without fear of the stigma of failure. When you attempt to modify a student's learning style, you must be sure that before you attempt to do so, you give the student your respect and the feeling that you accept and value him the way he is. Hopefully, you do. When the child feels secure in his relationship with you, you can begin to try to show him new, more efficient ways of doing things. If you are enthusiastic about new ventures, this enthusiasm will be contagious, and soon students will be eager to try things within the security of their relationship with you. Once you show students, through the freedom you allow them, that you are interested in the complete development of their personalities and intelligence, they will not be afraid to show you the many complex sides of their thinking.

Practice in convergent and divergent thinking can be taught effectively in the open classroom. The structure of the room will indirectly encourage divergent thinking, and your added encouragement for students to think in a divergent manner may produce astounding results from many children. Remember that the principles of the traditional classroom require convergent thinking in order for a student to be successful. Once this necessity for limiting their responses is removed, and you encourage them to give divergent responses, they will produce a remarkable proliferation of associations. After some practice in this area, you can help them to learn techniques for choosing the best answer for their purposes from the ones which have occurred to them. This is excellent training for taking tests and for understanding the relative value of different solutions to a problem. It is very valuable to have students read test questions and give as many answers as they can. Then you can have them narrow down their answers to two, and finally to the one they think the test requires for success. This will also help them to distinguish patterns in tests.

TYPES OF LEARNING STYLES

Some investigators have described general thinking and learning styles which seem to be consistent and well defined in some individuals. Kagan[16] defines the analytic and the impulsive child. The analytic child seems to reflect upon problems more thoroughly or for longer periods of time than does the impulsive one. The impulsive child tends to choose an answer immediately, without reflection. Because of this immediate or impulsive response, he often chooses wrong answers. The higher the intelligence of the impulsive child, the more likely he is to choose correct answers. The impulsive cognitive style has been associated with gross motor discharges, somewhat impulsive in nature.[17] The reflective child tends to choose correct answers more often, perhaps due to the prolonged consideration he gives the problem.

Rosenberg[18] describes the following discernible learning styles: rigid-inhibited style, undisciplined style, acceptance-anxious style and creative style.

Rigid-Inhibited Learning Style

The rigid-inhibited child has a strong need for structure and he dogmatically adheres to absolutist principles in dealing with his environment. Any new situation can be unnerving to him because of his desire to preserve the status quo. He may be passive, noncommittal, adhering to authority, rules and preestablished value systems. This makes him unable to evaluate situations objectively. He needs to preserve certainty at all costs. If he is confronted with an ambiguous or a very complex situation, he may become disoriented, confused and even withdrawn. He usually functions on a very concrete level of thinking and language development.

Undisciplined Learning Style

A child with an undisciplined learning style will seek immediate gratification of his needs. His behavior is usually serious, aggressive, competitive and critical. He will struggle grimly for anything he wants. He has weak tolerance for frustration. He is primarily interested in hedonistic gratification and is exploitive, coercive and manipulative in interpersonal relationships. He will tend to avoid situations which will make him responsible to others. He may appear happy-go-lucky and cheerful but has great trouble controlling his behavior, somewhat like the impulsive child described by Kagan. He will be non-analytic toward the environmental happenings, categorically accepting or rejecting things in terms of his own introjected negativity. He will most often interpret facts in a way which upholds his own views and beliefs. In class, this child will present problems in failing to do or to complete his work. He may have antisocial tendencies, will blame external circumstances when things do not go well, and tend to counter failures with the attitude that the task had no meaning for him. He usually functions on a moderately abstract level of language development.

Acceptance-Anxious Learning Style

In contrast to the undisciplined learning style, where the child is guided mainly by his inner needs, the child with an acceptance-anxious style is excessively concerned with the opinions others hold of him and his productions. This concern may take the form either of trying to be a good guy or of being extremely competitive. He needs constant affirmation of his worth from the environment. His self-esteem seems to hang on the opinions others hold of him. He will always conform to rules, holds back in any free play situation, and may appear somewhat isolated in the classroom. Sometimes he will appear aloof because he has not adopted defenses which will protect him from the rejection he fears, so he avoids as many situations as he can. He is usually anxious and somewhat obsessive in dealing with problem situations but his anxiety does not immobilize him. Because anxiety surrounds the learning process, he may get caught in a cycle of attempting to do a superadequate job. He may become lost in irrelevant details in his desire for perfection; he may withdraw, and after a period of time return to repeat the cycle. He never succeeds because of his ineffective strategies. He will be more comfortable with passive learning conditions in which he is given the correct answer and does not have to volunteer his own thinking, thus reducing the possibility of rejection. He becomes an expert at discerning what the teacher wants.

Creative Learning Style

A child with a creative style of learning is maximally open to perceiving his environment and his own feelings. He usually has reached a highly abstract level of language development. He is willing to try new things, contemplate alternatives and initiate new behavior. He is usually task-oriented, objective and self-critical. He is able to suspend his judgment when not enough information is available; he is able to seek more facts. He has no difficulty tolerating ambiguous situations. He can learn from mistakes and use failure as a means of adjusting his behavior so that he can be more effective on subsequent tasks. He is usually independent in his thinking. It is based primarily upon his own experience and not upon the thinking of others or upon strong instinctual needs. This child is able to suspend his judgment when not enough information is available and seek more facts. He is generally confident, trusting and enthusiastic. This type of child is probably the one who seems immediately happy in the open classroom where he can pursue tasks independently and freely.

Although many students will not fit neatly into these categories, the attributes described above are the kinds of things you will be looking for as you look for patterns in children's behavior. There is no reason to suppose that there are not all kinds of mixtures of these styles, i.e., forty percent anxiety-acceptance, mixed with sixty percent creative. It is also probable that many other styles exist which we have not been able to delineate. It is not necessary for you to know the exact categorical designation of each child. Categories in and of themselves are a dead end. The important thing is that you learn what kinds of traits and patterns to observe in students' behavior and that you attempt to modify those behaviors which are not successful for the individual child.

MODIFYING BEHAVIOR

Your knowledge of these factors of learning will help you to provide more valuable and specific learning situations within the classroom. You must always take into consideration the developmental level of the child. There is considerable evidence that we cannot advance children in the specific developmental aspects of their growth which seem to develop sequentially.[19] Most helpful in understanding the abilities of each child are the developmental stages postulated by Piaget.[20] In addition to deciding what kinds of situations will be helpful in modifying behavior or in learning new behavior, it is important that you be aware of what the child is developmentally capable of doing, and that you provide tasks which are compatible with this level. No one knows exactly how to create these situations within the classroom or how to modify behavior. This is still largely theoretical and experimental. Even though you have little idea of what to do, it is worthwhile to attempt things which will induce change even though they are based on incomplete knowledge. Although we know little about the learning process, that cannot be a reason to make us stop trying to teach! If you operate in the context of a warm and positive relationship with students, the chances of your doing any harm are slight, and the chances of constructive learning occurring should be high.

Using the description of the learning process and of specific learning styles as a guide, there are some possibilities for modification of individual behavior. I have suggested some examples although these are rather gross, as I cannot know the specific needs of individual children you will encounter. There are books available which elaborate various techniques of working with students in this way,[21] and they may provide a stimulus for you to experiment with techniques you can devise yourself in order to deal with your own particular students.

In dealing with typical learning styles, there are many learning situations you can employ as tools for modifying student behavior. In the case of a child with an impulsive kind of behavior, first you might try to make him aware of his tendency to choose answers too quickly. Next you can help him think through problems. Show him several times how you do it and then slowly encourage him to add his thoughts to yours and then try it by himself while you listen. You may eventually be able to teach him alternative solutions and to use some criteria to make choices. Your help will be most effective if you do these things with the child while he attempts to solve a real problem. Verbalize your perceptions of the situation, your analysis of the situation, and possible solutions or alternative actions. Eventually he will use you as a model for his own thought and will feel more secure in this type of thinking. As he feels secure in these new ventures, he will begin to try new variations of his own and perhaps eventually develop a more successful and individual style. We are assuming that many of his thinking procedures have been learned and that it is possible to reteach him more efficient ways to learn and think, as well as to expose him to additional techniques to supplement those he already has. It is possible that, for some children, much of this impulsive behavior is genetically determined or is the product of damaged or malfunctioning organic systems. In this case, you may see very little change in the student's behavior.

For a child with the rigid-inhibited learning style, you must grant the child the structure and security he seeks in your classroom. Do not make him try new things and do not challenge his absolutist attitudes. As he begins to trust you and to feel comfortable within the new situation (which may take some time since it is basically a new kind of structure and experience for him), you can try to encourage him to attempt new activities slowly. The open classroom is not the most comfortable atmosphere for this child, but it does hold many more opportunities for growth than does the traditional classroom. He will have many more opportunities to learn from concrete objects and real situations, which is appropriate and necessary for his concrete thinking level. In all instances, you should provide him with the control he seems to need. As his relationship with you grows and he ventures into new situations, you can begin to help him to learn more comprehensive ways of perceiving his environment. Try to provide simple situations at first, increasing their complexity and ambiguity only as the student is ready for it. This type of student may never be truly ready for ambiguous situations. Remember that he functions on a very concrete level of thinking and should be taught through the use of real things and situations. Your behavior can provide a model for new learning techniques which he can use in classroom situations. At the least sign of withdrawal or confusion on his part, try to simplify the material or the situation. If this is not possible or does not work, then discontinue your attempts for awhile and allow the child to gather his mental and emotional forces again before you start afresh.

In the case of a student with an undisciplined learning style, you must also accept him initially on his own terms. His main difficulty is his need to obtain immediate gratification despite the consequences. It is important to help him find constructive ways of obtaining this gratification when possible. This is made easier in the open classroom because all children are encouraged to do what they want to do. This means that this kind of child will not be coerced into unpleasant and meaningless situations. After you have modified some of his other behaviors, you can try to involve him in less gratifying tasks whose rewards may not satisfy his deep inner needs. It is important to emphasize the social results of his actions immediately.[22] This may help him to stop any antisocial behavior or persist in behavior which would antagonize you and the other students. After he sees that you are basically on his side in trying to help him gratify his needs, you will be in a position to help him to be more analytical in his approach to problems. You might try to help him to see several interpretations of the same situation or facts, helping him to become less self-centered in his interpretation of the world. You can also help him to view failures as being useful in learning how to deal with the same situation in the future, thus not damaging his self-esteem.

For the child with an acceptance-anxious learning style, your basic respect for him as expressed in many details of class organization and in your dealings with him should initially give him a feeling of security. However, the open classroom is always filled with new and unexpected situations without many guidelines for action. This will tend to make this child quite anxious. To counteract his anxiety, you can give the child a lot of reassurance (through your actions and your verbalizations) that he can do whatever he likes and that you are interested in and approve of his productions. You should encourage him to try, experiment, make mistakes and have fun. The little boy mentioned in Chapter 5 who thought of himself as a dead clown showed many characteristics of the acceptance-anxious learning style. He was unable to allow himself to feel or to express his feelings for fear of rejection, particularly by adults. You can help this kind of child begin to evaluate his own performance more realistically, rather than concentrating on the opinions of others. Begin by evaluating it yourself in great detail. Slowly ask for his thoughts about situations. If you are hesitant to give judgmental opinions to your students in general, this will help this type of child to feel less pressure to produce teacher-pleasing behavior, although in some cases your lack of clarity about what you want may make him overly anxious. In this case, you may have to reassure him that you are pleased with his work. You should constantly emphasize your hopes that he will do things to please himself. If the child has difficulty that stems from trying to achieve superadequate products, you can help him to plan more realistically, and you can work directly with him to achieve some end, making sure he does not become sidetracked by irrelevant details.

For the child with a creative style of learning, it is important to provide stimulating materials and situations from which he can experience and learn. He should be a great asset to any open classroom and should immediately feel at home there. A student who essentially displays the creative style may need help in some areas. Often these children are not task-oriented and need help in completing things, perhaps in developing the ability to use convergent thinking. Sometimes they are so sensitive to external happenings that they become a difficult problem in the classroom, since they notice every nuance of feeling and behavior. In this case, you will have to provide reassurance for them at difficult periods and help them to learn effective ways of dealing with their overly sensitive ability to perceive. This may mean avoiding certain situations, seeking the support of peers or teacher in others, etc.

Whatever the learning style of the child, you will effect little change unless you begin by accepting the total child as he is, realizing that he has made the most feasible adjustment to his world, given his temperament and the environmental opportunities available to him. You will not be able to significantly change a child's approach to learning or thinking unless you develop a warm, positive relationship with him, one in which he will feel secure enough to experiment and try new approaches to life. Any gap in your relationship with him (school vacation, illness necessitating absence) is likely to cause a temporary setback in whatever progress the student has made. When he fails, or tries too much before he is ready for it, he must be able to retreat to his relationship with you until he is able to venture forth again.

NOTES - CHAPTER 6

1. Harold W. Stevenson, "Learning and Reinforcement Effects," in *Perspectives in Child Psychology Research and Review,* Thomas D. Spencer and Norman Kass, eds. (New York: McGraw-Hill Book Co., 1967), pp. 326–329.

2. Robert D. Hess and Roberta M. Bear, eds., *Early Education* (Chicago: Aldine Publishing Co., 1968).

3. R. W. Gardner et al., "Cognitive Control: A Study of Individual Consistencies in Cognitive Behavior," *Psychological Issues,* Vol. 1, No. 4, 1959.

4. Robert Rosenthal, *Pygmalion in the Classroom.*

5. Benjamin Bloom, *Taxonomy of Education.*

6. Jerome Bruner, "Eye, Hand, Mind," in *Studies in Cognitive Development,* David Elkind and John Flavell, eds. (London: Oxford University Press, 1961).

7. Charles H. Rathbone, "On Preparing the Teacher: A Lesson From Loughborough," in *Open Education: The Informal Classroom,* Charles H. Rathbone, ed. (New York: Citation Press, 1971), pp. 155–167.

8. Doris J. Johnson, and Helmer R. Myklebust, *Learning Disabilities* (New York: Grune and Stratton, 1967), pp. 1–4.

9. Robert M. Gagné, "The Learning of Concepts," in *Human Dynamics in Psychology and Education,* Don E. Hamachek, ed. (Boston: Allyn and Bacon, Inc., 1968), pp. 13–21.

10. See Bibliography at the end of this chapter.

11. H. A. Witkin et al., *Psychological Differentiation* (New York: John Wiley and Sons, 1962).

12. J. McV. Hunt, *Intelligence and Experience* (New York: The Ronald Press Co., 1961), pp. 189–192.

13. Robert M. Gagné, "The Learning of Concepts," pp. 13–21.

14. Harry Harlow, "The Formation of Learning Sets," *Psychological Review,* 56, 51–65, 1949.

15. J. P. Guilford, "Basic Conceptual Problems in the Psychology of Thinking."

16. Jerome Kagan, Howard A. Moss, and Irving A. Sigel, "Psychological Significance of Styles of Conceptualization," *So-*

ciety for the Research in Child Development, Monographs, #86, 1963, 17:927–940.

17. Jerome Kagan, Howard A. Moss, and Irving A. Sigel, *op. cit.*

18. Marshall B. Rosenberg, *Diagnostic Teaching* (Seattle: Special Child Publications, 1968), pp. 38–63.

19. Lawrence Kohlberg, "Early Education: A Cognitive-Developmental View." *Child Development,* Vol. 39, No. 4, pp. 1013–1062, 1968.

20. Jean Piaget, *Six Psychological Studies,* pp. 3–71.

21. Marshall B. Rosenberg, *Diagnostic Teaching,* and L. E. Raths, A. Jonas, A. Rothstein, and Selma Wasserman, *Teaching for Thinking, Theory and Application* (Columbus: Charles E. Merrill, Inc., 1967).

22. Marshall B. Rosenberg, *op. cit.,* p. 43.

BIBLIOGRAPHY - CHAPTER 6

Books on diagnosis and techniques of dealing with individual learning styles:

Ashlock, P. and A. Stevens, *Educational Therapy in the Elementary School.* Springfield, Ill.: Charles C. Thomas, 1966.

Cults, N. E. and N. Moseley, *Providing for Individual Differences in the Elementary School.* New York: Prentice-Hall, 1960.

Gordon, I. J., *Studying the Child in the School.* New York: John Wiley and Sons, Inc., 1966.

Raths, L. E., A. Jonas, A. Rothstein and Selma Wasserman, *Teaching for Thinking, Theory and Application.* Columbus, Ohio: Charles E. Merrill, Inc., 1967.

Rosenberg, Marshall B., *Diagnostic Teaching.* Seattle: Special Child Publications, 1968.

Books discussing individual differences:

Bruner, Jerome, "The Course of Cognitive Growth," *American Psychologist,* Jan. 19, 1964, pp. 1–15.

Gagné, R. M., ed., *Learning and Individual Differences.* Columbus, Ohio: Charles E. Merrill, Inc., 1967.

Harvey, O. J., D. E. Hunt and H. J. Schroder, *Conceptual Systems and Personality Organization.* New York: John Wiley, 1961.

Kagan, Jerome, Howard A. Moss and Irving E. Siegel, *Psychological Significance of Styles of Conceptualization.* Society for the Research in Child Development, Monographs, Serial #86, 1963, 28:73–112.

Witkin, H. A. et al., *Psychological Differentiation.* New York: John Wiley and Sons, 1962.

CHAPTER 7.

CARRYING ON

7.

As you continue with the open classroom, you and your students will slowly develop new concepts of school and learning. As you gain insights into the abilities and interests of your students, how they work together as a group and individually, you are ready to begin an intelligent educational program built upon a foundation of skillful diagnosis.

Sometimes in the beginning stages of the open classroom, there is a feeling of exuberance which comes from the new-found freedom and involvement with learning and materials. The thrill of discovery, of experimentation and of enjoyment is an exciting experience. The first few weeks of your open classroom may be filled with this excitement. Unfortunately, this excess of feeling cannot be sustained for long. Unless you are observant and skillful and can help give focus and meaning to student interests and pursuits, this initial exuberance can dissipate into apathy or boredom. While many students are eager and capable of choosing their own activities and learning experiences, there will always come the time when students run out of ideas or seem to tire of whatever they do, no matter how stimulating it is. This is the time when you must be ready to move in and provide other kinds of learning situations. You may want to give some group lessons in one or more topics to stimulate individual learning and subsequent explorations. You may choose to introduce new materials which will challenge the interest and ability of students. Or you may plan a trip outside of the classroom to stimulate interest. Whatever your choice, do not be afraid to initiate new activities and take hold of the situation when you feel it is necessary.

HELPING STUDENTS TO SELECT CURRICULUM

As you encourage students to take responsibility for their own learning, you will meet problems. It is easy to say that we should let children do whatever they want to do, but sometimes this does not work out well in reality. Some children will find endless pursuits and never need your attention; others will find things to do for awhile, but then may feel bored and uninspired. A few students may never be able to find anything to do on their own. Sometimes students are so used to being guided and supervised by adults that they find it very difficult to suddenly take charge of their own learning or activities. Others seem to have few involving interests or ideas about how they might involve themselves or find anything in the environment to occupy their time. They seem to always want to be entertained or guided. It is hard to know whether this is the result of genetic predispositions or whether it is learned behavior. It is unlikely that we will ever know the answer to this question. But we can still try to modify such behavior if this seems needed and help children to develop new patterns of relating to their environment.

To help these students find things to do in the classroom in the interim period before you have been able to achieve any behavior modifications, and to help them learn to select their own learning activities, it is worthwhile to provide a focus or frame of reference from which they can operate. Their interests and curiosity can be aroused and focused on some topic through group lessons which use manipulable materials, and are presented with personal attention from you. By showing students how to investigate materials through group lessons, you will be teaching or retraining them to explore the environment through their senses. This will stimulate their curiosity spontaneously and naturally. Gradually they will pursue their unique interests and plans independently. If you find a student whose inability to select activities is connected with his basic learning style or personality problem, you may be unable to help him to make any significant change in his behavior. You may have to continue to provide more structured, teacher-selected activities for this child. A confused and passive child who is unable to make any decision will welcome your help.

Even if the majority of students do not become interested in the topic or question you choose to present to them as a group lesson, some will. It is possible to introduce a variety of topics until you eventually interest most of the students in some area. If you are a keen observer you can also note the interests of individual students and encourage them in their explorations. You can also bring in additional materials connected with the subject on the chance that this will involve them more deeply.

Curriculum List

When you want to select a subject or topic for individual students or for a group lesson, consult your list of curriculum topics and skills for your grade level and the one preceding and following it. I would also suggest you look over this list once a week all through the school year. Not only does it give you fresh ideas for lessons, but more importantly, it helps you to realize how individual interests fit into the suggested curriculum in a spontaneous manner. In most cases you will see that your students are going much farther than the curriculum guides suggest.

Your list will help you to get fresh inspiration for guiding and suggesting further activities to the children. For instance, if a few students have been busy weighing all manner of things on a classroom scale, you may notice in the curriculum outline that one skill is understanding the principles of a scale and being able to construct one. If the children are ready to move on to this activity, you can suggest it to them, or raise a question about how the scale works to see if they will take up the activity in response to your question. You may decide that another student who has been making great advances in addition is ready to move into some simple aspects of the concept of multiplcation. Until you become accustomed to the new manner of teaching in the open classroom, it is helpful to refer to your list for ideas and for reassurance that students are learning.

If you are following a more sequential type of curriculum plan in your classroom, with some traditional assignments or teacher-directed work, it is helpful to review the curriculum list also. In this case, you may want to make changes in the sequence suggested by the bulletins or planned by you originally. As students become interested in topics, it is more productive to follow their immediate interest. It may be a topic you had planned to teach in two or three months, but it should be easy to switch quickly if you are alert to the students' interests and to the demands of the curriculum. Curriculum guides are arranged with some logic and order. Students probably learn in some logically consistent way, but it may be different from that used in construction of the curriculum guides. You must be the interpreter of the course of children's learning, adjusting the plans to them, rather than making them conform strictly to predetermined plans.

OBSERVING STUDENTS IN ORDER TO EVALUATE LEARNING

Often the open classroom becomes so busy with so many different activities that you begin to feel as though no significant learning is occurring in any particular area. You will wonder where students are headed and what you are doing to facilitate learning. You may begin to feel as though you must introduce new materials or topics into the classroom to help students have some direction to their activities. Your feelings may be warranted, but often they will come from the lack of control you have over the learning situation. Students' energy will be diffused over a broad spectrum of topics and activities instead of being concentrated on one thing or area as is done in the traditional classroom. It is impossible for you to know every minute what each child is learning, and occasionally the whole situation seems to get out of hand and you have little idea what anyone is learning. Whatever the cause of your feeling may be, it is wise to investigate the overall involvement of the students in order to evaluate the truth of your feelings and to ascertain more specifically what is happening within your classroom.

You can observe students for the day, suspending your other teaching functions. Make a list of your students. Next to their names write the major projects they seem to be involved in during the day. Or you might use headings of the various subject areas across a large sheet of paper and everytime you see a child involved in an activity in a particular curriculum area, write his name under the appropriate heading, with a few words describing his specific activity. When you review your list at the end of the day, you will probably see that the students are engrossed in a number of activities.

Sometimes the activities become very individualized and diverse within the classroom. No two students may be doing the same things. If you find that this is happening in your room and you object to it, then you can use your observation sheets to see if there are any trends toward certain types of activities or toward certain subject areas. If there are trends, you might want to focus more of the students in the same area or type of activity by giving a group lesson which would direct their attention to specific areas and perhaps highlight shared interests. This should involve many students in similar activities and give a more clearly discernible pattern to their activities.

Your observations may reveal that a great deal of important learning is going on in the classroom. In this case, try to relax and do more observing than you had been doing. This will give you a better picture of what is happening and reassure you that the students are learning. At times all of us become edgy and driven to help students achieve more quickly. It is difficult to tell when we are reacting to our own drives rather than to a lack of activity on the part of students.

If your observations reveal that little meaningful learning is occurring, then you will need to resort to some stimulation. Allowing students free choice is never a guarantee that they will learn. If you feel certain that nothing is happening, do not hesitate to act as the catalyst who makes learning happen. If you are mistaken, and are interrupting some valuable learning activities, the children will react badly to your interference.

MEANINGFUL LEARNING ACTIVITIES

In order to make the judgment that learning is or is not significant, you must have some criteria to use. Or lack of knowledge about the learning process makes it difficult to know all the activities which might be worthwhile for students, but we do have some guidelines. One important sign that something of significance is occurring is the child's absorption in his task. Although we may not know exactly or even grossly what is happening, a high degree of involvement in a task indicates that it has great personal significance for a child. When a child explores materials, he is gaining valuable learning also. He learns about the environment and about his own ability to handle and manipulate parts of it.

Any creative play situation is usually an attempt to master

some situation or learning which has occurred to the child. These are usually important learning situations because the child makes several attempts to reorder his environment in acceptable ways, making it essentially a problem solving behavior. Other problem solving behavior is always valuable, whether it is trial and error or hypothesis testing. It should be encouraged. There are many instances of problem solving which take place in the area of emotional and social learning. Learning to talk or work with other students on many levels is a valuable learning activity for all students.

Collecting information is also a valuable learning activity. In the open classroom it can take many forms and may not always be obvious. Collecting information includes the whole spectrum of perception as well as the more formal aspects of it which we are accustomed to seeing in traditional classrooms. Sometimes just "messing around" can come under the category of collecting information. If the messing around seems to be leading nowhere and student interest is obviously lagging, you may be able to step in to give some organization to the situation. A well-timed question or suggestion may help students begin to classify their observations, and increase their meaning.

A vital aspect of learning which is given little notice in most classrooms is thinking or reflecting upon things. A child may need to sit quietly reviewing his experiences in order to integrate them in some satisfactory way which will solve or satisfy his problem or interest. He does not help us to recognize this by putting his hand to his brow and bending his head in deep concentration. Some children may need to engage in a meaningless or mindless activity such as bouncing a ball or doodling while they think. You may be able to discern individual patterns in the way students choose to meditate.

Another associated facet of thinking or gathering information is the act of watching or listening to other students or to an adult. Many children learn easily through imitation or through using their observations of others to make deductions in an indirect manner. A child with a rigid-inhibited learning style usually enjoys vicarious experiences in the classroom. Often he will learn from them or try them later by himself.

It is unlikely that any student will spend every minute of the day engaged in vital learning activities. All of us need breaks in activity, rest or play periods during the day, in order to gather our energies for new ventures. This is one of the things which can be disturbing to visitors in your classroom (or to you sometimes). While many children are engaged in worthwhile activities, others seem to be doing nothing or engaging in activities which seem to have little connection with any valuable learning. For this reason, a brief observation of the open classroom cannot give a very valid picture of what is occurring in it. In a traditional classroom, we expect all students to think or rest at the same time and we usually don't give them very much time to do either. Realizing the individuality of students, this is a foolish and ineffective practice. Various students may be more or less involved in learning at different times during the day. This can be a function of the available activities, the child's interest or his energy level. As in other areas of learning, you should look for patterns or regularities in the behavior of each individual. One or two observations will not give you a very reliable picture of what is occurring.

MATERIALS

As time goes on, you will find it necessary to vary the available materials. As students become involved in lengthy projects as the weeks progress, you will be replacing some of the initial types of materials with tools and instruments to facilitate their projects. Often when you introduce a new topic, or the students do so through their interest, it will be necessary to bring in more or different materials. Do not ignore the school storeroom. Often its contents are unknown to even the person in charge of it. Students will be valuable sources of materials if you encourage them to help gather materials. Appeals to administrators to use special funds set aside for such needs may also be productive. Parents can be a wonderful source of supplies. Send notes home when you need specific things. Parents may have access to many interesting materials through their jobs and their acquaintances. If you live in a city you can become a scavenger in industrial areas which contain surpluses of fascinating "garbage."

Materials serve the needs of the child's interests and curiosity, becoming versatile instruments which he can adapt to meet the needs of his own explorations and learning. Materials become the instruments to further learning. The cardboard box that becomes a space ship or a secret cave in which to hide treasure is essential to the learning taking place at that moment. Bottles, eyedroppers, spoons and similar utensils which allow a child to mix and measure become vitally important equipment in the classroom when this type of active learning is taking place.

As you continue the open classroom you will be able to observe the importance of materials to stimulate students. We all respond to the sensory stimulation of the environment and the objects it contains. In the classroom, interesting things combined with the stimulation of peers and an alert teacher combine to keep a child's interest in his world very high. We know today that humans deprived of sensory stimulation suffer extreme anxiety and even begin to hallucinate to replace the missing environmental stimulation.[1] This sensory contact with the world makes a vital link with life which children seek out and need. The more stimulation a child receives, the more likely he is to grow and become more sophisticated about and involved with his world.

One of the best learning experiences my first graders ever had occurred when they opened a large box of sunflower seeds (gerbil food) by mistake and began running their fingers through them and spilling them around the floor. The feel and the sound of the smooth hard seeds intrigued the children and brought forth a wealth of visual and auditory analogies. The seeds sounded like "thousands of tiny raindrops," "piles of money falling." They were like "shiny beads," "drops of sunlight," and "satin buttons." Although these are the types of responses every first grade teacher would like to elicit, not many of us would encourage their natural, spontaneous development within the classroom through a purely sensory experience shared with others. If anything, the traditional classroom is notable for its lack of shared sensory experiences. We constantly ask children to cut off all sensory contact and imagine something. Next we ask them to produce analogies which are pleasing to the teacher. This type of distortion of a child's natural desire and ability to relate his immediate sensory experiences to past ones can only cripple the natural development of such skills as well as convince most children that the things he learns in school are quite bland, useless and unrelated to real experiences. Real sensory experiences should have as prominent a place in the classroom as exercises in the use of the imagination.

The exploration of materials allows a child to measure the dimensions of reality in a variety of ways. It also helps the child measure himself in many ways. He learns how skillful he is in handling some materials and that he needs some practice or help in handling others. He learns which materials need care in handling and which ones can be manipulated easily and even played with carelessly to make interesting situations. Learning which things are too heavy for you to move and which things you can move with ease is the kind of experience which defines the self very clearly and concretely for a child. As the child grows stronger and more capable, he is able to see his own growth through his advanced ability to deal with the same materials in his environment. There can be no more certain affirmation of one's abilities and growth than this basic relationship with the stuff of a child's world.

If you notice students are not using some materials, remove them for awhile. If you bring them back in a few weeks, or when an appropriate situation for their use occurs, the students may see them in a fresh light. Or you may wish to use them in a group lesson which will encourage students to use them initially and perhaps continue to use them individually. When you find some materials which students find consistently interesting, you might want to bring in similar materials which present slight variations of the same principle.

Occasionally a group of students will abuse delicate materials or instruments. If this happens, discuss it with them, pointing out the consequences of their behavior. If it continues to happen, it is best to remove the materials or instruments from the room. Children may, for some reason, not have sufficient control to use them. They become frightened by their own destructive behavior and will need the reassurance of your willingness to control them when their own controls fail. If they begin destroying other things when you remove the materials, then they may be acting out against you in some way, and you will have to give the situation closer scrutiny in order to determine what the problem is. You may be too rigid in your demands regarding use of the materials, or clean-up. Or you may be too lax in giving students direction in their use of some materials. Experiment with different ways of handling the situation.

LOCATING TROUBLE SPOTS

Whenever you find things do not seem to be running smoothly or not the way you want them to, you can look to several sources for the difficulty. One of the main sources of a problem such as this is how the behavior of the class meets with your expectations. Do you have a clear view of the behavior, learning and general atmosphere which you expect? Sometimes we have an unconscious expectation which is vague and unconnected to any reality, and which may be impossible to fulfill. These expectations can make us feel uneasy and dissatisfied in a real situation because their roots are not in reality. If you are comparing your class to some mystical class in your mind, try to specify for yourself exactly what behavior you expect to occur in the class at various times. Often what we have in our minds is far too demanding and perfectionistic to ever be achieved by real, live children. Compare your expectations to what really does occur and then try to adjust your instructions or class organization more closely to the desired situation.

As you consider your expectations, you should remember that things will appear quite different in the operation of the open classroom than you would expect them to in a traditional classroom. Being used to the atmosphere of a traditional classroom, it is often difficult for us to accept that of the open classroom for a number of reasons. We usually feel unable to take in all that is going on in the open classroom because of the diversity of individual activities. In a classroom where important learning is occurring, one child literally may be jumping for joy over a discovery. Another may be loudly provoking a fight with a neighbor, and a third may be running around discharging energy. Others may be quietly reading or writing stories, while some are deeply engrossed in working with the tape recorder or various art media. To observe and judge this behavior without some deeper or more complete knowledge of what is causing it gives a distorted view of the open classroom. Occasionally we all respond to these superficial and somewhat meaningless aspects of the open classroom. Often there is a natural movement or flow to the events which occur in the open classroom, but this does not mean that things will run smoothly. There may seem to be confusion or disorder within the group when in fact there is important movement toward the solution of some problem. Usually strong and vital feelings are expressed in all learning which occurs. This adds to the superficial appearance of disorder or uncontrolled activity. Be sure that you focus on the deeper and more significant aspects of your classroom when you compare it to your expectations.

Sometimes you may find things are not running as they should because you are not being explicit enough in giving students directions, or in communicating expectations of behavior and learning. When this happens, students may be confused about their objectives unless they are very independent and self-motivated. Most students interpret the clues from their environment and incorporate them as part of the information which guides their behavior. Your communications will be important clues to most students. If they are unclear or ambiguous, students will have difficulty acting within the classroom and their confusion will create an uneasy atmosphere.

If you think that you are not making yourself understood clearly, try simplifying your instructions and comments. Give them in very concrete terms; do not use compound words and try not to be redundant. Experiment with different kinds of directions or rules, such as verbal, written and symbolic ones. At the end of a learning sequence, you and the students might try to evaluate how well they interpreted the directions. This can lead to valuable discussions about the qualities of the instructions you give and often will pinpoint the problems you or the students are having with the directions. Your directions may prove to be too complicated. You may be assuming experience and verbal sophistication which your students do not have. Their interpretations of simple directions may be faulty for a number of reasons, and these reasons might become apparent through repeated analyses of their interpretations.

Another source of dissatisfaction with the overall learning can stem from your expectations about the kinds of learning which do and will occur. You may be forgetting about the multiple ways a child can demonstrate learning and growth, and may feel that students are learning very little. Your feelings may be based upon your feelings relating to standard types of learning expected in traditional classrooms, such as content retention and speed of recall. The ability to assess problems, select materials which will solve them, and try different paths in attempting to find a solution are all important learning activities. They are often time-consuming, look like "messing around," and may produce few noticeable results, but they are nonetheless the means of acquiring valuable intellectual skills.

Trouble with routines may develop anytime during the year. Sometimes routines which have worked fairly well seem suddenly to go sour. Perhaps this occurs because of a sudden spurt of maturity in students, which makes old ways too simple or meaningless and unchallenging for them. Or new needs may be emerging in the group as a whole, making new routines necessary. It is difficult to know what happens in these instances. Try to be flexible when you detect such a problem; change the manner in which the routine is carried out. You can do this by your own decision or by a group decision following a class discussion of the problem.

If you feel that something is wrong and you cannot pinpoint what it is, try to delineate the time during the day or week when you feel uneasy. This may give you some clues about the problem. If the difficult period is before or after the students leave the room for some reason, search into the situation outside and inside the room for difficulties. There may be problems with a specialist, gym or lunchtime. Try to change the activities and routines before they leave or after they return if the problem seems to be something within the room. You may have misjudged their interests and/or capabilities at these times.

Problems can arise from too much or too little freedom. The needs of the group for freedom and for structure can fluctuate over the year. You will gradually grow sensitive to this, but in the beginning weeks or the first year you teach the open classroom, it may simply manifest itself as a problem to you with no apparent cause. If your class is very unstructured you might try to provide more focus and direction for students and see how they respond. Conversely, if it is very structured or if you have been intent on pursuing some particular curriculum topic, you may need to provide more freedom and leeway for students in their choice of activities. You must remember that the needs of the class as a whole will change from time to time, just as the needs of individuals do.

When things seem to be going badly, do not hesitate to discuss your feelings with the students. This will encourage them to express their feelings about the general operation of the class and will provide many valuable insights into what the individual students and the class as a whole think and need. It will also communicate to students that you care about their feelings on this subject and that you are willing to act upon their suggestions. This will encourage them to spontaneously express their ideas and feelings in the future, which will enable you to correct unsatisfactory situations more quickly.

SOCIAL VALUES

One of the most important elements of your classroom will be the overall atmosphere which is created. You help to create it by the materials you supply, the activities you encourage and the social values you display and encourage in students. The students will contribute to the atmosphere by their individuality and their social values. Some of their behavior within the classroom will be influenced by you. There is an abundance of evidence[2] which suggests that teachers promote more social, concerned student behavior when they use democratic, learner-centered approaches than when they use autocratic, teacher-centered approaches. The democratic teacher produces students who are more concerned about their fellows, are not fiercely competitive, and who fight and argue less than do those students of autocratic teachers. The open classroom provides the optimum environment for democratic teaching methods.

I think we have a responsibility to help children learn how to get along together as free and independent individuals living within a democratic community. We have the perfect chance to do so within the classroom, where children can learn through real experiences how to get along with each other in real situations. Since children may bring a very diverse set of values and behavior for relating to others from their home, it is necessary for you to set some common standards within the class which will help students to work together. This may mean learning new ways of getting along together.

Encouraging Group Cohesiveness

One of the pitfalls in the open classroom, where everyone is working individually, is that the group spirit of the class will deteriorate. Children tend to lose touch with each other as they work on individual learning projects and, except for a few friendships in the class, there may be very little real group spirit or feeling of common goals. In the traditional classroom, where children are pitted against one another in competitive situations, there also tends to be little group spirit. But because of the commonality of experience and assignments, students can have a feeling of working together in the same way, although they may not feel any particular fondness for their fellows.

There are certain common events which occur within the open classroom which will tend to give some feeling of group togetherness. Having one or two group lessons a week, or one a day, will keep the students working on similar aspects of the same topic, increasing the possibilities of their communicating with each other in common work situations and discussing common interests and findings. Group meetings to share experiences and activities may also help. Trips, experiences within the classroom, assemblies, etc. will also add to this feeling of common experiences. If you rely only upon these events to give a group spirit to your class, however, you will probably find that it is a weak one. Just as you set the pace for intellectual striving and investigation through your use of rewards and emphasis upon these things, you will also be able to set the tone of the group interaction. If you express pleasure every time one student helps another to learn (not giving the answer, but showing ways of finding the answer), soon you will find that this is one of the values held in high esteem within the group, and that examples of it will occur frequently.

Personal Values

To derive the most benefit from your position to develop these social values, you should be clear about what values you feel are important. The ones which you select will grow out of your own life experiences and value system. They should also be influenced by the values of the students you teach. You must respect their values even if you do not feel you want to reinforce them in the class. If students in very poor neighborhoods are reluctant to share their food at snack time or lunch time, respect this attitude. It grows out of the life they must live every day outside of the school room. If you are in a position to change that life so that this kind of non-sharing becomes unnecessary, then you can try to change their attitudes also. If you are not in such a position, then you should respect a value and attitude which has grown out of the reality of their everyday existence. From a very practical point of view, students will trust and respect you less if they think you are so foolish that you can not understand that it is not good to share your food. This can alienate them from you in many ways. This does not mean that you cannot show them other ways of personal relating, but you must first respect their value system.

It is possible to help children use different values for different situations. If you create situations within the class where children will have an opportunity to share food and other things, you can demonstrate to them that it is all right to share within the controlled atmosphere of the classroom. In this way you gradually can enlarge the possibilities for different behavior and for the development of the children's value systems without putting yourself in direct conflict with strongly reinforced personal values.

Since most of us who teach come from the same educational experience, we tend to identify with the middle-class values inherent in that system. It is essential to being a good teacher to be just as observant of the values and attitudes your students hold, and to respect them whether or not you agree with them. Just as it is quite legitimate to attempt to enlarge the perspective of lower-class students who have had different experiences than you have had. It is also desirable at times to change and enlarge the perspective of middle-class children who may also hold limited values. Surely it is helpful to middle-class students to be involved in situations within the classroom where competition is undesirable and where the smartest child may not be the one who is the most successful in a situation. Or where the quiet child is in control of a situation because of his calmness or knowledge, instead of the popular, manipulative child who usually dominates activities.

Influencing Student Values

Whatever the background and values of your students and yourself, it can only benefit them and you to try to enlarge their store of values and attitudes. This way they will become more aware of themselves as individuals with a particular set of values, as well as learning about other people who may have values different from their own.

Your position in the classroom as a model for the children to follow in their social behavior is especially important because so often these values are intertwined almost imperceptibly with our every action. Your awareness of your own values and attitudes will help you to realize what you may be communicating to students in thousands of little, unconscious ways. For the values you wish to emphasize, you will be able to use more direct, conscious ways of communicating them to students. You will thereby increase the possibility of their learning them and using them with some awareness, rather than blindly in an attempt to imitate someone they are fond of and respect. Children always learn best through real experiences. There are ample opportunities to encourage them to solve social situations within the classroom if we encourage them to do so. Just as you encourage intellectual experimentation, you should also encourage students to experiment socially, testing the limits of their own personality in this sphere and that of their social group.

The open classroom and the philosophy embodied in it are particularly suited to developing respect for others and for individual needs of each member of the group. Many people give lip service to these values but practice them minimally. In the open classroom, they are essential to the actual operation of the class. Another essential value is the feeling of responsibility for the shared property, the materials and tools within the classroom. There will be ample opportunity to develop these values in situations which occur daily in the room. You can do this by

1. respecting and using these values in your own behavior toward students
2. verbalizing your belief that these values are important
3. making the assumption that they will operate in all situations.

If you seem surprised, even mildly shocked, when students do not behave in accord with these values, they will soon take their cues from this and try new behavior more in line with your expectations. Your verbalization of values in the midst of a situation in which they are or should be used will be especially valuable in the beginning weeks of the class. Once the values take hold, students will verbalize them for one another.

In addition to these values which are really basic to the operation of your class, you can introduce any others you wish. I have always felt that a feeling of responsibility for one's fellows and for their learning is an important value. This, along with attitudes of fairness, sharing, compromise and all the values which help people to live together peacefully can be frequently demonstrated and experienced within class situations.

LONG RANGE PLANNING FOR STUDENT LEARNING

One of the most important differences between the duties of a teacher in a traditional classroom and a teacher in an open classroom is the type of planning which is done. The teacher in the traditional classroom concentrates her attention on lesson plans which will provide the entire class with the same educational experience. Although the teacher may be aware of individual differences in ability, she is mainly concerned with keeping the entire class moving along at a certain pace, learning the same skills and topics. All students are presented with standard curriculum, workbooks, textbooks and lessons that should help them to learn at the same pace.

In the open classroom, the teacher plans for each student, rather than for the class as a whole. After obtaining a wealth of diagnostic information about each student, in the beginning weeks of class she makes long range learning goals for each student. The formulation and pursuit of these goals will compose the bulk of the teaching activity during the school year.

In the open classroom, a steady progression of development in general ability is more important than a concentration upon specific subject matter. Ability and skill do not develop in a vacuum; they must be exercised upon subject matter of all kinds. Because of this, students in the open classroom do not usually suffer from a lack of information or knowledge. The important thing is that a student has access to whatever subject matter will meet his needs at particular times. It will not be identical for each student in the class; in some cases, it may be very different.

The beginning weeks of school should have provided you with ample information about your students. Their choices of activities, interests, patterns of dealing with learning situations and of responding to them, have all provided a rather full picture of each child. If you have given group lessons which were climaxed by encouraging each child to develop the topic in his own way, you may have even more specific information about how children deal with learning material. You should be able to describe certain patterns of learning for each child which will provide the basis for your long range plan. Your long range plan will be for the modification and/or enhancement of each student's learning style, for providing appropriate materials and experiences to match the child's developmental level, and for helping him to develop those skills and knowledge which are appropriate to his ability and his needs. Your planning will have little to do with grade level expectations. Students who are developmentally ahead of their fellows will do more complex work, while those far behind will do less difficult work. Your plans will not consist of specific subject matter unless children have very special interests or become quite involved in certain topics over the year. Obviously you will not ignore subject matter, since it is the means and substance of learning. But you will be allowing the student to choose his own subject matter.

Working with individual learning styles, to modify them or to help a child increase his learning tactics, is discussed in detail in Chapter 6. Understanding the developmental level of the child will help you to make appropriate materials available to him. If a child who is in the preoperational stage[3] becomes interested in airplanes, you would not supply him with books on airplanes which contained few pictures. You would know that he still needs real things and materials to work with whenever possible, and you would supply materials with which he could construct some planes and perhaps hangars and airports. You would try to help him find books with many pictures of airplanes in them.

Based upon already existing skills and knowledge, you can make a tentative plan of skills and abilities you hope to teach the child over the year. For instance, the child mentioned previously, who developed the interest in airplanes, might need some help increasing his overall verbal ability and his every day vocabulary in particular. This would be one of your long range plans for him. When you notice his interest in planes, you can begin to emphasize the names of different kinds of planes, equipment, buildings and personnel connected with them as you encourage or provide real and play situations around the child's interest. You will be following your plans for him but will use subject matter selected by the child himself. For a child with a different need who also became interested in airplanes, you might want to emphasize writing stories or poems about them in order to develop his writing and spelling skills.

Your long range plans for an individual child will help you to know what kinds of questions to ask him about his work, and in which direction you want to focus his attention or expand his activities. They will provide a basis for giving small group lessons, or if enough students need the same skills, perhaps for large group lessons.

These plans will be modified as the year proceeds and students change. They may mature more quickly than you had anticipated, so that more advanced planning must be added to your original plans. Or you may overestimate the ability and experience of students initially and have to narrow the scope of your plan for their learning. Depending upon your students, you may want to discuss these plans with them periodically in order to evaluate their progress and let them know how you feel about their work and what you think will be helpful for them to concentrate on in the immediate future.

It is essential that you keep a record of your plan and a record of progress for each child. Records do not have to be exhaustive to be effective. They do have to be taken at regular intervals and reviewed periodically in order to give you and the student adequate information about the process of his learning. If your students are old enough, they can help to keep their own records by detailing activities and skills learned. Even young children can keep records by learning to file their written or drawn work in folders.

How you keep records is a very personal matter. Some of us need to include extensive details in order to consider them worthwhile, while others of us may do a fine job with only a few cryptic comments recorded every week or every month. Your impression and evaluation of the student at the beginning of the year is of special importance in this record. You will want this in some detail so that you will be able to compare his growth over the year with this initial showing.

Since the open classroom is still in the process of being accepted in this country, records are particularly important to help you and others demonstrate the progress or lack of it which each student makes in this kind of atmosphere. If the open classroom is superior to the traditional classroom, records of individual student progress will eventually be the things which prove the point. As a parent, I would want to know that a teacher is knowledgeable enough to keep intelligent records and plans for my child.

THE TEACHER'S ROLE IN HELPING CHILDREN TO LEARN

Some advocates of the open classroom insist that the teacher has no role, that if she only relates naturally and warmly to students, they will learn and thrive. It is pleasant to think that just being full of love, interest and respect for children will give them the optimal learning situation, but I think this is too romantic a notion to accept seriously. Others suggest that the teacher's primary role in the classroom is to structure the environment for students in such a way that they learn under optimal conditions. While the environment is very important in controlling the kinds of learning which occur, it is only one factor in a child's learning. Many children are exposed to unusual and stimulating environments, but if no one focuses their attention and learning during this exposure to the environment, their learning may be inconsequential.

I think we must insist that warmth and respect for children is a prerequisite for any teacher or teacher trainee. Without it, a nourishing educational environment will be deeply lacking. However, it is naive to believe that we need only be warm and natural with students to help them learn. We must also have an adequate knowledge of child development and of the essentials of the various subject areas in order to structure the student's environment effectively. We do have some knowledge about what kinds of teacher behavior facilitates learning. This knowledge, although small compared to the teaching task and the activities involved, provides guidelines for us to view teaching as a purposeful rather than as an accidental or random activity.

Flanders[4] found that successful teachers are able to provide a wide range of roles in their teaching. They ranged from dominative supervision to discriminating support. A successful teacher must be able to make diagnoses, think of possible courses of action and be enough in control of her behavior to switch from role to role. She must understand the principles of teacher influence and be able to make reasonable assessments of current conditions in the classroom. Except for the principles of teacher influence, these abilities have been discussed earlier.

Methods of Influencing Students

One of the most powerful influences a teacher has in the classroom is her ability to reinforce certain behavior by personally rewarding it. The reward may consist of a smile, a nod, an exclamation. Whatever the form, students will be sensitive to the behavior which is rewarded and will tend to repeat it. As the students' relationship with you grows over the weeks and months, your rewards for their behavior will become more valued. If you react positively to their learning, experimenting, exploring, sharing and helping, these behaviors will increase within the classroom. In traditional classrooms, teachers often become so preoccupied with discipline and superficial behavior, that these are the things which they reward and which achieve importance and prominence in the class, rather than learning and thinking, which should be the important activities.

One of your most active influences upon students will be your attempts to focus their attention and learning. You will do this through group lessons and through planning with students. On a more informal basis, you will be doing it constantly. As students work at self-selected tasks, it will be important for you to watch them and to be ready to move in with a question, a suggestion or added materials. Any of these will focus students' attention in one particular direction or on a specific aspect of a problem or situation. To ask a child who has been constructing model boats how to make them actually move in water, should focus his attention on sources of power. To place a magnifying glass next to a student who is intent on examining leaves and flowers can open up new discoveries and questions. When you see a child struggling to make a workable elevator out of cardboard and string, you can make sure that pulleys are within his view without saying anything to him. Or you might suggest he use some metal or wooden supporting pieces for braces. This will focus his attention on the foundation and supporting structure of his construction. Or if you see students carrying heavy blocks across the room, you might ask them if they can find some way to transport them more easily. You might also suggest that they try getting some wheels; then let them go off on their own and try to solve the problem of utilizing the wheels. If you see students making some elaborate constructions from wood, you might give them some sandpaper or files to encourage them to finish off the pieces.

How do you know in which direction to focus children's work? Often you will intuitively know when to step in and what to do. However, it is foolish to rely only upon your intuition. Your long range plans for each student and your list of curriculum topics and skills which are recommended for coverage during the year will give you the frame of reference and specific ideas which you need to focus students' interest and activity. If you consult these two things frequently during the beginning months of teaching the open classroom, you should have an abundance of ideas about focusing the individual student's work.

If you are used to more direct teaching in which you pass information on to students, directing their activity and their thinking along preplanned paths, then this will mean you must learn new approaches of more indirect teaching. It will take time for you to learn when to ask a question or make a comment, and when to say nothing. About the only concrete guideline we have to offer is that children should not be interrupted in any way when they are deeply absorbed in an activity or in solving a problem. It is usually good to focus students when they seem to have no particular purpose in mind, or seem to be fooling about aimlessly with materials or each other. If you want to make a comment or ask a question about something in which a child does seem deeply absorbed, you should always wait until he is at a stopping point in his work. This will prevent you from interrupting whatever purpose he has in mind at the moment. Materials which will facilitate student explorations can be supplied by you at any time. When students are deeply engrossed in their work, you can simply place the new materials or tools at hand without interrupting their work.

You will facilitate students' learning by clarifying situations, checking work, and demonstrating how to do certain things or how to use certain tools. In this way, you will be constantly providing students with added insights into learning situations. Your long range plans for individual students will provide a guide to help you know immediately which child you will give help to and which one you will encourage to work independently. In most cases, when students ask you for help, you should try to encourage them to think through their problem themselves if possible. For students who have particular difficulty because of their learning style, you may want to work with them when they summon you for aid, so that you can provide more successful ways for them to work out the problem.

You will be a resource to students in several ways. Initially, you were the source of stimulating and involving materials. As the depth of students involvement in learning increases, their need for more complex and more abstract resources will also increase. You will be a valuable source of reference for them, guiding them to needed information. This does not mean that you need to know everything the students want to learn about. It does mean that you must know how to find specific information and how to get needed materials.

In the case of younger children who are less able to manipulate and move about freely in the world outside the home and classroom, you will remain a primary source of materials, information, etc. The desire of young children for factual information about their world is striking in the open classroom setting. Unfortunately, the books they can read or understand through pictures are not very informative, and you will have to interpret for them books of greater complexity in order to get the information and facts they seek.

It is always helpful if you are knowledgeable in a subject students become interested in, because then you are in a better position to structure group lessons and learning experiences. However, you should not let yourself get into the position of directly giving students information. You should always try to help students find their own information. This is learning and learning how to learn at the same time. Sometimes information may be unavailable to students or you may be at a loss for further sources. In this case, certainly do not withhold information you may have personally accumulated.

A rather mysterious source of influence will come from your opinion of each child, his ability, his talents, his shortcomings, and his potential for growth. Rosenthal[5] conducted some interesting studies in which teachers were given advance information about students' potential for development. The students had been randomly assigned to groups of normal children and "late bloomers." The teachers were encouraged to help these late bloomers to fulfill their potentials. After two years the researchers found that all the late bloomers were doing superior work despite the fact that they had, in fact, been identical to the group termed "normal." Other studies have demonstrated beyond doubt that teachers who have classes of students thought to be slow or backward, generally produce students who are slow and backward by the end of year. This occurs despite the fact that the students may have been quite normal or above average. Conversely, students given labels of superior or above average will generally be just that, although they may have entered the class at the beginning of the year with normal or below normal records of achievement. It is frightening to think that we have such power over the development of students.

It is often difficult to remain unbiased about student ability and potential. All of us like some students more than others and probably always will. Even with supreme attempts to control these feelings, it is difficult to never express them within the classroom. In the open classroom you have such a variety of situations in which to see students operate, that you get much broader views of a single child's ability than you would ever get in a traditional classroom. This will tend to give you a better chance to appreciate all students instead of only some of them. As you realize how different they are from one another and how each child excels at something, you feel less judgmental about individual students.

BEHAVIOR PROBLEMS

Advocates of the open classroom often claim that there are no behavior problems when students are allowed to pursue their natural interests in their own way. In one sense this is true. Many of the discipline problems which result from constricting children unreasonably do disappear. Students who are problems because they cannot sit still or keep quiet in traditional classrooms are not problems in open classrooms, where they are encouraged to move and talk freely. Students who develop problems because of boredom or complete lack of understanding of what is occurring within a traditional classroom are not problems in the open classroom because they are able to choose interesting activities corresponding to their ability and understanding.

Behavior problems do occur in the open classroom. It might be more correct to give them different names because their sources are different, but basically there are some students who will have special problems and who will require more effort to deal with in the classroom. One source of such problems is a poorly organized classroom which does not provide enough variety of activities or enough social structure. Another source of problems is the type of adjustments an individual child makes to the world. Some children have problems relating to their peers, to adults and to materials. We have discussed the former problem in great detail in this book so I will not consider it here. The latter problem is one which teachers will always have to face, no matter what type of classroom they have.

In the open classroom personality problems tend to become more prominent because students are constantly faced with relating to materials and to other students. They must do these things in a setting which provides less external control than do most social situations. The continual need to test oneself against the environment and to relate to others puts the student under pressure which he may not experience in other situations. This will tend to aggravate any existing emotional problems. A child with problems usually has adopted patterns of behavior which are inadequate for his needs or which cripple him in some way. In the case of the child who has inadequate defense mechanisms, these soon will be broken down in the open classroom because of the constant pressure on the student to relate. For those students who have crippling defense mechanisms, the areas in which they cannot function will soon become glaringly apparent. He may choose to give up some of his crippling defense mechanisms. He will then be faced with the original problems. The freedom of the open classroom will encourage all students to express their feelings more honestly. For students who have severe problems in handling their feelings, this can be upsetting and difficult to deal with.

Handling Problems in the Beginning Weeks of School

Each child has achieved a certain balance between his needs, the demands of the outside world and his potential for various responses. This balance is important in maintaining him in the world in which he must live. When he first comes into your class he will present a true picture of how he functions in new situations. After he has been with you for awhile and feels more secure, his behavior may change somewhat from what it was in the first days of school. Whatever his needs appear to be in the beginning, try to meet them if you can without disrupting the routines of your class. For children who appear to need lots of attention, give it to them. For those who need to maintain control over situations, let them have it whenever possible. For children who want to withdraw, do not coax them. Include them in general invitations to do things but do not single them out for special attention from you. The only kind of behavior which you cannot go along with usually is the aggression of children who act out their hostility in some way, abusing other people or materials. For this child, you can always try suggesting that he hit, pinch or do whatever his specialty is to something which is not alive and which cannot be damaged significantly. You should supply a punching bag or a pillow for such purposes. If he is reluctant to switch to inanimate objects, get him started by doing it with him and agree that it sometimes feels good to get your anger out by hitting a pillow. Make it clear that he is always welcome to hit the pillow but not people. You will be showing him a permissible way he can express his aggression instead of merely making him try to control it. Obviously, if he was able to control it he would have done so originally.

For students who seem very confused or frightened in the initial days of school, it may be that the change of structure and outward functioning of the class is frightening. It is best to keep these students near you if possible and to structure their activities or give them specific assignments. You might have small group lessons for them on and off during the day if you have several students like this. This will provide them with some structure, familiar activities, and your personal control.

By immediately responding to the emotional needs of your students, you will be communicating to them that you recognize and accept their needs. You will be showing them that you can accommodate yourself to meet their needs. This is a good beginning for the development of a warm relationship with students. Surely, as adults, we should have the knowledge and the emotional control necessary to accommodate immature children who need our help. Too often in traditional classrooms the child must accommodate himself to the adult completely or be branded a misfit in the educational situation. Eventually you will be able to help the children who need it to learn new ways of satisfying their needs and coping with the world using less destructive, less crippling, and more socially acceptable defenses. It is just as important that you accept children's emotional styles as it is that you accept their intellectual styles. These styles children develop are the most efficient ways they have been able to find to function in their world. If you immediately tell them by your rejection of their behavior that you will not accept their particular styles of dealing with the world, you will also be rejecting them as individuals. It is essential that we accept the basic right of each child to cope with the world as best he can.

As your relationship with the students grows over the first few weeks, you will learn more about their emotional needs and reactions. Then you will be in a position to try to help them to learn new patterns of behaving to satisfy their needs and deal with their world. For students whose styles are already successful and satisfying, you can provide the atmosphere and the situations which will encourage them to add to these successful modes of action.

Unless a student presents a serious management problem in the class, it is a good idea simply to observe his behavior in the first weeks and sometimes months. The atmosphere of the open classroom is usually enough either to weaken the defenses of a child or to solidify his problem in some way so that it becomes very clear to you what the difficulty is. The types of students who will present management problems in these first weeks are the aggressive child, the hyperactive child, and the child with few inner controls over his feelings. The aggressive child needs as many outlets for his aggression as possible, because he has developed no effective means of controlling it. You must make it clear to him that he cannot take out his aggression on others or on the materials. At the same time you must help him to find outlets. Any activity which involves physical activity will usually provide an outlet for aggression. The more wholeheartedly the child can throw himself into the activity, the more satisfying it will be. Hammering, pounding, cleaning, cutting, jumping on something are all things which will help the aggressive child. As the class proceeds, he will be able to select the activities which seem most satisfying for him to use to vent his feelings. They will act as his controls until he matures enough to develop restraint and inner control over his feelings.

Hyperactive children can present a problem in an open classroom. Although they do have freedom to move about and go from activity to activity, their behavior may prove distracting to other students. Often you can observe particular activities which seem to engage these students for longer periods of time or which seem to calm them in some way. They may respond to music, to water or sand play, or to painting or drawing. When you notice these children becoming unduly agitated, try to lead them to the activity which seems most calming for them. You can also enlist the aid of the class as a whole in dealing with these students. After a good group feeling has been developed, you can suggest that students try to help the hyperactive student by encouraging him to play with them, by realizing that he may not be able to pay attention too long to things, etc. The students will easily adopt the same attitude you take toward these children. If your attitude is understanding and helpful, theirs will be also.

For students who have very few inner controls over their behavior, you will have to supply control and support. When a child appears grossly confused, disoriented or agitated within the classroom, try to provide as much structure for him as you can. Your control and ordering of his activities will reassure him that you will be able to provide the control over the environment and over him which he does not have. If he does not respond to your attempts to structure his environment, it may be necessary to move him into a more traditionally structured class. Some students simply cannot tolerate the emotional and social pressures of the open classroom.

Sometimes you will have students who present problems for other reasons. Perhaps they are quite withdrawn or act in such a way that they interfere with the functioning of the class as a whole. In the case of the withdrawn student, it is helpful if you can convince yourself to leave him alone. Many children who exhibit this kind of behavior are quite manipulative and use their withdrawal as a means of controlling others. Obviously this is a very self-destructive means of control. If you do not respond to their attempts to passively control you, they will eventually be forced to communicate in other ways. First, they usually tell another student what they want and the student tells you. If you pay scant attention to this maneuver, within a matter of weeks they will begin to talk to you directly. If a withdrawn student does not respond at all in several weeks, then you should explore the family situation and the child's behavior at home to try to assess more clearly what the problem is and what can be done.

With students who severely interfere with the operation of the classroom, it is worthwhile to invest considerable time with them in the beginning days and weeks of class. Stay close to them and attempt to help them to find ways of spending their time constructively and interestingly. This may mean literally showing them and suggesting to them how they should act for several days, giving them a very clear framework from which they can operate. You must leave no question in the student's mind about what kinds of behavior you expect from him. When he is able to function without disturbing others, then you can slowly encourage him to use some free choice, but not before. This is purely a matter of retraining a student with as little ambiguity as possible about what he can do in various situations.

If you teach younger children, you may occasionally find a student who is autistic or one who presents unusual problems with which you are unable to deal. In this case, it is wise to refer them to the school social worker or psychologist for a thorough evaluation. There are students who should be in specially structured classes for brain damaged or emotionally disturbed children. In these classes teachers are specially trained to deal with the specific problems of such children. The open classroom is not a panacea for severe problems in behavior anymore than the traditional classroom is. We simply do not know the effect of open classroom techniques on disturbed children at this time. My guess would be that the social and emotional pressures within the open classroom would make most students of this type very agitated. We will have to have more evidence in this area to evaluate its effects fairly.

Modifying Emotional Behavior

After several weeks have passed, you will be ready to make long range plans for the emotional and social development of your students at the same time you make them for their intellectual development. As problems begin to crystallize within the classroom, you will be able to think in terms of helping the child to change or add other means of dealing with his environment. Just as you assess intellectual functioning, you will be simultaneously assessing emotional and social development. It is helpful to know the common defensive tactics which children use to cope with their world.[6] But even without this knowledge their problems usually become quite apparent. They may have difficulties relating to other children or to you in very specific areas or ways. You will be in a position to observe this. Students may have problems of self-direction or of expressing their feelings. All of these problems will be intimately connected with their intellectual development and will change as their styles of dealing with the world change. You can provide the security of your relationship and new avenues of behavior which will help them accomplish this change.

When you feel sure that you have spotted some particular problem, you are ready to begin plans for changing the student's manner of dealing with it. You can help him to grow emotionally and socially in the same ways you help him to grow intellectually. Communicate your thoughts about his problem. This may be through verbalization, play situations or nonverbal ways. By formulating the problem and expressing it to the student in some manner, you will make the child more aware of it and aware of the fact that you know about it and want to help him. For the student who constantly tries to relate to others by teasing or provoking them in some manner, you can mention to him that he does this, and that it does not seem to work very well. The next step is to begin suggesting or demonstrating alternative ways of dealing with the problem. For the teasing student, you can suggest that he try asking a question about what another student is doing, instead of making some teasing remark. For a student who complains that no one ever wants to play with him, you might suggest that he relate to others in parallel play for awhile and observe how the students interact with one another. Then he can slowly try to join in the play unobtrusively and gradually as the others accept his participation fully. This operation needs constant evaluation, discussion and support from you. The more you treat the situation as a problem solving situation, the less emotionally involved you become in it, the more successful the student is likely to be in resolving the problem.

You do not need to have extensive training in emotional development and methods of dealing with emotional and social problems in order to deal with the types of problems you will encounter in the classroom. The open classroom atmosphere will in itself encourage students to explore and experiment rather freely with their feelings and with ways of expressing them and of relating to others. In this atmosphere of exploration, students will often begin to try new methods themselves. For those whose problems prevent them from doing so, you can suggest alternative behavior.

You should remember that behavior changes occur over long periods of time and, in between the transitional periods, you may have to deal with difficult and stormy incidents and behavior. Growing and learning are often painful and hard. You and your students will have to adopt an accepting attitude toward difficult periods of learning and growth if effective changes are going to occur. By encouraging experimentation in the emotional and social realms as fully as you would do in the intellectual area, you will allow students to find the most satisfying and socially acceptable means of relating to others and of dealing with their feelings.

NOTES - CHAPTER 7

1. Charles A. Brownfield, "Deterioration and Facilitation Hypothesis in Sensory-Deprivation Research," *Psychological Bulletin*, 6:304–13, 1964.

2. Ned A. Flanders, *Teacher Influence, Pupil Attitudes and Achievement* (Washington, D.C.: U.S. Dept. of H.E.W., 1965). Cooperative Research Monograph, No. 12.

3. Preoperational as defined by Piaget.

4. Ned A. Flanders (1964).

5. Robert Rosenthal, *Pygmalion in the Classroom*.

6. James C. Coleman, "Types of Adjustive Reactions," in *Human Dynamics in Psychology and Education*, Don E. Hamachek, ed. (Boston: Allyn and Bacon, Inc., 1968), pp. 617–641.

BIBLIOGRAPHY - CHAPTER 7

Books dealing with the teacher's role and relationship with students:

Clayton, Thomas E., *Teaching and Learning.* Englewood Cliffs, N.J.: Prentice-Hall, Inc., 1965.

Ginott, Haim G., *Teacher and Child.* New York: The Macmillan Co., 1972.

Flanders, Ned A., *Teacher Influence, Pupil Attitudes and Achievement.* Washington, D.C.: U.S. Dept. of H.E.W., 1965, Cooperative Research Monograph, No. 12.

Moustakas, Clark, *The Authentic Teacher.* Cambridge, Mass.: Howard A. Doyle Publishing Co., 1967.

Taba, Hilda, "Teaching Strategy and Learning," *California Journal for Instructional Improvement,* Dec., 1963.

Books with helpful ideas for curriculum, lessons and emotional learning:

Allen, Marjorie, *Planning for Play.* Cambridge, Mass.: M.I.T. Press, 1968.

Biggs, Edith E. and James R. MacLean, *Freedom to Learn: An Active Approach to Math.* Ontario, Canada: Don Mills, Addison-Wesley (Canada) Ltd., 1969.

Brearly, Molly, ed., *The Teaching of Young Children: Some Applications of Piaget's Learning Theory.* New York: Schocken Books, 1970.

Davitz, J., ed., *The Communication of Emotional Meaning.* New York: McGraw-Hill, 1964.

Marshall, Sybil, *An Experiment in Education.* Cambridge: Cambridge University Press, 1966.

Moffett, James, *A Student Centered Language Arts Curriculum, Grades K–6.* Boston: Houghton Mifflin Co., 1968.

Rioch, D. and E. Weinstein, eds., *Disorders of Communication.* Baltimore: Williams and Wilkins, 1964.

Rogers, Vincent R., *Teaching in the British Primary School.* London: The Macmillan Co., Collier-Macmillan, Ltd., 1970.

Weber, E., ed., *Primary Education: Changing Dimensions.* Washington, D.C.: Association for Childhood Education International, 1965.

CHAPTER 8.

EVALUATION

8.

As your class proceeds you will probably be evaluating yourself and your students spontaneously. You will want to be sure that you are providing them with optimal educational opportunities and that they are able to take advantage of these opportunities. You will need to constantly evaluate individual progress in order to anticipate the learning needs of each child. You will also need to evaluate the overall operation of the class periodically to insure continued successful operation. You will want to determine group needs and accomplishments to evaluate your own success in running an open classroom. You may also want to share this type of evaluation with administrators, colleagues and parents. The more we can learn about experiences with the open classroom, the better all of us will be in understanding and improving our teaching techniques.

ORIGINAL OBJECTIVES AS BASIS
FOR EVALUATING RESULTS

All the tools currently used to evaluate children will be helpful to you: standardized tests (which do measure some aspects of learning), classroom observations, class projects and activities, performance on workbooks, homework, performance within and without the classroom, etc. Plus these things, you will have to do some creative thinking in terms of your specific educational objectives. If you know what you are testing, and construct an adequate test or task of some kind to measure the quality and evaluate performance carefully, you will have resulting information which may be just as valuable as standardized test results. The difference is that from your results, you will not be able to evaluate how an individual child compares to others of his age level across the country. You may not care. If you do construct your own tests, it is important to record them and the results as part of your record of individual students. You may find some test situations more valuable than others over time, but you can only judge this realistically if you can check records. Again, these records do not have to be exhaustively detailed in order to be effective.

RELIABLE METHODS OF EVALUATION

If you want to test the independence of students in their approach to problems and finding solutions, you might suggest or create a problem within the classroom and encourage all students to solve it. The number of times a student comes up to you to ask for help or suggestions will be an important measure of his independence. The kind of help he asks for will also be significant. A child who asks how to find the answer is approaching a problem very differently from a child who asks if there is a magnifying glass in the classroom. In constructing test situations, remember that the more ambiguous you make the test situation, the more unique will be the behavior you elicit from each student. In the lack of external directions, the student's own mental organization and structure takes over and you have a better opportunity to observe the student in action in a natural way.

RANGE OF ABILITY WITHIN THE CLASSROOM

As you make individual evaluations, you will find the spread of ability within a subject area (such as reading or math) will widen as your class continues. When you truly allow students to learn and progress at their own pace and level, they do just that. When activities are teacher-directed, students tend to be kept at a similar level, brighter ones not working to their capacity and slower students not understanding what they are doing, although they can produce the superficial aspects of the learning task. You may have a spread of reading ability ranging from first through eighth grade in your second grade classroom. This is usually dismaying to teachers, but if you are truly individualizing, it will happen. There is no reason to be dismayed about this, since you are teaching individually also, and so you will not have to teach students with such widely varying ability levels only as a group. Neither will you have to evaluate them with group-oriented tests.

REALISTIC EXPECTATIONS FOR STUDENT CHANGE

It is important to have patience as you do your evaluations. It has taken children a long time to develop their styles of dealing with the world. You will not be able to change these patterns significantly over a period of weeks or months. If you make substantial changes in the course of the entire year you can consider yourself quite successful. Your goals in the open classroom are more difficult and far-reaching ones and they will consequently take longer to achieve.

PERIODIC EVALUATIONS

When it comes to evaluating the class as a whole, you will have to do this periodically in order to keep the class running smoothly. Assessment of current problems and functioning of the class as a whole is part of your everyday routine. Besides this, you will want to periodically assess and evaluate the overall learning which is occurring within the room. You may find that reading seems to be neglected in your classroom or that students are not progressing in this area as you would wish them to. You are then in a position to look into some of the possible causes for this situation. If you wait until the end of the year to face the reality of this kind of situation, it will be far too late to do anything about it.

As you put together your evaluative material, remember that it is a good idea to maintain a schedule for evaluating progress and classroom climate. You can do it monthly, and if necessary more often. If things are not going the way you want them to go, or if students are not learning in some areas and they are learning in others, you should change your schedules, routines or individual learning plans and try to bring the situation closer to your ideal. At times you may have to overhaul your entire classroom organization in order to achieve the kind of classroom you feel is best. If it seems necessary, do it.

There are more general things which will indicate to you the overall success of your classroom at any given time. Perhaps the most important of these is whether or not the children are enjoying school. Do they come early if they can and linger after class when possible? Are they taking things home to continue working on them? Do they try to prolong the school experience by lingering at the end of the day? Do they find holidays and vacations unwelcome? All these things will indicate the success of your efforts to make learning and school enjoyable and exciting.

Another important sign that your efforts are successful will be demonstrated when students relate their learning in class to their life away from school. Do they bring in things from home to use in the school situation? Do they discuss things which happen outside of school in a way related to things which have happened in the classroom? Often there is a wide split in students' minds between what happens at home and what happens in school. If an effective connection is being made between the two environments, then you truly have made school an important experience—a place to learn what life is all about, rather than a place to put life aside for six or seven hours a day.

OUTSIDE SOURCES OF EVALUATION

Objective evaluations of how your class is operating are always valuable, whatever their source. You can give them the same weight as you would give any opinion from the same source. If you can have colleagues and friends visit your class and tell you their impressions, this will be helpful in assessing the functioning of your class. Administrators and supervisors usually come whether you want them to or not. However, their opinions are valuable if you do not overestimate their value or lack of it. The open classroom is often disturbing to view since the viewer can never be fully aware of all the currents of action, and therefore cannot fully appreciate what is happening. If you keep in mind that you will get biased opinions and views, and take them as constructive views which will give you added insights, they can help you become aware of things which occur in the class which you might not notice yourself. It is frequently the most obvious things which we fail to notice.

Another valuable source of evaluative material is to leave a tape recorder running all day in your classroom and then listen to it in order to evaluate your interaction with the students. You may find that you can notice particular patterns of behavior in your verbalizations to the students. Or you may find that you are talking too much or not enough.

Since you will be helping students to learn to use their mistakes as learning blocks, you should be willing to do the same thing. An effective teacher is a teacher who can change when change seems warranted, and who can remain firm and steady when that seems justified. An effective teacher is one who uses imagination and flexibility to obtain the best possible results from open classroom techniques.

BIBLIOGRAPHY - CHAPTER 8

Baron, Denis and Harold W. Bernard, *Evaluation Techniques for Classroom Teachers*. New York: McGraw-Hill Book Co., Inc., 1968.

Cass, Joan and D. E. M. Gardner, *The Role of the Teacher in the Infant and Nursery School*. London: Pergasson Press, 1965.

Furst, Edward J., *Constructing Evaluation Instruments*. New York: David McKay Co., Inc., 1958.

Nelson, Clarence H., *Measurement and Evaluation in the Classroom*. London: The Macmillan Co., Collier-Macmillan Ltd., 1970.

INDEX